Arctic Circle

ICELAND

·ɤ Faroe Is.

Shetland Is⌐

NORWAY

Bergen
Oslo

Stavanger
Christiansand

Skagerrak
Kattegat

DENMARK

Baltic Sea

North Sea
Cuxhaven
Kiel
Bremen

Danzig

GERMANY

English Channel
Brest
Paris
Lorient
Carnac
FRANCE
Bay of
Biscay
Bordeaux
Cape Ortegal
Biarritz
Gijon
Santander
El Ferrol

T · I · C

PORTUGAL
SPAIN

Azores
· ·

Cadiz

Gulf of
Cadiz
Gibraltar

⁊ · N

Madeira ·

Casablanca
MOROCCO
Agadir

Canary Is. · ·ₒTenerife ·
Las Palmasᵒ

A F R I C A

Cape Verde Is.
· ·
· ·

Dakar

Freetown

Gulf of Guinea

HIRSCHFELD

HIRSCHFELD

The Story of a U-boat NCO
1940–1946

as told to
Geoffrey Brooks

by
WOLFGANG HIRSCHFELD

NAVAL INSTITUTE PRESS
ANNAPOLIS, MARYLAND

First published in the United Kingdom in 1996 by
LEO COOPER, an imprint of Pen & Sword Books Ltd.

Published and distributed in the United States of America and Canada
by the Naval Institute Press,
118 Maryland Avenue,
Annapolis, MD 21402-5035

Library of Congress Catalog Card No. 96-70117
ISBN 1-55750-372-9

This edition is authorized for sale only in
the United States, its territories and possessions,
and Canada

Printed in England on acid-free paper

For my son Louis Brooks

'Tis all a Chequer-board of Nights and Days
Where Destiny with Men for Pieces plays:
Hither and thither moves, and checks and slays,
And one by one back in the Closet lays.

RUBAIYAT OF OMAR KHAYYAM

CONTENTS

ACKNOWLEDGEMENTS

The author wishes to acknowledge the assistance of the library of the Institute of Marine Engineers, Mark Lane, EC3: the German Historical Institute, Bloomsbury Square, WC2, and the Science Museum Library, South Kensington, and extends his thanks to Professor Dr Jürgen Rohwer, the naval historian, who supplied much useful information with regard to the question of the uranium oxide aboard *U–234*: to Jak Mallmann-Showell, the U-boat historian and author, who checked the manuscript for error and pointed out a number of avenues the author had carelessly left unexplored. Finally to Brigadier Bryan Watkins and to my ex-MN friend Philip Oastler a special note of gratitude for invaluable comments, suggestions and encouragement.

Geoffrey Brooks
London 1996

FOREWORD

by Jak P. Mallmann-Showell

This book, based on a secret diary of a U-boat radio operator, ranks as one of the most outstanding documents of the Second World War. It is unique inasmuch as it is probably the only German diary written by a non-commissioned officer as the events unfolded. The keeping of private records was so strictly forbidden that discovery would have resulted in a court martial.

Wolfgang Hirschfeld witnessed almost the whole period of the Battle of the Atlantic and his position enabled him to be better informed than many officers. What is more, he served under three unusual commanders. The first, Fischer, was unjustly dismissed for incompetence. The second, Bleichrodt, one of the famous 'aces', was probably the only German naval officer to have resigned in mid-operation on the high seas and to have broadcast his intention for all to hear. The third, Fehler, joined the U-boat Arm after having served as Demolition and Explosives Officer aboard the legendary ghost cruiser *Atlantis*, which remained at sea for 622 days without putting into port.

Hirschfeld's final voyage is of special interest because many aspects of it are still shrouded in mystery. The submarine surrendered on its way to Japan. When the Americans unloaded it, they found amongst its cargo of war material an Me 262 jet fighter and, even more intriguing, radioactive substances.

Another great virtue of this book is that Wolfgang Hirschfeld is a natural writer of great ability. Not only does he bring the past alive by illustrating hard facts with fascinating anecdotes of seaboard life, but he slots the events he is describing into the overall picture of the war.

This brilliance has been well translated, making the English version just as compelling as the original German.

INTRODUCTION

This is the story of an enlisted naval rating who served as a telegraphist in the German Navy for the ten years from 1935–45.

Wolfgang Hirschfeld was born in Berlin on 20 May, 1916, the only child of Margarethe (1893–1987) and Eugen Hirschfeld (1882–1972). The father, who was a qualified pharmacist, was serving as a conscripted infantryman at Verdun. Previously he had been on the Somme, where he had been wounded in the lungs.

After the war, the father's study accommodated a large selection of war books, among them the personal records of the U-boat aces Hashagen, Valentiner, Hersing and De La Perière, which the boy Hirschfeld later read with special interest, since he felt the inclination to join the Navy. However, he had no desire to become a submariner, for this seemed to be an unpleasant and somewhat eerie form of existence. At the age of ten he attended the Hindenburg-Oberreal school in Berlin Lichterfelde, and his political philosophy was moulded at this precocious age when he joined a youth organization known as the *Deutsche Freischar*, which was modelled on the *Freikorps* of the immediate postwar period. The *Freikorps* was a body of well-equipped and disciplined veteran soldiers opposed to demobilization and harnessed to what was left of the High Command.

In January, 1919, when communist revolutionaries and Spartacists, led by Karl Liebknecht, attempted a *putsch* in Berlin with the intention of proclaiming a soviet republic, they were decisively and brutally routed by the *Freikorps* under the leadership of the Minister of Defence, Noske. Later, the *Freikorps* was employed to resist Polish attempts to seize Silesia.

During school holidays, the junior version of the *Freikorps* made long excursions to West Prussia, Upper Silesia, Memel and Posen.

Germany had been deprived of these eastern provinces by the Treaty of Versailles. They had retained East Prussia, but only with land access through the Polish Corridor, a state of affairs which had last prevailed in the 17th Century. The purpose of these visits can be guessed at. The *Deutsche Freischar* was a political nursery, strongly anti-monarchical and a flower which blossomed in the War Guilt Clause of the Treaty of Versailles.

Even today, Wolfgang Hirschfeld has not forgotten the insult and injury heaped on Germany in the aftermath of the Kaiser's defeat. The American President, Wilson, had led Germany to expect a peace of reconciliation, but had instead offered only a peace of revenge, dictated chiefly by the United States and France. In addition to the loss of their eastern territories already mentioned, the Germans had been compelled to surrender Alsace and Lorraine permanently, and the Saar temporarily, subject to a later plebiscite; and all the colonies of their overseas Empire. Their overseas investments were held forfeit, and Germany had had to pay reparations of an undefined amount sufficient to redeem all Allied war costs. The reparations clauses were intended to ruin Germany financially and to reduce the German nation to a permanent state of impotence.

The Chancellors of Germany in the Weimar period guaranteed the reparations, but only at an economic and human cost of seven million unemployed. The alleged assistance of the United States Government amounted to little more than an extension of the period of German indebtedness, since the Dawes Plan of 1924 and the Young Plan of 1929 merely reduced the instalments and increased the term of payment. If the Young Plan had remained in force, the last instalment would have been due in 1987. Despite the collapse of the German economy, the Versailles *Diktat* was not revised, and the corollary was a strong resurgence of the extremist political parties.

It was in this sense that the victors of the First World War, and particularly the United States, created the circumstances for a new war in which the losers would attempt to rectify matters. In 1933 it was the memory of the political turmoil of 1919, and the belief that the victors of the First World War had deliberately perpetuated it by economic means ever since the end of the fighting, that won for Hitler a substantial proportion of the seats in the Reichstag.

Although not eligible to vote in 1933, because he had not attained his majority, Hirschfeld confirms that he would have voted for Hitler had opportunity allowed. He did not subsequently become a Nazi Party Member because only an elector could join, and German military law forbade an enlisted serviceman from engaging in political activity, whether National Socialist or otherwise.

In 1932, at the age of sixteen years, Hirschfeld had been offered the opportunity of an apprenticeship at the Prussian Institute for Fisheries in Berlin Friedrichshagen. Even in those years of savage unemployment no school leaving certificate (*Abitur*) was required to enrol, and he accepted one of the five annual vacancies. The post of Master Professional Fisherman, which he had hopes of achieving within five years, was a civil service position offering financial security in a nation which had not known it since the war.

In a former royal hunting lodge at the State Fishery School, Sacrow, near Potsdam, he spent a year learning the fish catching methods of the Havel and other lakes surrounding Berlin, followed by two years at Timmendorf in Holstein where he trained as a cadet in the Kiel trawling cutters of the western Baltic.

In the Nazi Government, Hermann Goering was not only *Reichsluftminister* but also *Reichsjägermeister*, to which office the national fishery was subordinate, and in 1934 Hirschfeld received notice of redundancy: the apprenticeships were now to be offered to men demobilizing after serving a term of 12 years with the *Reichswehr*.

When Hirschfeld asked the Senior Fishery Officer at Kiel for his advice, he was handed an application form for the German Navy and told, 'Serve your twelve years in the *Reichsmarine*, then you can resume your training with the Institute.' He was happy to consider this, and dreamed of the voyages he might make to far-flung parts of the globe aboard one of Germany's new light cruisers which annually made the circumnavigation. Early in 1935 he applied, and this is the point where Wolfgang Hirschfeld's narrative begins in this book.

Shortly after he was compulsorily transferred to the U-boat Arm in 1940, Hirschfeld began to keep a diary, even though this was a court-martial offence if discovered.[1] His observations were committed to writing mostly during the long night watches when there was little radio traffic, the papers secreted between the pages of old signal logs kept in the confidential document safe. The radio team of a U-boat occupied two small rooms on the starboard side immediately forward of the control room bulkhead amidships. On the opposite side of the central corridor was the captain's tiny cabin, his privacy guaranteed by a green curtain. The telegraphists were, whether they liked it or not, party to all of the captain's conversations conducted above a whisper. Not only did Hirschfeld also see all signals except those designated 'Officers Only', but, as the captain's secretary, he spent much time typing up the captain's private notes for the boat's war diary. I have based this book on Hirschfeld's private war diaries as well as on conversations and correspondence between us, and I have found it convenient to cast the narrative in the first person as Hirschfeld related it. He sketched a picture of U-boat life from the point of view of a Senior NCO, and apart from the partisan slant which inevitably creeps into any personal account, there is nothing political or glorious about his story.

Perhaps it would have been for the best if the submarine had been outlawed for warfare from its inception, as for some time it was proposed. After the appalling carnage on the seas during the Great War, the victorious nations, Britain, France and the United States, had the opportunity to legislate to restrict the worst excesses but apparently they were satisfied that it was unnecessary.

Accordingly, the harrowing catalogue of grisly killings which the world had experienced in the Great War continued, on an even greater scale than hitherto, during the Second World War, in the Battle of the Atlantic and in all other theatres where the submarine was deployed.

A case in point is that of the Norwegian motor ship *Tirranna*, 7230 BRT, which had been captured by the raider *Atlantis* and sent to France as prize with a German crew of 18 and 274 civilians, mostly British, including six women and children. In September, 1940, she arrived off the Gironde, where she was torpedoed and sunk without warning by a British submarine. The British commander made no attempt to rescue the survivors. Sixty persons, all civilians, including the children, lost their lives.[2]

This was legitimate submarine warfare as the British Admiralty understood and accepted it. And two years later, the Americans showed in the *Laconia* incident that a submarine commander exercised humanity at his own risk and that the very concept of the temporary truce at sea to save civilians was anathema.

Therefore I depart from the tradition of apologizing when introducing the personal account of a German serviceman of the Hitler period. Hirschfeld enlisted in the German Navy in 1935 intending to enjoy a quiet twelve years with the surface fleet and was pressed into U-boat service. Although U-boat men were supposed to be volunteers (*Freiwillig zur U-boot Waffe!* as the recruiting posters urged), Hirschfeld had no choice, being pressed into U-boat service almost as if it were a kind of disciplinary measure, and he would never have volunteered on principle if asked to do so since that would have conflicted with his personal motto *Never volunteer!* It was merely his duty.

G.B.

— I —

EARLY DAYS AT SEA

Early in 1935 I applied for the signals branch of the Navy because a technical training was offered. The recruiting officer, Captain François, advised me to request training as a telegraphist. 'Not only is it the finest branch in the Navy, but the time will come when you will go down on your bended knees to thank me for recommending it,' he told me. I stared at him for a few moments and then agreed to take his advice; I never regretted this decision for an instant and if I met him today I would go down on my knees to thank him as he had prophesied.

After six days of intensive intelligence and psychological testing at Berlin Tempelhof, I was accepted. Yet if I had known then the psychiatric opinion of my qualities, my enthusiasm might suddenly have palled, for when I saw my personal file during a visit to the U-boat Personnel Office at Kiel in 1944, I noted that I had been classified as 'specially suited for small units with unsupervised responsibility, e.g. S-boats, R-boats and the Wireless Monitoring Section.' Wandering around the world in a small light cruiser was therefore a dream unlikely to have been fulfilled during my twelve years of peacetime service.

Following the basic three-month infantry induction period at Stralsund in early 1936, I was posted to Flensburg for the first of numerous courses in telegraphy at the Naval Signals School. After a spell with the Wireless Monitoring Section (B-Dienst), I had my first sea time aboard the minesweepers *R-15* and *M-102* and earned my first promotion, to Leading Telegraphist (*Stabsfunkgast*) in October, 1938. In April, 1939, I sat for a further promotion to Junior Petty Officer (*Funkmaat*). The rank of *Funkmaat* did not have an exact English equivalent; it was intermediate between Leading Telegraphist and Petty Officer in the Royal Navy. All German ratings and NCO's

I

below the rank of Warrant Officer wore the square rig. In my new rank I was appointed senior telegraphist aboard the old torpedo boat *T-139*.

T-139 had sailed for many years under the name *Pfeil* with the Remote Control Group, where she had done service to the former Imperial Navy pre-Dreadnought *Zähringen* as a tug. This great hulk was stuffed with cork to make her virtually unsinkable and used by the fleet for artillery practice.

One day in 1938 *T-139* had had a head-on collision with a quay which had demolished part of her forecastle. After the rebuilding, she was the only torpedo boat in the German Navy with a clipper bow. She was attached to the 24th Flotilla, and we were always being given special tasks on account of having the most modern hydrophone and radio equipment aboard. Our first wartime mission was the hunt for the Polish submarine *Orzel*, which was attempting to flee the Baltic for England. We got a fix on her off Trelleborg in southern Sweden but couldn't depth-charge her because we were all in Swedish neutral water, and so she escaped.

Besides the new bow, *T-139* had been restored to her former glory as a torpedo boat, except that she had no torpedo tubes and no gun. We procured a specimen of the latter from the stock of impounded Polish weapons at Gdynia, and then received orders to begin patrol duties in the Kattegat, searching Scandinavian merchant ships for contraband. Whenever an illicit cargo was discovered, the arrested ship would be escorted into Kiel. We also had a long run to the Soviet Union, escorting the new *Admiral Hipper* class heavy cruiser *Lützow*, which had been sold to the Soviets.

I was the only non-reservist aboard *T-139*. The Captain, Lt Cdr (Reserve) Schwarten, the only officer, had been demobilized from the Imperial Navy with the rank of midshipman in 1918 and had been a director of I G Farben in civilian life. The NCOs and most of the crew had sailed for the Kaiser, and some had even been aboard units of the Fleet for the mass scuttling at Scapa Flow in 1919 and had never trodden a ship's planks since. The boatswain, who until recently had been a Bailiff of the Supreme Court, was the watchkeeping officer and coxswain and was such an expert at the wheel that the Captain left him to do all the tricky steering and harbour manoeuvres. It was remarkable how these older men and reservists, who had been away from the sea for twenty years, could so readily bring a naval unit to preparedness as though their absence had been mere weeks.

My relationship with the Commander was excellent: *T-139* was my finest sea posting and I cherished hopes of spending the remainder of the war aboard her in the Baltic. But it was not to work out like that.

During the early months of the year 1940 *T-139* acted as torpedo retrieval vessel to the 24th U-boat Training Flotilla at Warnemünde, and in March entered the Deutsche Werft shipyard at Kiel for overhaul. Returning from a fourteen-day furlough, I found the boat still in the yards with machinery and cables strewn around the decks. The Captain beckoned to me to come aboard at once and with some emotion imparted the news that I had been drafted with immediate effect to the light cruiser *Karlsruhe*.

Now this was a most unwelcome development, for I was a small-ship man and it was quite against all my instincts to join a floating barracks. My Commander certainly wished to retain me, and asked if there wasn't something that could be done, to which I replied that, with three gold rings on his sleeve, the Captain might attempt to intercede with the 2 AdO, the office of the Admiral Baltic.

Lt Cdr Schwarten took the communications pinnace to Wik and I watched him go with the feeling that he was unlikely to achieve anything. However, contrary to all expectations, he returned triumphant with an assurance that the transfer had been cancelled. A stone fell away from my heart. I did not want to leave Kiel for another reason: I was in love with a pharmacist's assistant there by the name of Ilona.

One afternoon I called into a saloon by the name of The Patzenhofer on the Dreiecksplatz which was highly popular with the naval men, and there I encountered a row of familiar old faces from my training days. They greeted me most heartily. They had recently completed a course in Flensburg and whilst waiting for a ship had been employed as writers in the Draftings Office of the 2 AdO. Now they had been assigned *en masse* to the light cruiser *Karlsruhe* on which many of them had seen service in peacetime, when she had been a coveted posting because of her overseas cruises.

When I explained to them how I had been assigned to the cruiser myself but had managed to get the transfer reversed, they all laughed and stared at me with meaningful grins on their faces. Now it became clear to me that I had these well-intentioned friends to thank for my posting. And, worse still, they told me with glee that the cancellation had been cancelled and that I was due to report aboard the cruiser by 5 April, 1940, at the latest, that being the following Friday. I was so shocked that I needed several large tots of rum to recover my composure, but I could not be angry with them, for they were such good types and had only intervened on my behalf because they thought they were doing me a great favour.

Accepting the inevitable at last, I devised a scheme. 'Listen, cover for me until next Monday,' I told them, 'I want to take a proper farewell from my girl-friend Ilona.' This they could understand, and they departed for Wilhelmshaven with a '*wiedersehen*' until we should meet the following week aboard the cruiser.

Next day Lt Cdr Schwarten showed me the new movement orders without speaking and then said that he would go to the 2 AdO to attempt to reverse them again, but when he returned from Wik I could see by the expression on his face that he had not succeeded. 'Sorry, Petty Officer, there was nothing that could be done this time. The cruiser is at Wilhelmshaven with readiness to sail. Gate Four. You should leave today.'

I implored the Captain to be allowed to stay until Sunday in order to be able to take a proper farewell of my fiancée, and the Captain gave me a sharp look and said, 'I didn't know you were engaged.' There was a significant pause and then he decided, 'On Sunday evening you will go without fail, and don't let me down or I'll get angry.'

I gave him my promise, but there was no discussion about the engagement. That Sunday I threw a farewell party for myself aboard the torpedo boat, the whole ship's company attending. There was a tremendous mood. In the afternoon I sent my junior telegraphist to Kiel railway station with my sea bag and effects, instructing him that it should be addressed care of the cruiser, Gate Four, Wilhelmshaven. Once that had been done I settled down to enjoy the party.

The last connection for Wilhelmshaven was scheduled to depart from Kiel at 2014 hrs, and I left at the last possible moment, reeling and stumbling down the road which led to the Kiel-Gaarden ferry. To my consternation and dismay, I saw the vessel sail one minute early by my watch. I was only a few yards short of the boarding ramp when it was slammed shut in my face.

I took the next ferry, sprinted up the steps of Kiel station and caught sight of the three red tail lamps of the express slowly diminishing in the distance. I chased after the train until pulled back by several military policemen. How slender the thread by which a man's destiny hangs! Or does Fate intervene to ensure that a man's life follows a certain predetermined course? I did not know it then, but this was the turning point of my whole life. If I had caught that train, it would eventually have taken me along the road to an early death.

I slunk back to the torpedo boat to be beerily greeted by my shipmates. I confided to them that I would be in a most ticklish situation if the commander were to discover my presence. I was proposing to conceal myself aboard until the morning, when I would

4

take the first connection for Wilhelmshaven, but for that I needed a travel order. In my capacity as quartermaster, I had kept a stock of blank orders in the radio room; after having gone there and filled one out for myself, I was about to leave when the shadow of the Captain fell across the doorway. He was lost for words at the sight of me. I poured out the whole sorry story, to which Lt Cdr Schwarten listened patiently and then said in annoyance, 'I hadn't expected this of you, Hirschfeld. You missed the train because you were drunk.'

'But no, sir, that is not the case. The ferry sailed a minute early.' Schwarten stared at me with a troubled mien and it pained me to have so disappointed my Captain.

'You will leave tomorrow by the first train. Now go to your bunk. This is an order.'

I went dutifully to my bed, passing through a gang of my shipmates who were still seeing to what was left of the alcohol.

The new radio operator was already installed: his previous experience was with the Imperial Navy and he was openly doubtful as to whether he would be able to cope with modern telegraphy and the new types of cipher machines. At about 2200 hrs the Captain visited the NCO's room to satisfy himself that I was in my bunk, and afterwards he lingered a little while with the boozers. As he rose to leave, a boatswain on the staff of the 2 AdO arrived. He was carrying under his arm a red-backed chart, which signified an operation of the highest level of secrecy. Amidst general speculation, the captain and the boatswain hurried away and after a short while I was summoned to the radio room. It suddenly fell quiet in the NCO's quarters.

Lt Cdr Schwarten came directly to the point; he had received orders for *T-139* to participate in a large-scale military operation and it was essential for him to have an experienced senior telegraphist aboard. My erstwhile successor had packed his kit and was on his way back to the shore barracks.

'Now go and have a proper sleep and don't let it disturb you when you hear us putting to sea. We will also be loading fuel, ammunition and depth charges. Early tomorrow, after we pass the Kiel lightship, I will expect you in my cabin having slept it off. I won't open the orders with the new radio frequencies until then.'

When I returned to my bunk, I was deluged with questions but I merely told them that they would find out in the morning.

Operation *Weserübung*, the German invasion of Norway and Denmark, began on 7 April, 1940. *T-139* docked at Warnemünde to embark troops for Norway and we landed them there without incident. During the main operational landings, the Fleet sustained serious losses, including the light cruiser *Karlsruhe*, which was torpedoed and sunk by a British submarine.

Before her return to Germany *T-139* was detached to act as security boat for the new U-boat *U-122* which was carrying out deep dive trials off the Baltic island of Bornholm, and it was late in the month before we put back into Kiel. On arrival, I picked up a letter from my mother in which she told me that I had been listed as missing in action aboard the *Karlsruhe*. I considered it likely that this was a clerical mix-up which would sort itself out in time and so I did not bother to see the 2 AdO to put the record straight myself.

It transpired that my name had been included on the muster of the *Karlsruhe* which had been handed ashore as the cruiser cast off from Wilhelmshaven. My friends had reported me present as they expected me to put in an appearance at any moment and Lt Cdr Schwarten had forgotten to notify the 2 AdO of his own action in retaining me.

Shortly afterwards, I had to visit 2 AdO in my capacity as boat's quartermaster to request extra personnel. A Writer NCO by the name of Helbig asked me what an enlisted *Funkmaat* was doing aboard a reservist's boat. When I replied that I had been aboard *T-139* since the outbreak of war, Helbig drew my personal file and read through it.

'It states here that you were on the *Karlsruhe*. You're supposed to be missing in action.'

'Yes, I know, my mother told me in her last letter.'

Helbig gave me a devastating look. 'You seem to be taking a very light view of this, Petty Officer. I shall be asking for a full report from your commanding officer. You will be hearing from me again.'

A few days later when perusing Baltic Station Orders I saw my name listed for the U-boat Arm. There was no appeal against this drafting: my pleasant career aboard the old torpedo boat *T-139* had come to its close. Meanwhile, all the surviving radio crew from the *Karlsruhe* had been transferred *en masse* to a capital ship. When I met them later in Hamburg, they expressed sympathy that I had been dumped into the U-boat Arm, where my prospects of a long life were not very promising. They, on the other hand, had been blessed by Providence. They would be safe and sound aboard an unsinkable battleship. They had all been drafted to the *Bismarck*.

* * *

The U-boat Arm seized its volunteers swiftly and by 1 May, 1940, I had begun four months' U-boat signals training at Pillau and

Mürwik which was followed on completion by a posting to the 1st Flotilla (Personnel Reserve) at Kiel.

Here I was given a choice, the only one I can ever remember being offered in my service with the U-boat Arm: did I want to sail Type VII or Type IX? Other U-boat veterans urged me to opt for the former: 'Man, take the Type VII, they give you a better chance of surviving. They submerge ten seconds quicker and the voyages are shorter.'

But, simply because I like a bit of comfort, I chose the larger boat, and when I saw the cramped conditions with which the crews of the Type VII boats were expected to put up I had no regrets. In October I was told to join the new submarine *U-109* completing at the Deschimag Yard, Bremen.

2

U-109: WORKING UP

The Type IXB submarine *U-109* was commissioned on 5 December, 1940, alongside a rainswept wharf at the Deschimag Yard. The crew paraded in three ranks on the aftercasing and the Captain Lt Cdr Hans-Georg Fischer, a gaunt youngish man with a hoarse sounding voice, addressed a few pithy words to us from the bridge.

The brief ceremony concluded with the raising of the German battle flag at the ensign staff and, on receiving the order to dismiss, the crew poured down the hatches into the snug interior of the boat, where the event was to be marked with a small celebration.

In the NCO's mess, drinks in hand, we gathered round two ageing survivors from the Kaiser's submarine *UB-109*. These men had a harrowing experience to relate. During a patrol off the Dutch coast in 1916 the exterior controls of their boat had become entangled with the mooring wire of a mine and, in their struggle to get free, the mine had touched the hull. The explosion blew the boat apart. They were only at sixty feet, but even so pitifully few of the crew had managed to reach the surface alive.

'Well, at least that sort of thing won't happen to this boat,' I said, 'we'll be in the Atlantic with thousands of feet of water beneath the keel.'

'Don't think you're safe yet,' one of the old hands retorted, 'you've got to survive the training in the Baltic first.'

After an eastwards transit of the Kiel Canal the next day, the boat called in at Kiel for fuel and to embark the training officer, Captain (Reserve) Hashagen, a renowned U-boat ace of the First World War. The initial period was primarily concerned with boat handling techniques and to test the mettle of the officers.

The three watchkeeping officers of *U-109* were Lt Volkmar

Schwartzkopff and Sub Lt Siegfried Keller, and the coxswain, Warrant Officer Bruno Petersen, the most senior enlisted man aboard, who also navigated the boat. The Chief Engineer was Lt Martin Weber.

On the first day of trials off Heikendorf, the Chief made a complete mess of the trim after a dive and the bows ploughed into the mud of the sea bed and stuck there. As I watched the two engine room artificers manfully struggling with the blow-valves, depth rudders and propellers in the effort to wrench the boat away from the grasp of the bottom, I remembered HMS *Thetis* and realized that it might be just as dangerous during the working-up period in the calm waters of the Baltic as actually fighting the enemy.

Lt Weber received a stern reprimand from the training officer in front of the whole crew for endangering and damaging the boat, which needed some minor repairs in dock. The Chief Engineer was incompetent and he tended to rely very much on his Senior NCO's to cover for him.

We left Kiel for the Bay of Danzig; the cold was more piercing there but naval traffic was scarce. We practised alarm dives, simulated emergencies in all departments and fired practice torpedoes. One morning Lt Cdr Fischer called me to the bridge and, indicating a grey patrol vessel passing on a parallel course, asked me, 'Isn't that your last ship over there?'

I studied the aged torpedo boat for a few seconds and nodded. When Fischer suggested that I might like to send her a message, I scribbled one down, and he had it flagged across for me;

Petty Officer to Commander. Glad to see the old bucket is still afloat. Best wishes from your former senior telegraphist.

There was a pause and then an Aldis lamp flashed back an answer.

Commander to Petty Officer. I wish you a long life.

Fischer turned his head to me. 'He doesn't think you're going to have one,' he said with a sad smile.

The grey dawn of 23 January, 1941, revealed many ice floes stretching broadly out across Danzig harbour: the flotilla of U-boats under training lay huddled together coated in a mantle of frozen snow. Torpedo practice had been cancelled for the day. As senior telegraphist of *U-109*, I was also responsible for stocking the food store and I took the opportunity to go ashore to order the meat supply from a Neufahrwasser butcher, taking with me my towel and a bar of soap. Only my Number Two, Bischoff, knew of my absence. After concluding my business in the town, I slipped aboard the Flotilla depot ship *Hertha* and found a bathroom. Within minutes I was dreamily soaking in the steaming water of a full tub while outside, beyond the iced-over porthole, the muffled sirens of the harbour tugs and the ice floes scraping alongside the hull were but barely audible.

My occupation of the bath was a longish one, and it was not until I perceived a certain ominous motion of the *Hertha* that I hurriedly dressed and made my way to her radio room. The operator, a classmate from my 1936 training days, listened sympathetically to my story and then explained that the order confining the depot ship and U-boats to port had been rescinded because the Danzig Bight was ice-free and the Flotilla Commander thought that U-boat officers should learn to aim and fire torpedoes even in snow storms. Glumly, I watched the harbour receding astern, and then settled down to spend the remainder of the day in the radio room of the depot ship.

In mid-afternoon the radio operator handed me a decoded signal:

To 25th Flotilla. Have rammed submerged submarine. Probably *U-109*. From *T-156*.

'Oh my God,' I thought. For several hours I waited to hear the worst and it was dusk before *U-109* surfaced and signalled that a patrol boat had sheared off her periscopes, but that she was otherwise not seriously damaged. The exercises were then abandoned because of the danger of further collisions in the poor visibility. When I slunk back aboard at nightfall, Bischoff told me that my absence had passed unnoticed.

The next day, while the boat was in the repair yard, I discussed the incident with the Captain over a bottle of wine.

'I'd have written you a really nice obituary if the boat had been sunk,' I told him.

'And what makes you think you'd have been a survivor?'

'I wasn't on board.'

Fischer stared at me with large eyes as I recounted my misfortunes of the previous day, then suddenly burst out laughing, clapping me on the shoulder like a brother.

'Have you thought this thing through, Hirschfeld? If we'd been sunk, nobody would've known you weren't on board. You could have gone home and laid low until the war was over.'

I shook my head. 'No, the telegraphist of the *Hertha* knew.'

'Well then,' Fischer said with a grim smile, 'you wouldn't have survived us long after all. They would merely have given you a transfer to another U-boat.'

The winter of 1940 was a gruelling and bitterly cold one, and the pack of training boats was frozen up in Danzig harbour for much of January and February 1941. During this time the crews were accommodated on the *Hansa*. On the morning of 25 February the meteorologists forecast something of a thaw and we were awoken well before dawn and told to report to our boats for torpedo practice in the Bight. It was still pitch dark as we tramped through the thick snow to the harbour.

U-109 was moored alongside Kleinschmidt's boat, *U-111*, which was the outer boat of the two. *U-111* cast off first. 'Have a nice exercise!' her men shouted back at us.

She had already vanished into the darkness by the time *U-109* put out. After a few minutes Walter Gross, our duty boatswain, who had been at the bows to cast off the mooring warps, shouted up to the bridge that he had found a large field kitchen lashed to the deck between the base of the conning tower and the gun pedestal. The Captain leaned over the bridge mantle and tried to make it out in the gloom. 'Damn,' he said loudly, 'how did that get there?'

'Perhaps you should ask Kleinschmidt,' Walter Gross called back. Lt Cdr Fischer descended to the foredeck to inspect the field kitchen, which had a tall chimney and appeared to be the property of the *Reichs Arbeits Dienst*. 'We've got to get rid of it quickly,' Fischer told the boatswain. 'If the *Hertha* sees that thing on the forecasing when it gets light, we'll be the laughing stock of the flotilla.'

The boat ran into Neufahrwasser and we manhandled the offending object ashore and dumped it in a disused coal store. Then the boat surged off after the pack and at first light we were on station when *U-111* loomed up nearby, her bridge and gun platform crowded with her crew. All their binoculars were trained on our foredeck. Lt Keller glared indignantly at the grinning faces on *U-111* and said, 'Can you imagine it if we had had to dive with that thing on the forecasing?'

'Kleinschmidt would have laughed till he cried,' Fischer told him.

* * *

That evening we docked in Neufahrwasser. There was a hard frost and a thick carpet of snow lay underfoot. Our accommodation ship *Hansa* was not available and we had been told to spend the night on the *Hertha*. An icy coat glistened on the sides of the depot ship and an arctic wind whistled through the cabins. To spend the evening in quarters like this was such an intolerable proposition that a pub crawl was decided upon. We dressed in our U-boat leathers and a blue bobble hat so as not to make it so obvious that we were naval men, and then set out.

By midnight a party of five of us was still on its feet and gracing a saloon by the name of The Lighthouse. After a few boisterous rounds, the innkeeper closed the bar on the grounds that we had had enough, but when Eduard Maureschat, one of the boatswains, told him in confidence that I was Germany's second most successful U-boat commander, mine host was so impressed that he relented and reopened the bar. This coincided with the arrival of the Captain and Lt Keller, who were dressed in similar fashion to the rest of us, and when the innkeeper introduced me to the two newcomers, they told me how honoured they were to meet me, since they had heard so much about me and could wish for nothing more than to be so famous themselves one day. Naturally we now invited them to join the boozing, which then continued until interrupted at two o'clock by the arrival of a military police patrol and instructions to get back to our ship.

Kuddel Wenzel was hopelessly drunk and declared that under no circumstances would he return to the stinking rat-ship *Hertha*, smashing his fist down on a counter display for emphasis, breaking the glass and cutting his hand so badly that an ambulance had to be sent for. The captain had to reveal his true identity and guarantee to reimburse the inn for damage and then we tottered through the cold, starry night towards the harbour.

Bischoff discovered a toboggan and the five of us climbed aboard it, Fischer insisting on steering since he was the Captain. We set off down a slope, but because of our condition we were unable to exercise full control over the vehicle and an accident occurred, the commander being hurtled into a barbed wire fence, with all of the passengers landing on top of him! Fortunately, we could assure Fischer that the damage to his face and head was not as serious as it had seemed at first, and we all staggered back to the *Hertha* on foot. To the right of the gangplank we found Maureschat sleeping in the snow. We dragged him on board and threw him into a cabin, but when I visited the outside head an hour later I found the boatswain sleeping on the deck. He said it was warmer there.

The next morning *U-109* sailed to Gdynia to join the 27th Tactical Exercise Flotilla. Our new depot ship was the modern U-boat tender *Wilhelm Bauer*.

The tactical exercises were feared because they drove crews to the very limit. Commander Ernst Sobe was our examiner, a man said to have special qualities. Lt Cdr Fischer told us that he had known Sobe in 1926 when they were sea cadets together and had had serious differences.

I went aboard the *Wilhelm Bauer* and the senior telegraphist, Hein Walter, showed me round a large and well appointed radio control centre behind the wheelhouse equipped with the most up-to-date radio and direction finding devices.

It was explained to me that the exercises were simply an endless series of convoy attacks. The group of training U-boats formed a broad scouting line 100 miles long and searched for a 'convoy' consisting of a steamer and two banana boats escorted by a couple of escort vessels and the *Wilhelm Bauer*. When a U-boat detected the convoy it kept contact and transmitted regular homing signals to the pack which closed in and attacked when told to do so by Cdr Sobe in the control centre of the U-boat tender, where all radio traffic was collated. A Luftwaffe colonel directed the anti-submarine aerial activities from the bridge of the *Wilhelm Bauer*.

'But if the colonel is on the bridge, surely he can find out where the U-boats are, can't he?' I asked Hein Walter.

'Sobe doesn't tell him, but he pays a telegraphist to slip him a note of the coordinates where a plane can find a U-boat.'

'But that's not fair.'

'It's only an exercise, Hirschfeld. They haven't got enough fuel to fly around all day looking for U-boats. And if you're not buzzed by them here, you won't have a clue when you get to the Front.' My companion handed me a thick block of message pads. 'Sixty percent of the signals are reprimands for the Commander,' he said, 'but the training is not only for them. Even the radio crews can flunk it.'

On 3 March, 1941, the squadron of training U-boats dieseled out into the Bay of Danzig and formed up in line. A torpedo boat approached and the submarines dived to 100 feet.

In *U-109* the loudspeakers clicked on and Fischer announced that a demonstration would now be made of a depth-charge attack.

The torpedo boat sailed on a parallel course about one hundred yards distant and dropped two charges to sixty feet. A giant's fist suddenly shook the boat, violent hammer blows slammed against the hull and a horrendous thunder growled through the depth. It sounded like the dissolution of the universe. I looked along the central corridor and saw the appalled expressions on the faces of the Captain's runners. Never once from all the descriptions of it had they ever conceived such a noise. It drilled into the very marrow of the bones.

Walter Gross stood near the hydrophones room. 'Yes, Wolfgang, just imagine that noise, hour after hour, sawing away at your nerves. When I was with Weingärtner in *U-14* off Norway last year . . .' He intended to describe it, but evidently he found the memory too fresh.

The squadron spent the next fortnight at sea. For the telegraphists there was no rest. A flood of signals pattered down on us incessantly. Each one had to be taken down, decoded, entered into the signals log and placed before the commander. Then his response had to be written down, encoded and the message morsed out. Meanwhile radio direction bearing had to be taken at set intervals on the homing signal of the contact boat and the information passed to the coxswain at the chart table in the control room.

When the Luftwaffe was spotted we had to dive. Whereas this gave us a welcome respite, eventually we had to catch up on the signals we had missed by tuning to the programme of signal repeats continually broadcast on the long wave frequency.

The telegraphists hated it most when the boat was the contact keeper at the convoy, because that required the combined endeavours of both radio watches.

Towards the end of the second week the weather improved and the sun broke through. One morning, when the convoy was many miles away, Lt Keller had the bridge watch. I was quietly basking in the warmth with a fat cigar for company when a shout interrupted my reverie; the after lookout had seen an aircraft coming towards us out of the sun. It was far too late to dive. The four lookouts ducked for cover behind the bridge mantle and I pressed myself against the periscope housing, crouching. The motors of the floatplane screamed as the aircraft pulled out of its plunge and flew down the centre-line of the boat, depositing two sonar buoys either side of the conning tower with a gentle splash.

The huge voice of the bosun, Maureschat, yelled up at them from the interior of the boat, 'You useless bums! Can't you keep a better lookout than that? If that had been the real thing, we'd all be dead now!'

The Captain, who had been sleeping in his tiny compartment, sprinted up the ladder to the bridge. 'What was that, Keller?' The Second Lieutenant gave him an embarrassed smile. 'An Arado 196, sir.' Fischer glared at him. 'It came directly out of the sun, sir,' Keller explained.

Fischer stared wrathfully out to sea, where the aircraft was no more than a mere point on the horizon. 'So, an Arado. Then we've been bombed. If Sobe hears about it, it's curtains for us.'

I sat in the radio room waiting for the signal and, after a few minutes had elapsed, *Wilhelm Bauer* asked us to report our position. As soon as we had complied, Sobe signalled:

To *U-109*. Fischer, you were bombed and sunk at 0932.

When I went to the bridge to commiserate with Lt Keller, he pointed to the retractable wireless aerial, which had been bent forward by a float of the aircraft. 'That really *was* a mad dog,' Keller remarked, 'he could easily have sunk himself coming in that low.'

I went below and reported the damage to the Captain, adding for good measure how the Luftwaffe colonel on the *Wilhelm Bauer* corruptly directed his aircraft. Fischer gave me a pained smile. 'I thought as much. But there's nothing we can do about it. He wiped us out fair and square.'

Nevertheless, the exercises continued without remission, continually extending us to the very limit of endurance, and gradually we began to appreciate what a convoy battle was like. It was worst of all for the Commander, who rarely slept, and who was faced with the decision, on every occasion when the situation changed, either to remain on the attack or turn away. At the Front, the lives of all of us would depend on such a decision.

The exercises finished on 16 March, 1941, and the Captain attended the conference for commanders aboard the *Wilhelm Bauer*. When he returned he tossed his cap towards his bunk, cursed and glared around him with an angry frown. 'Petty Officer, get me a double whisky,' he said.

I turned to go, but Lt Keller had anticipated the Captain's order and had taken the bottle and some glasses from the drinks cabinet. Then the two watchkeeping officers stood at the entrance to the Captain's tiny cabin.

'Yes, gentlemen,' Fischer said calmly, taking the bottle and glasses from Keller's hands, 'we've failed. We've got to do it all again.'

'What, the whole thing?' asked Schwartzkopff.

'But surely they would want us at the Front as soon as possible?' protested Keller.

'The tactical exercises all over again,' Fischer growled. 'Apparently we're not yet fit enough to be allowed to go to the Front. Cheers!' He downed a glassful of liquor in one gulp while his officers stared dejectedly at the floor plating. The coxswain had quietly joined the mournful little group and the Captain said to him, 'Well, Petersen, and what have you got to say about it?'

'Ah, Captain,' he replied with his disarming smile, 'we shouldn't be too upset about it. I'm sure that the war will last a few more months yet.'

Fischer laughed. 'You're right, Petersen. I bet Kretschmer and Prien will leave a few steamers over for us, won't they?' He poured himself another drink, took a second glass and filled that too. Then with a glass in each hand, he crossed to the radio room. 'Well, the radio crew did us proud, I hear, Hirschfeld.'

'Yes, sir, we got a "Very Good".'

Fischer nodded, handed me a whisky and said, 'Bottoms up!' The glasses were quickly drained. 'The crew of *U-109* all passed as competent; everyone, that is, except the commander . . .' His voice trailed away and he shook his head sadly.

U-109 went through the tactical exercises once again. This time our examiner was Captain Hans-Gerrit Stockhausen, who as commander of *U-65* had won the Knight's Cross whereas Sobe had never seen a torpedo fired in anger. Stockhausen actually spent the entire course aboard *U-109*. Fischer had also known him in his sea-cadet days and the two men were on the friendliest terms. On 2 April Lt Cdr Fischer was informed that he had qualified.

On my next visit to the *Wilhelm Bauer* I found out that three leading U-boat aces, Kretschmer, Prien and Schepke, had all been sunk. At a stroke the U-boat Arm had been deprived of its heroes. Whether the British had developed a deadly new counter-measure to the U-boat was not known, but the losses were so secret that even the majority of U-boat officers had not heard about them. When I returned to the boat, the Captain called to me from his cabin. 'Well, Hirschfeld, all OK?'

'Yes, sir, we're ready. Or shall we do the tactical exercises once more for luck?'

Fischer looked at me with curiosity. 'Why, do you want to?'

'Perhaps. In the Atlantic, it seems that the devil's loose.'

Fischer stood up and came to the radio room. 'So, you've heard? You telegraphists get to know everything, don't you? But you mustn't speak of it. Mum's the word, right?'

The boat left Gdynia for Stettin the following day. There was a stiff breeze and the sea foamed across the forecasing. When the lookouts pulled their collars up, I went below into the snug interior of the boat. The heating system was full on and an aroma of fresh coffee wafted down from the galley. The crew was in good spirits, for we had a leave to look forward to before the first Atlantic patrol. I sidled up to the cook for a private word.

'Järschel, we've got to hand in all the unused food supplies when we get to Stettin. Is there going to be much?' The cook grinned.

'There's going to be nothing over. The boys are going to take the whole lot off in a handcart. All except the grapefruit: nobody will touch it.'

'Well, don't make it so obvious that someone notices.'

'No, I won't. Everything has been divided out fairly. I've put yours in your locker. All except the coffee. I'm not sharing that out until tomorrow.'

'Right, I've heard and seen nothing.'

I was returning to the radio room when the Captain's runner called me to the foot of the tower ladder and Fischer, who was on the bridge, asked whether I would be able to hear anything in the hydrophones. I shook my head and said that the noise of the diesels and the crash of the waves against the hull would make it impossible. Fischer came below and said, 'Right, we'll dive. Alarm!'

The bells shrilled and Otto Peters, the Control Room Petty Officer, who had been quietly sipping a cup of coffee in the NCO's room, came to the command centre cursing and complaining that the training was over and you still couldn't get a quiet moment to yourself.

The lookouts came tumbling down from the bridge and the boatswain and an ordinary seaman sat at the depth rudder controls while Lt Keller operated the dive valves. Even before Lt Keller had wound the tower hatch wheel tight, the vents had banged open and the bows cut deeply under. At least that's one thing we've learned to do well, I thought.

The hiss of the sea along the outer skin of the submarine ceased; a few waves slapped against the tower, and then it was quiet. 'One,' said the Chief through the loudspeakers. It was the order to open the last vent at the stern.

I sat at the hydrophones and made a sweep. The audibility was excellent: straight away I picked out the propeller noises from a couple of steamers and trawlers and one very big ship. I consulted with Bischoff.

'Listen, she's got at least three screws. I've never heard anything like that before, have you?'

The Commander poked his head through the control room doorway. 'Well, what have you got for me?'

'Apart from some steamers and fishing vessels, there's a very fat tub at 70°. Several propellors. I would guess at a battleship, sir.'

The Commander put his hand out for the headphones and listened in with interest. 'Take a note of that noise. It *is* a battleship. That is the *Bismarck*.' Returning the instrument, he added, 'I'm very keen on battleships.'

On reaching the Oderwerke at Stettin for fitting out, we learned that the lay-up would last about a month. During this period Fischer was promoted to the rank of full Commander and a 10.5cm deck-gun was fitted on the forecasing. Boatswain Maureschat was appointed gunnery petty officer.

When I returned from furlough Bischoff was no longer on the muster. One evening he had fallen down an open hatch on deck. Exactly what he had broken nobody could say, only that he was in the hospital at Kiel and that a permanent replacement had been requested.

The coxswain approached me with a worried expression. 'Let me explain something to you, shipmate,' he said gravely. 'When someone drops out just before an important voyage, that frequently means something. Either we're going to get drowned and Bischoff survives, or we will come through and Bischoff will be sent on a boat that gets sunk.'

'But Coxswain, surely that is pure superstition,' I replied. 'I believe that we will certainly be coming back.'

Petersen stared at the disbeliever with his guileless blue eyes. 'Yes, yes, you youngsters all think like that. But if you live long enough, when you look back, you will see that more often than not it works out as I have said.'

My replacement Number Two, Ferdinand Hagen, had previously been with the heavy cruiser *Admiral Hipper* and was not a small-boat man, but soon adapted. On 2 May, 1941, we set out for Kiel to take on provisions and fuel for the Atlantic patrol. On completion, we would put into Lorient on the Biscay coast, attached to the 2nd Flotilla.

Fischer was given orders to sail on 6 May. It was sunny and cloudless. That morning a rating was taken to hospital with appendicitis. Bruno Petersen tapped me on the shoulder with a meaningful stare.

'Coxswain, you mustn't take everything as a premonition,' I told him with a laugh.

Shortly before the midday meal the Commander returned on board bringing with him an ordinary seaman from the Flotilla Reserve. 'He just begged me to let him sail with us,' Fischer said, 'so I brought him along.'

After the new man had been kitted out in a set of new grey U-boat leathers he was served a meal, which he ate like a horse. The coxswain shook his head as he watched the new arrival. 'Here's another volunteer for death,' he said, 'Can you understand it, Hirschfeld?'

'No, I can't, but I do know he's absolutely mad about U-boats,' I told him.

At 1330 hrs we paraded on the broad afterdeck of the submarine. From the conning tower a boatswain's whistle piped 'All lines cast off'. The electric motors hummed and music swelled up from the military band on the quayside: '*Wir fahren gegen England.*' The long steel body of the boat, newly painted in a green-and-black-striped camouflage dazzle similar to a mackerel, parted from the Tirpitz Mole, and then the exhaust nozzles snarled as the diesels cut in, pushing the boat out of the U-boat basin at half speed ahead. Rounding the Mole, we waved to onlookers lining the decks of the former liners *St Louis* and *Weichsel*, and along the Hindenburg Promenade.

As we approached the Holtenau Lock I ran my eye over the numerous neutral steamers lying at anchor in the Kieler Förde, head to wind at straining cables, mostly Swedes, Danes, Russians and Finns.

For a time we made a fast passage westwards through the Kiel Canal. The pilot stood beside the Commander on the bridge, slurping coffee, and I was perched on the circular railing surrounding the Winter-Garden (the anti-aircraft platform abaft the bridge) and studied the pilot, who was regularly casting concerned glances at the high surf washing over the embankment in the wake of the boat.

Suddenly the pilot put down his cup and said to Fischer, 'What speed are we doing, Captain?'

The Commander took out his cigar and said with a grin, 'It can't be more than eight knots, surely?' Naturally, he had noticed much earlier the gradual increase in the engine revolutions, which was aimed at getting the boat into Brunsbüttel as early as possible for a last night ashore, but he couldn't pull the wool over the eyes of the shrewd old pilot. 'Your speed is too high, Captain. Decrease your revolutions by ten per minute, if you please.' With a sigh of resignation, the Captain obeyed.

At Rendsburg young ladies attending the Colonial School would often present themselves at the French windows for observation through binoculars whenever a passing naval vessel gave a blast of the siren, but on this occasion *U-109* was out of luck. It was a bad omen.

We tied up close to the Brunsbüttel Lock at 2030 hrs that evening and were informed that as no North Sea escort could be arranged until the next day we should make the best of the opportunity to spend a last night ashore before the first Atlantic war voyage began. Upon receipt of this advice the Captain invited the whole crew, with the exception of a small shipboard watch, to accompany him to a bar-cum-eating house close by the main lock, which was a traditional last port of call for U-boat crews before sailing for distant parts.

I had been given a few signals to despatch to Flotilla announcing the safe arrival of the boat at Brunsbüttel and this delayed me for about half an hour. When I eventually joined the party I found the beer flowing freely and the tavern keeper, who was proudly sporting a Party badge, perched on a large barrel and exhorting his guests to perform great deeds at sea for the Führer.

Next he produced a thick guest book in which we were supposed to inscribe something suitable. I knew these books from Flotilla days. One of the crew drew a caricature, then wrote the boat's number in large numerals on one page. The boat's crew would then autograph the facing page. The owners of these books were aware of the future historical value they might have, on which naturally there would be a good price.

Fischer gave me the tome and told me to do a caricature as I had done several times previously during the tactical training. I flicked through the pages. They were all there, the names of the greats: Hartmann, Prien, Schepke, Bleichrodt, Lemp, Suhren and many others. Five days previously, the last entry: *U-111*, Kleinschmidt.

In large letters I printed on the next clean page *U-109*. This is an enormous breach of security, I thought. Then I saw the leering grin of the tavern keeper in the shadows and the will to draw deserted me.

'What, no picture?' said Fischer.

'No, I haven't got a fresh idea.'

'It's rubbish anyway,' Fischer said beerily, and raised his glass.

When the boozing was at its height, there was an air raid alarm. The bombers had approached from the sea undetected and were almost overhead. The night sky was raked by the probing beams from the searchlight installations at Hamburg while the anti-aircraft batteries at both Hamburg and Brunsbüttel had engaged the intruders. Led by the Commander, the crew of *U-109* sprinted back to their charge through a hail of metal splinters, and all arrived surprisingly unharmed.

Reclining on his bunk shortly afterwards, Cdr Fischer discussed the events of the evening in the most concerned tones with Lt Schwartzkopff.

'That that innkeeper should have such a guest book,' Schwartzkopff said. 'He could photograph the pages and get it to some British contact.' Fischer nodded. 'Yes, a man is not necessarily a loyal German just because he wears a Party badge. And I didn't think much of the send-off with the brass band playing on the Tirpitz Mole either. From the Hindenburg Promenade anyone could see that a U-boat was on its way to sea. We will have to be very careful in the North Sea. Nearly every boat there is attacked by British aircraft.'

These were laudable sentiments indeed. But, unfortunately for him, it was not in the nature of the Cdr Hans-Georg Fischer to be cautious in such matters, and therein lay the seeds of his downfall.

3

FIRST PATROL: AN EVENTFUL FAILURE

U-*109* steered a northerly course towards the Shetland-Bergen
Narrows. That morning the deeply laden submarine had
wallowed her way through the yellow waters of the Lower
Elbe in fine drizzle and mist and then waited off Cuxhaven for the
escort vessel. Eventually a squat, grey-painted merchant ship
appeared, bristling with flak guns, and Fischer was peremptorily
ordered to follow.

Towards evening a stiff north-westerly breeze set in, sending low
inky cloud scudding across the darkening sky, and the first white
curling crests came foaming along the forecasing to thump against
the tower. The exhaust ports of the diesels gurgled and gasped
whenever a sea washed over them. When it was dark the escort
blinked a message of good luck from her wheelhouse and turned
back for the German coast.

Within the belly of the submarine it was warm and soft music
played through the loudspeakers. Boxes and crates of provisions
were tucked away in every free corner, and bunches of bananas and
long lengths of German sausage swung from the overhead piping. It
was homely below and the war seemed very far away.

U-boats proceeding through the North Sea between the German
coast and the latitude of Stavanger in Norway were required by
standing orders to travel submerged by day because of the danger of
air attack.

Commander Fischer's first serious error of judgement was to
disregard this instruction. On the first two days of the outward
passage it was relatively safe because the conditions were fully
overcast and extremely windy, but on the third morning the wind
weakened and the cloud cover began to disperse. I liked to spend
time in the company of the four lookouts on the bridge, where I

customarily took my leisure leaning against the periscope housing, quietly smoking a pipe, and early that afternoon, when the coxswain had the watch, I decided to take the air.

As soon as I was comfortably settled, Petersen said to me, without ever for an instant lowering his binoculars, 'This Skagerrak is damned dangerous. Last year we got a terrible pasting here in *U-14*. It will be a miracle if the British simply let us sail through in this sort of weather.'

I went below to answer a call of nature and so I was not on the bridge when the expected attack arrived at about 1430 hrs. A British bomber on patrol had spotted the U-boat through a partition in the clouds and, swooping low across the ruffled water, dropped a bomb into the boiling patch of ocean where *U-109* had submerged seconds before.

Three factors contributed to our salvation. The aft lookout, boatswain Walter Gross, had seen the plane as soon as it began its descent through cloud; Lt Weber had got the boat under within 35 seconds and the bomb had exploded dead astern where the structure of the submarine was strongest. Otherwise we would certainly have been sunk.

Ferdinand Hagen said to me, 'That last evening in Brunsüttel was sheer madness. I bet the crew of that aircraft even knew this boat's number.'

After half an hour Fischer gave the order to surface. The coxswain shook his head vigorously and Lt Schwartzkopff immediately protested.

'But we must get on, Number One,' the Commander explained, 'we must get to the Front as quickly as possible.' A number of glances were exchanged between the control room hands at this remark; it seemed that Fischer was risking all our lives in order to get to the Atlantic in seven days instead of nine for no obvious reason, and this sort of zeal usually meant that a commander was on a personal quest for the Knights Cross.[4]

The subject of these suspicions had raised the sky-periscope and quickly spotted the circling bomber. He instructed Lt Weber to hold the boat at periscope depth since he thought the plane was just departing.

'Now that really would surprise me,' Petersen whispered over his charts. There followed a long, pregnant pause after which Cdr Fischer closed the periscope handles and told the Chief Engineer to take the boat down to 180 feet. It was not safe on the surface as he had first imagined.

On the evening of 10 May Fischer reported to U-boat Command

by short signal that *U-109* had passed the latitude of Stavanger and the boat turned towards the Shetland-Faroes Passage. On the bridge I heard Petersen and the third boatswain, Wenzel, discussing the horrors of their earlier voyages on *U-14* and *U-16* in these parts: it sounded like two housewives gossiping across a garden fence and I laughed at the lugubrious tone of the conversation.

The boat was cracking on despite squalls and winds gusting to storm force: when Petersen called down that visibility was now less than a mile, Fischer joined him for a look at the conditions. The rollers were coming on at the slight angle to the bow in a series of steep, white-capped ridges, and *U-109* had begun to lurch and roll her way westwards through them.

Wenzel drew the attention of the Captain and the watchkeeper to a shadow emerging from a squall; it was undoubtedly a trawler on patrol duty and Fischer told the helmsman to steer west-south-west to avoid it. He gave a push on the helm button and the rudder indicator wandered slowly to the required bearing; below, the crew swiftly began the task of stowing all loose gear.

The First Lieutenant inquired from his bunk the reason for the change in the course, and when I told him it was only a fishing boat, he lay back and drew his green curtain.

By afternoon the waves were climbing to a great height under the storm-force winds and had begun to sweep over the conning tower. Suddenly the watch came tumbling down into the control room, the alarm bells rang and the submarine set off for the deep, the incline of the bows being so steep that I had difficulty making my way uphill from the NCO's mess to the hydrophones room.

The loudspeakers announced that a destroyer had been sighted emerging from the murk about two miles on the starboard beam, heading directly for us, while another destroyer was lurking on the horizon off the port bow. *U-109* would proceed at 250 feet, silent routine. Undoubtedly the trawler had seen the boat and reported it.

Cdr Fischer said to me, 'You should have seen them rolling. Probably all their guns manned and couldn't get a shot off.'

'But they could still drop depth charges, sir.'

'No, I don't think so. They can't get up the speed, nor get a good fix on us, the sea's too rough.' Evidently neither of the destroyers had Asdic, otherwise we would have heard the pings.

U-109 crept forward for several hours at four knots until from right abeam the two destroyers had dropped so far astern that the listening microphones of the U-boat could scarcely detect the sound of their propellers.

When Fischer gave the order to surface, the duty lookouts cursed, for it was much nicer submerged. Now they would have to stand on the bridge in freezing water, harnessed to a hasp on the inside of the bridge coaming, and duck down for cover whenever a comber crested above the conning tower, which was often. But we had beaten the British blockade and the broad Atlantic now lay outstretched before us.

When Hümpel took down the signal repeat programme, I saw that Fritz-Julius Lemp in *U-110* had failed to report his position despite several requests to do so. When Lt Schwartzkopff saw the signal log he shook his head and said, 'Yes, this Lemp, he's a goner. Just like the other aces. Their success made them careless.'[5]

On the afternoon of 12 May the storm died away and the sun shone down on romping green waves with white crests to the limits of visibility. 300 miles to the south west, Wohlfahrt in *U-556* had reported a convoy. While Fischer was tossing up whether he ought to make for it, the BdU[6] ordered him to proceed to a point off Greenland and await further instructions.

Although Fischer did not make his disappointment known, it must have been a rather bitter pill to swallow to find that nothing had been achieved by his fast and unorthodox passage through the North Sea a few days earlier.

For the next three days we continued westward on a bearing towards Greenland. The pace was leisurely, the skies clear and the boat rolled heavily in the north-westerly swell. At dusk on 15 May we made a torpedo run against an unlit merchant vessel and Fischer was ready to loose off a salvo of two when the freighter set her navigation lights and illuminated the Finnish flag on her hull. She was the *Hogland* of Helsinki; another five seconds would have been too late.

The following day the wind eased and thick banks of fog began to gather. By noon neither end of the boat could be made out from the conning tower. U-boat Command ordered Fischer to report the weather.

A weather balloon about six feet in diameter was inflated on the Winter-garden under the supervision of the civilian meteorologist Dr Schröder. A delicate array of thermometers was attached to a miniature radio transmitter and secured to the balloon, which was then released.

It rose slowly and, once it had cleared the fog, emerged into the sunshine. It looked like a large yellow moon. The lookouts perused its ascent through their binoculars.

'Damn it, you can see that for miles,' Fischer groaned.

The boat had been stationary during this exercise. While it was going on, an empty American milk can bobbled past and Walter Gross fished it up with a net. The can had been punctured to make it sink and had not been in the sea long.

We submerged for a hydrophone sweep and I reported at once that I could hear a battle group, probably consisting of two battleships and three destroyers, on a bearing to the east. They weren't German and, as the commander suspected that they might be an enemy group, he brought *U-109* back to the surface.

The diesels sprang to life and the boat leapt forward powerfully.

I saw the coxswain standing at the door to the hydrophones room shaking his head. 'Honestly, Hirschfeld, this is sheer madness. Full ahead through the fog.'

The boat careered blindly into the impenetrable mist at 18 knots. A full hour passed with the crew in a high state of tension, fearing a fatal collision at any moment. Then the boat was stopped, submerged, and Fischer asked me for the new hydrophone bearing. I reported that the battle group was now broadly astern.

'Good, we passed right through them,' Fischer exclaimed. 'Surface!'

The bridge watch scrambled up the conning tower ladder closely followed by the Commander. The diesels started up and at slow speed we turned about and headed towards the foe. Below, the hands were at battle stations and the caps to all four forward torpedo tubes had been opened. We cruised through the dripping mist for a few minutes and then the fog cleared a little, giving Lt Keller a misty view of the battle masts of a large naval unit dead ahead.

Emergency orders were bellowed out and the boat heeled violently as the diesels were thrown to full ahead and the helm was put to port, bringing her broadside to the swell, the exhaust outlets spluttering as the sea swept across them. The Captain yelled down for even more revolutions and the diesels began to hammer furiously, plunging the bows deeply into each wave; then the alarm bells rang and the watch came tumbling down to land in a heap on the control room grating. Fischer slammed the tower hatch lid shut as the submarine went down at a steep angle. Through the loudspeakers the calm voice of the boatswain, Maureschat, ordered the bow caps closed and stated the trim depth as 180 feet.

I asked him what was going on and he said that as far as he knew we had been spotted.

Lt Keller joined me in the hydrophones room. 'They're Americans,' he whispered. 'The mist got patchy suddenly and I saw their typical bar-masts. We turned away at once, but one of the destroyer escort made towards us.'

'Bearing?' asked the Captain from the control room.

'Destroyer at 190°,' I called back, and then continued in a low voice to the Lieutenant, 'If they're Americans, they can't touch us.'

Keller cast me a pitying look. 'You're soon going to find out.'

U-109 was turning to port while the destroyer was approaching fast overhead from astern, her propellers thrashing at a tremendous rate.

'Full ahead.'

'Take the hydrophones off,' Keller told me, 'we can all hear him now.' The men in the control room were all staring at the deckhead as though there was something to be seen there. A few seconds after the escort vessel had cleared us there was a somewhat muted explosion in the sea some distance abeam and the shock wave rolled the submarine once or twice.

'Are you sure these are Americans?' I asked Keller.

'Certainly. I got a glimpse of the battleship myself for a moment. An old type, *Arizona* or *New York*, but definitely not British.'

I reported that the destroyer was making off to starboard, the noise of its propellers gradually diminishing. The remainder of the battle group was loitering nearby. Our control centres reported no damage.

Fischer appeared from the control room and sat on his bunk. 'There you are, Keller, that's neutrality for you.'

'Perhaps we should have had a pot at the battleship, sir.'

'No, no, Keller, remember your *Führerbefehl*. We must avoid incidents with American naval units at all costs, no matter what the provocation.' He drummed his fingers on the surface of his writing table in agitation. 'The question is, why are they here, right on the edge of the declared blockade zone of Great Britain?'

He thought about this for some considerable time before explaining to Keller:

'I think that either they are waiting here to escort a convoy, or they are inviting us to take a pot at one of their warships. In the latter case they would have their excuse to come into the war against us.'

When *U-109* came up to periscope depth a few hours later to take down the signal repeats on the long wave, it was noted that Kentrat in *U-74* had earlier reported two *New York* class battleships and three *Dunlop* class destroyers from an adjacent position.[7]

On 17 May, 1941, *U-109* was drifting 600 miles off Labrador in a glassy sea with visibility to the farthest horizon. The BdU was preparing a scouting line several hundred miles in length but as all U-boats were not yet in position Fischer had to be patient.

The radio direction finder aerial, a large metal loop which was retained in a slot within the bridge coaming when not in use and was raised and lowered hydraulically, had jammed. It was an essential instrument for convoy location work. Schewe, the senior engine room artificer, said that the problem lay in the upper stuffing box and he cut a hole in the bridge coaming with the oxyacetylene burner in order to gain access to it. He now unscrewed the retaining cheeks and the aerial extended. Next he placed a greased leather cuff around the tube and, holding the retaining cheeks apart with his fingers, told me to go to the control room and slowly lower the aerial. I refused because I knew that there was a tendency for the air pressure to escape during the operation which usually resulted in the heavy aerial suddenly dropping without warning. This could result in the loss of fingers or a hand.

The red-headed Schewe told me that if I wouldn't do it, then he would get the most junior engine room hand to assist him. He could look after his own fingers, thank you very much. I went below and instructed little Wüsteney in what he had to do. The control room petty officer, Otto Peters, turned away shaking his head. I asked Wüsteney if he understood and the freckle-faced youth scratched his head in embarrassment and went to the direction finder. I emphasized that he would have to keep his attention riveted on the air pressure gauge; if the air pressure suddenly fell, he was to inject a fresh cushion of air immediately.

I went to the radio room and listened to the hiss of escaping air with disquiet. Suddenly there was a dull thud as the direction finder dropped down. I sprang to the control room doorway. Wüsteney was a shade paler then before and was staring at the direction finder with large, frightened eyes. For a few moments it was all quiet above and I was just about to remark that Schewe seemed to have got away with it when I heard Lt Schwartzkopff, who was the bridge watchkeeper, begin to curse so loudly that every word could be distinctly heard in the control room.

'Oh shit! Schewe, what have you done to yourself? Go below at once!' The bridge manhole darkened and a figure made its way slowly down the ladder. Schewe stood in front of me and, with an embarrassed smile, showed me his hands. He had lost half the thumb and three finger tips of his right hand, and had crushed the tips of the fingers of his left.

'What did I tell you?' I said. Together we went to the dispensary beside the Captain's compartment. Because I had passed a short medical and first-aid course, I was the ship's doctor. I sent for the coxswain's mate, Hein Jürgensen, for advice: Jürgensen had a master's ticket in steam and as a ship's captain was well versed in the treatment of injuries. The stump of the thumb wasn't bleeding and Jürgensen explained to me that the veins had sealed themselves off; I should just smear some cod liver ointment over the wounds and bandage them.

The tube of lanolin was similar to the cod liver ointment and I spread the wrong salve over all the injuries of the right hand before I noticed my error and had to scrape it all off again with a wooden spatula. Schewe wanted to strangle me, but couldn't do so because of the state of his fingers. Jürgensen calmed the engineer with a story.

'Did you know that I was once master of a ship which sank because of a boiler explosion? The stokers came up out of the engine room like monkeys. Someone was screaming for help down below and I grabbed the Chief Engineer and told him to come down with me to help whoever it was. The cowardly dog refused: it was only a black, he said. So I went down myself. The poor sod was trapped by his foot under an iron girder which I couldn't lift. The ship was sinking and the boiling water rising swiftly. There were only seconds remaining. I took a heavy iron coal shovel and with a blow hacked his foot off, put him over my shoulder and carried him up. He's alive to this day!'

'Shut your trap,' said Schewe, 'I feel ill.' Hein Jürgensen laughed. 'I just wanted you to know that there are far worse cases at sea than your fingers.'

*   *   *

Late the following day the BdU finally managed to assemble around Newfoundland a reconnaissance line approximately 200 miles in length and consisting of eight boats including *U-109*. This wolf pack was collectively known as the '*Westboote*.'

Bruno Petersen would have said in retrospect that there was a certain grim predestination about the chain of events which now unfolded over the course of the next eight days. It began with two apparently unrelated occurrences on 19 May, 1941.

The great battleship *Bismarck* sailed from Gdynia in Poland for Norway on the first stage of her intended commerce raiding cruise in the Atlantic, and off Newfoundland Kuppisch in *U-94* sighted a convoy in grid square AJ 6636 heading north at 8 knots and consisting of fifteen merchant ships and one armed merchant cruiser as escort.

To Fischer it was quite clear that he should join Kuppisch for the attack and the coxswain was given a course to steer to the northwest. The boat trembled as the engines surged to full speed ahead. I grinned at Otto Peters as I saw all the heads appear over the sides of the bunks.

Peters asked me what was up. 'Kuppisch has reported a convoy, Otto, and we're going for it.'

'Oh shit.'

'There's only an armed merchant cruiser escorting it, no destroyers.'

Peters looked sceptical. 'Well, don't be surprised if some turn up.'

Once he had gone, Maureschat asked for the estimated time of arrival at the convoy. 'It will probably be tomorrow evening, if we can keep this speed up,' I told him.

'These bloody useless diesels,' he muttered. He had previously been on E-boats in the English Channel, where things happened much faster than this.

Cape Farewell is the most southerly tip of Greenland. Even in the early summer it is a dreary waste of water, continually lashed by long-drawn-out Atlantic gales, often heavily overcast and swept by icy blasts of wind and rain whenever the weather has anything northerly about it.

The eastbound convoy HX126 was shadowed by Kuppisch for the whole morning of 20 May. The BdU had confirmed him as the contact boat, which meant that every thirty minutes he had to transmit a long homing signal and every hour broadcast the speed, course and position of the convoy. When the visibility was reduced by mist and hail to one mile, he was told to begin the battle by himself.

Shortly after, Wohlfahrt in U-556 signalled that he was close to Kuppisch and at about midday Kentrat in U-74 and Korth in U-93 both informed U-boat Command that they were about to attack. When he read this signals traffic in the log Fischer fell back on his bed with a groan of despair. We were still a hundred miles short of Kuppisch. 'Oh God, they're simply going to massacre the convoy,' Fischer wailed to me. 'What will there be left for us?'

At about 1800 hrs that evening, during a break in the hail, the bridge watch spotted smoke trails from a number of ships close to Cape Farewell. Fischer said he expected the convoy to be in the process of scattering and this opinion seemed to be confirmed when an independent steamer was briefly exposed to our view several miles dead ahead during her passage between squalls. Once the officers had calculated the steamer's true course and speed Fischer turned the boat to the east. Tactically, the attack had to be made from a point forward of the target's bow and this often required a circular manoeuvre which could take time.

U-109 had been stalking her prey for no more than a matter of minutes, however, when there was some alarmed shouting on the bridge, the bells rang and the lookouts arrived in a sprawl of bodies at the foot of the conning tower ladder. Even before the hatch lid had been properly secured, the vents were open and the boat cut under at a steep incline, the Chief eventually achieving trim at 200 feet.

Through the hydrophones I could hear a destroyer's swirling propellers growing ever louder on the starboard bow. The noise became audible with the naked ear and then the escort vessel passed overhead, dropped her group of depth charges with a splash and then made off at full speed to avoid being blown up from underneath by her own explosive. Depth charges sink at fourteen feet per second: we counted ten seconds before the sea erupted nearby and the hull of the boat reverberated as the shock waves of the thunder-claps shook the hull and growled off menacingly through the depths. These were the real thing, quite different from the dummies which the Americans had dropped to aggravate us a few days previously.

The destroyer's screws thrashed away to port.

'Where is he?' asked the Captain.

'Port bow, sir, and apparently continuing with his voyage.'

Fischer nodded. 'The swine came out of a squall. If he had been a bit smarter, he could have got a couple of rounds off at us.' The British vessel appeared to have other business to attend to and had departed smartly without troubling us further. Within half an hour I was able to report to the Captain that the escort vessel was no longer in the vicinity.

'How far away is he?'

'I can't tell you that, sir. In these parts there are no water layers to distort the transmission of sound, so we should be able to hear him even when he's below the horizon.'

'Can you still get a fix on the steamer?'

'310° and weak, sir.'

'Good,' said the Captain, 'we'll surface and get after him.'

On the destroyer's last bearing there was a large black rain cloud, but of the warship itself no sign. *U-109* now hared off after the steamer, her bows cutting through white-capped ridges of ocean, the spray from the crests whipping raw the faces of the forward lookouts. Towards dusk Fischer was rewarded when we began to catch glimpses of the quarry through driving rain.

By 2230 hrs the boat was positioned ahead of the freighter and Fischer took us down to prepare for an attack in sixty minutes. I grabbed a roll of bread and large German sausage and went to the forward torpedo room to watch the missiles being placed ready for the reload. The torpedo handlers were packed like sardines into the torpedo room, which also served as their quarters, and every torpedo loosed off gave them that much more square feet of living accommodation. Therefore they looked forward to the attack for a motive unconnected with the Tonnage War. On my return to the hydrophones room Ferdinand Hagen handed me the headset: the steamer was approaching at a steady nine knots, blithely unaware of the killer lurking off her bow.

When the merchantman was within two miles, Fischer shot off two torpedoes at her. The stop watches were set in motion and those without them counted the seconds softly to themselves. After three minutes there were two explosions in quick succession.

'Hit amidships. Hit astern,' said the Captain and retracted the periscope.

The steamer's screws continued to turn for a minute or two and then petered out. There was a massive explosion followed by a series of spluttering detonations rather like machine-gun fire, from which we assumed that her cargo had probably been munitions. There wouldn't be any survivors after an explosion like that, we said. Then came a groaning, grinding sound as the ship went down. Engineer Warrant Officer Alfred Winter, who had made a large number of U-boat voyages, remarked to me, 'Listen to that sound, that's the sound of a ship dying. The noise is the water pressure bursting the bulkheads.'

'Reload torpedoes,' Maureschat said unemotionally through the loudspeakers.

U-109 turned away from the scene of the sinking[8] towards where the sound of underwater explosions in the distance indicated that other U-boats were still busy mauling the remnants of the convoy. Either that or the destroyers were mauling the U-boats: it was difficult to say which.

After midnight we surfaced. The wind had risen and the boat rolled heavily in the long, confused swell. The lookouts and the commander pulled up the collars of their oilskin coats, pulled down their sou-westers and peered into the blackness through Zeiss binoculars. Fischer knew that the convoy was very near, because I had reported that, whenever the homing boat transmitted, I had to turn down the volume of the receiver, it was so loud.

'Destroyer, sir, collision course ahead,' said Lt Keller.

'Yes, I see him,' murmured the Captain, 'we'll turn off a bit, he can't see us.'

The helmsman put the rudder ten degrees to starboard so as to bring the submarine clear of the destroyer's stern.

'Another destroyer, sir, parallel course, starboard,' said the boat-swain. The Captain swore quietly. 'Where the hell are they all coming from?' he said. The second destroyer was less than a mile away.

'First destroyer turning towards us!' warned Lt Keller. The Commander spun round and stared; we all knew the choice that now confronted him. Should he dive or run for it on the surface? He had only seconds to decide which.

'First destroyer coming straight for us!' screamed Keller.

For long seconds Fischer held the foaming bow-wave in his Zeiss, frozen in indecision. Already the destroyer was too close for an attempted escape on the surface. 'All below,' Fischer said and, passing the helmsman in the tower, added, 'Sound the alarm.'

We crash-dived to 120 feet. On my first hydrophone sweep I detected a third destroyer coming up fast on the port side, while the first two were now just drifting. The Captain stood by the doorway shaking his head in disbelief. I gave him the parallel headphones and, when Fischer had put them on, circled the indicator round the scale.

'That's them, sir. Do you hear their auxiliary machinery? The transmission of sound in these waters is damned good.' I made another sweep. 'Now all three have stopped in the water, listening out for us, sir.'

In the submarine it was deathly quiet. The only audible noise was the soft whirr of our own propellers rotating at 90 revolutions to maintain the trim. 'Fourth destroyer approaching from 300°.' The Commander whipped off the headphones with a gesture of annoyance and crossed the narrow corridor to his compartment, where he sat on the end of his bed, elbows on his chart table, his head cradled in his hands.

'Fifth destroyer approaching from 90°.'

Suddenly the Captain sprang up in a rage. 'This is all rubbish you're feeding me, Petty Officer. These are echoes you're hearing. Do you mean to tell me there are five destroyers up there, all hanging around concentrating on us while seven other German U-boats are tearing their convoy apart?'

I was stung by the implied censure. 'The noises are quite definite, sir. I don't think these can be echoes, not with a depth of six thousand feet beneath the keel.'

Fischer threw me a murderous stare and disappeared through the control room doorway. A few minutes later the imperturbable Bruno Petersen, who was the most experienced U-boat man aboard, slipped quietly alongside me.

'Can you imagine it,' he whispered. 'The Captain is thinking about breaking out of the ring by sailing beneath them.'

'What, at 120 feet?'

Petersen nodded. 'He won't go any deeper.'

'But that's madness; if we go beneath them, they'll simply get a fix on us and blow us out of the water.'

'I think so too.'

The fifth destroyer had started to close in very quickly. Petersen was listening through the parallel headphones. 'This one's really shifting,' he hissed. 'He's going to drop!'

I called out a warning that the destroyer was on a course to pass directly overhead. Now Fischer had to make his decision. It was all a matter of simple geometry; he had to put the submarine on an evasion course in the few minutes during the destroyer's run-up at speed when the enemy vessel could not maintain a definite fix on the U-boat. He was now approaching like a steam train. Petersen nudged me and nodded towards the compass-repeater: the boat was turning to port. The crew stared upwards, their eyes large and fearful: the Captain was in the control room, bent over the chart table, apparently unconcerned. I went cold as I remembered that we were still at 120 feet. If the depth charges were set deeper, the explosion would hit the boat from below, at the very least driving us to the surface for a leisurely destruction from the guns of half a dozen destroyers.

The attacker passed overhead. In our fear we ceased to draw breath. The thrashing propellers passed quickly to the other side of the boat, then all hell broke loose. With an unbelievable violence, the depth charges exploded with a sound like the crack of doom and five mighty hammer blows pummelled the pressure hull. The men ducked involuntarily at each blow, the lights flickered and then, as the terrible thunder growled through the depths, the heads slowly came up. It was a miracle that we could have survived such a bombardment unscathed.

As the damage control centres reported that the boat was still watertight, the Commander asked me, 'What's he doing now?'

'He's on a bearing away from us. Because we turned, he's now astern, sir.'

Fischer nodded. 'And the others?' The hydrophone indicator made a revolution.

'They're all still hove-to, sir.'

Fischer grunted as if he did not believe this information. I followed the track of our attacker for a few moments and then said, 'The last one has now stopped as well, sir.'

The Commander turned away without a word and Petersen, who had been listening to this exchange from a discreet distance, rejoined me. 'He doesn't want to believe they're stopped up there in a ring around us,' I whispered to him.

'Just wait till it gets light,' Petersen replied quietly, 'then he's really going to have something to worry about.'

'Navigator report to Commander.' Petersen gave me a meaningful glance and was soon involved in a long discussion with Cdr Fischer across the chart table, after which the Captain ordered the conning tower surfaced. No doubt he had good reason for this course of action, I thought, but if any of the idling destroyers began an attack run now it would be fatal. But the British vessels remained adrift, their presence betrayed only by the low hum of their auxiliary machinery.

The Chief Engineer reported in a low voice that the bridge manhole had come clear and the Commander unwound the securing wheel, opened the lid, and went alone to the bridge. A draught of fresh sea air surged through the interior of the boat while the sea thumped against the tower; the hull wallowed just below the surface.

'Telegraphist to the bridge!' he bawled down.

With mixed feelings, I climbed the ladder and stood beside Cdr Fischer.

The Captain kicked the manhole cover shut and placed a hand on my shoulder.

'See anything?'

I grasped the bridge mantle to steady myself against the wilder lurches and peered in vain into the black belly of the night. 'No, sir.'

'Let your eyes get accustomed to the darkness first.'

After a few moments I glimpsed a greyish outline dead ahead. The Commander passed me the binoculars and I saw that the shadow was a large destroyer with four smoke stacks.

'That's one, and another there, and another there. Five in all. You were quite right. They are around us in a semi-circle.'

I returned the binoculars. 'Now, go below and tell the Chief Engineer to steer through 180° to port and then get us out of here without blowing the tanks. I shall remain up here alone.'

When Lt Weber received these instructions he shook his head.

Sweat stood on his forehead. He went to the foot of the tower and shouted up, 'I can't hold the boat at 90 revolutions, Captain.'

Fischer gave him permission for 250 revolutions and the U-boat began to creep away on her electric motors. It was the greatest hour of trial for the boat since the Captain had taken over his command, an hour of unbearable tension. Forward she crept at a few knots, trickling a small wake behind the partly submerged gun platform, while the seas broke occasionally over the low freeboard of the bridge coaming. Our departure was not noticed by the destroyers, which I found incomprehensible, for it should not have been possible for us to simply slip away from the trap in such excellent waters for hydrophone audibility. After sixty minutes Fischer gave the order to blow tanks and proceed at full speed with the diesels, and came down below.

Throwing his cap into his compartment, he stretched out on his bed with a look of triumph.

'Well, Hirschfeld, we really shit all over them, didn't we?'

I laughed at the incongruity of the remark. 'I can't understand how they managed to let us escape, sir.' But Fischer appeared highly pleased with himself. 'Thing is, Hirschfeld, where did they all come from? And where's the convoy now?'

I passed him the latest position report from Kuppisch in *U-94* and the Captain took it into the control room. On the half-hour, when I took the direction finder bearing on Kuppisch's homing signal, I noted with some apprehension that the line between *U-109* and the convoy passed directly through the position of the five destroyers from which we had so recently escaped.

'Well, unfortunately it can't be avoided,' Fischer remarked when he was shown it, 'but we've just got to get at the convoy tonight.' So saying, he passed the new course to the helm, the diesels bellowed and *U-109* set off to the west at full ahead.

There were now some very sour expressions in the control room. The coxswain's mate, Hein Jürgensen, stood looking at the chart and shaking his head. 'I can't believe we're going straight back to where we've just come from,' he muttered to me bitterly. 'Those British destroyers are going to be absolutely delighted when we show up there again.'

Thirty minutes later I took a revised bearing on Kuppisch and obtained the Captain's permission to come up on the bridge. Fischer curtly accepted the fresh information and turned away.

I tucked myself into a corner between the loop of the direction finder and the third boatswain, who had the starboard bow quadrant. Without looking away from the eyepiece of the Zeiss, Maureschat whispered, 'Have a look at the eastern horizon.' I had already noticed: astern it was dawning, while ahead, where lurked the five waiting destroyers, it was still night, black as pitch.

'Sir, we are silhouetted against the sky to the east,' Lt Keller said. The Commander ignored him and continued to stare ahead through his binoculars.

After a few anxious minutes, Maureschat shouted, 'Shadow ahead, 30°!' Keller and the Captain spun round in dismay.

'Damn, two destroyers,' said Keller.

'Those will be the rear sweepers,' the Captain replied.

All at once the sea was illuminated with a reddish-yellow light; on the port bow a tanker had exploded, flinging up burning oil in a giant plume which, when it collapsed, spread over the sea and burnt fiercely. Next, the destroyers started firing up star shell, looking for surfaced U-boats.

'Flood!' screamed the Captain. The bridge party tumbled below without ceremony and the churning sea closed over the sinking deck casing. Somewhere in the distance a depth charge pattern roared through the depths.

I took my seat at the hydrophones and Lt Keller joined me. I made a quick sweep and located a sharp, harshly metallic propeller noise which sounded extremely close.

'Where did this destroyer come from, Lieutenant?' I asked Keller, pointing to a bearing on the scale.

'We didn't see that one until the tanker blew up,' Keller told me, 'and he would probably have rammed us, which was probably his intention.'

I went hot and cold at this admission. 'Have a little listen, you'll probably find a few more,' Keller added. I steered the pointer round in a circle, briefly pausing five or six times. 'My God, they're coming from all directions,' I gasped.

Keller nodded grimly. 'They saw us coming against the dawn,' he said.

'Whoever torpedoed the tanker saved us; he must have attacked from the west and seen where the destroyers were against the lighter sky.'

Gradually a hush had developed inside the boat. I plotted the hydrophone fixes.

'Well, Petty Officer, what can you hear?' enquired the Captain.

'On the port side, destroyers at 290° and 310°. A tanker with a few revolutions at 350°. Dead ahead a diesel, probably a departing U-boat. To starboard destroyers at 17°, 25°, 40° and another some way off at 75°.

37

Fischer stared at the instrument, but this time he could not doubt the report. 'We've got to sail under the tanker to escape this time,' he said to Keller.

'And what if he sinks on top of us?'

'Well, we don't actually need to pass beneath his keel.'

'That will take a few hours at minimum revolutions. We can't surface, it'll be light soon.'

'Yes, you're right, but we'll keep on this course for the time being.'

'May I suggest we go deeper, sir?'

Fischer laughed. 'What difference does it make, Keller? They drop their depth charges to explode at between 60 to 90 feet and we're at 180 feet. That's deep enough.'

The Captain turned away and lay on his bunk. Keller looked at me with a shake of his head. 'The convoy must have been wiped out,' he whispered, 'otherwise they wouldn't be concentrating all their energies on us.'

Meanwhile, above us, all the destroyers had slunk up appreciably nearer: one after another they moved closer to the submerged U-boat and then stopped. It was the old game. After an hour a tight ring of six destroyers was encircling the boat. The silent routine on *U-109* was first-class; all talk was whispered, the propellers whirred slowly and softly, all tools were placed with the utmost care on work surfaces when not required.

Suddenly a fine chirping began and I felt my scalp rise.

'Asdic, sir,' I called across to the Captain.

'Nothing we can do about it.'

'Asdic impulses!' cried the helmsman in the tower.

The Captain turned the page of the crime novel he was reading. He was addicted to them. After a while, the rate of the pings accelerated: they had obtained an accurate fix on the lie of the boat. The hated propellers began to thrash the water.

'Destroyers at 290° and 310° approaching!' I shouted.

The Captain put his paperback aside. 'Control room, full ahead!' he bellowed from his bunk.

The sound of the pounding propellers filled the boat. The first enemy vessel crossed overhead. The Commander rested his head in his hands. The coxswain was drumming on the chart table in the control room with a pencil. I saw the waxen faces of the meteorologist, Dr Schröder, and Lt Schwartzkopff staring at me from their bunks. Their features were dead, graven in stone.

The inferno broke loose with such devastating violence it seemed that a volcano had erupted around the boat. I wondered how the pressure hull could possibly withstand it. The main lighting slowly

38

failed. The unbelievable din of fifteen great thunderclaps one after the other shook and rolled the submarine, an endless cascade of almost unendurable sound. Then the reverberations growled away and the emergency lighting flickered on.

The damage centres reported in: astern, the starboard propeller shaft, the stuffing boxes and the diesel exhaust caps were letting in water. One of the stern torpedo tubes was flooding through the outer cap. A thin jet of water was hissing into the engine room through the diesel hatch.

'Go to 240 feet, creeping speed,' ordered the Captain. He looked at me questioningly.

'All destroyers stopped, sir. They're searching for us with their Asdic.'

'Those depth charges were dropped well astern of us because of the 8 knots we were doing. We'll maintain this course.'

The minutes dragged by. Nobody spoke; we were all waiting for the next attack. When it came, three of the destroyers were involved, passing overhead in a criss-cross pattern, but the ferocious storms rolled away without inflicting further damage. The escort vessels repositioned and stopped their engines, the fingers of their Asdic beams feeling for the U-boat in the depths. Fischer took the boat to 300 feet and, when the third attack came, the destroyers misjudged the position of the submarine and dropped their cargo of death hopelessly wide. An hour of silence passed. The British vessels were having a problem it seemed, and they did not mount another attack. But time was on their side; provided there was no serious deterioration in the weather, they knew that eventually the submarine would have to surface to recharge the batteries. I noticed that it had become so unusually quiet outside the boat that I could no longer track the enemy by use of the hydrophones. I took out a number of microphones from the starboard boxes and played a hair drier over them to evaporate any moisture in case that should be the cause of the trouble, but it did not appear to improve the reception. Many of the exterior vents were leaking seriously and there was already a lot of water sloshing around in the boat. The Captain had shut down the control tower and the helmsman was steering from the control room.

Lt Weber reported to the Captain. 'We'll have to start pumping, sir. The water in the control room is up to the floor plates.'

'But that can be heard for miles.' The Captain wrestled with the problem for a few seconds before giving his consent, but he had little choice in the matter, for the bilges were full.

Scarcely had he given Weber the nod than the pumps started up: the racket was appalling. It made the stomach contract in fear; never before had we realized how loud the main pump was. The destroyers also heard it and, once the pumps had stopped, they launched a fresh attack.

The blast of the explosions struck the hull with tremendous power and they were certainly better on accuracy than the last group.

I wondered why the British had given up with their Asdic. I knew that the device was very sensitive, and I was hoping that the depth-charging had put the instruments out of commission. For the latest attack the destroyers had obtained their fix from a noise made inside the boat and this gave us some room for optimism.

The air in the boat was very foul and the fug was being circulated from bow to stern by the fans; we all knew the effect that this would be having on us. Järschel had made a strong bean coffee, but despite this I had already begun to experience a lassitude that was impossible to shake off. The Commander was of the opinion that we could remain below for two more days and he had given orders for potash-cartridge breathing sets to be distributed. All off-watch men were confined to bed: all unnecessary lights doused: all duty men were to wear slippers. There was probably enough oxygen in the boat for 48 hours, although this was being held in reserve, but it was doubtful if the batteries could last that long. Once the charge was exhausted, the propellers would no longer revolve and the boat would sink.

More long hours passed. The water level was again rising danger-ously. The Commander lay on his bunk staring at the deckhead. I was slumped almost in stupor at the hydrophones; although wrapped in a sheepskin jacket, I was chilled to the marrow.

The destroyers began a new approach overhead. The men waited for the depth charges, but none came down. The noise of the propellers ebbed away, became softer, then louder, then much softer until the naked ear could no longer detect them. Strange.

After being relieved, I staggered to my bunk and slept the sleep of the dead. When Telegraphist Hümpel shook me awake I was completely disoriented. 'No depth charges for two hours,' he whis-pered. I nodded, took a can of Shoka-Cola and padded off unsteadily to the hydrophones room.

'They're still there,' Ferdinand Hagen informed me, 'they just keep steaming up and down. Perhaps they can't find us. The Captain discharged some *Bold*[9] earlier. That might have irritated them.'

The depth gauge showed that we were still at 300 feet. I thought it odd that the vents were letting in so much water at that depth, but I attributed it to the blast damage. The destroyers dropped some more depth charges and the ocean was pervaded by the waves of rolling thunder, but the explosions were nowhere near the boat.

'Do you notice, Petty Officer? The *Bold* seems to have helped.'

I was sceptical. Our 90 revolutions per minute had brought us no great distance from where the cloud of aluminium strips had been released. The British were sending down no more than six depth charges per hour at most and it seemed much more likely to me that they couldn't track the boat for some reason.

When we had been under siege for sixteen hours Keller relieved the entire radio crew. I slept heavily, perhaps for many hours, and dreamed of death. I knew that we were going to die. We would all just fall asleep. Perhaps Otto Peters had already forgotten the oxygen. He was supposed to have started using it and, if he had forgotten, then we would all fall into the final slumber without realizing it. I wanted to get up to remind him, to check up, but my limbs were so damned tired I couldn't move them.

I heard a whisper. Was someone else still alive then? With a great effort I forced an eye open. Behind the bow-room pressure doorway Leading Machinist Kaufmann was tapping the small depth gauge and shaking his head.

I cast aside my potash breather and stumbled to the doorway.

'What's up, Kaufmann?' The engine room rating looked at me with fearful eyes. 'This depth, Petty Officer, I can't believe it.'

'How deep does it say we are?'

'Over 600 feet.'

Suddenly I was wide awake. 'What?' I shouted.

'More than 600 feet.' My God, no submarine had ever visited such a depth and returned to the surface to tell of it, I thought.

'Kaufmann, call the control room and report it.'

'But we are not allowed to use the telephone,' he whispered. And it was also forbidden to walk through the boat during the emergency. I glanced along the darkened central corridor and saw the message relay party slumped together in a deep slumber on the plating.

'Ring them up! I'll take full responsibility.'

Kaufmann did as he had been instructed. The telephone snarled. Kaufmann reported his finding. They made him repeat it, then he hung up, 'The control room says our depth gauge is wrong. We're still at 300 feet.'

'Well, they should know, they're supposed to be running things,' I said, and went back to my bunk.

The telephone snarled again. Kaufmann answered. 'Yes, over 600 feet. The indicator is in the blank, resting against the stud.'

I got up again. Kaufmann was standing behind the pressure doorway in a state of confusion, the receiver still in his hand. 'They rang the stern room. Their depth gauge is reading the same as this one.' I went cold: the master gauge in the control room was reading false and nobody had noticed.

Suddenly the bow began to rise; evidently the Chief Engineer was attempting to get the boat to rise by using the hydroplanes in combination with the motors. Kaufmann looked around in alarm because it wasn't working; the bow was rising towards the vertical. Already the water from the bow bilge was washing around the rim of the pressure door forward of the control room.

The loudspeakers clicked on. 'Everyone to the bow!' screamed the Chief Engineer. There was panic in his voice. Suddenly a wild scramble forward began. I dived for my bunk as the men came stampeding through the boat from the stern. It made no difference; the bow continued to rise. At an angle of 40° the contents of the bow room began to cascade aft; first the loaves from the hammocks, then the boxes of oranges, the eggs and the cutlery. At 60° the bilge water poured down in a giant brown waterfall.

This is the end, I thought. The boatswain, Maureschat, was standing on the bulkhead, holding himself upright with both hands clasped round the deckhead piping, jovially roaring in his tremendous voice, 'We're going to the bottom, comrades.'

'You shut your filthy mouth!' they screamed back at him.

The civilian meteorologist, Dr Schröder, gripped my arm. 'Think of it, I have five small children at home,' he sobbed. 'I know. I'm so sorry,' I said in as comforting a tone as I could manage in the circumstances.

'Electric motor is on fire!' came a shout from the stern. The bilge water had swamped the anchorage of the equipment; a few seconds later a long-drawn-out grinding and tearing noise began aft; it was the same death rattle that the sinking freighter had made two days earlier.

'Stern room flooding!' the loudspeakers reported.

Yes, I thought, this is logical. The stern, which was much deeper than the bow, would be crushed first by the water pressure. Probably it was already at a depth of something like 900 feet. I hoped that drowning would be a quick death. I heard the rattle of the compressed air in the piping: they were blowing the tanks. A glimmer of hope flickered across the faces of the condemned; all eyes were watching Kaufmann standing at the depth gauge in the bow room. The indicator was still right off the scale and resting against the retaining stud. The air was hissing through the pipes into the dive tanks, but the indicator didn't budge.

'Damn,' shouted Kaufmann, 'the boat's not rising.'

The hissing stopped. 'Why don't you keep blowing the tanks?'

Maureschat shouted down to Keller, who was sitting below him astride the control room doorway.

'They're only blowing the stern tanks because the air's escaping from the forward tanks,' Keller explained.

'Boat's still not rising,' said Kaufmann. The lighting was slowly failing; the main electrical plant had had it. The emergency lighting was still intact, but it was weak, and I thought about how pallid the faces of condemned men become in the final seconds before death. In the bow some of the hands had torches, and the beams of these were all focused on the depth gauge.

The Chief Engineer had abandoned hope. He had confessed to Otto Peters that there was nothing further that could be done to save the boat. Every possibility had been exhausted and he had reconciled himself to death. Upon hearing this, Otto Peters decided to take charge of the blow valve panel himself in a last desperate attempt to save us.

Because air was escaping from the forward dive tanks, Weber had blown all the stern tanks only in the effort to get the boat to rise. When he saw that this was unsuccessful, he had seen no other possibility. Petty Officer Otto Peters reasoned that if all the available compressed air in the stern tanks could be transferred to the forward tanks, which were presently at a depth of at least 150 feet less than the stern tanks, then the air might expand just sufficiently to buoy the boat upwards despite the leak. If that happened, the speed of ascent would swiftly increase as the air in the forward tanks continued to expand under the diminishing atmospheric pressure.

On the other hand, if this did not work, the boat was doomed. Otto Peters juggled with the valves: in the stern they heard the compressed air roar through the piping and, seconds later, five voices cried out in unison, 'Boat's rising!'

'Call out the depth,' Keller yelled, 'the stern's not reporting any more.'

'They're probably drowned in there,' someone said.

'600 feet,' said Kaufmann; '550 feet.' Our hearts beat faster as we realized that we were saved. '450 feet.' It was like being in a fast lift. As the boat went through the 300 feet mark the Captain bawled, 'Flood! Or we'll break through the surface!'

'I can't flood,' the Chief Engineer shouted back, 'there's too much water in the boat already!' *U-109* continued to spear upwards like a rocket, her engine room afire in the stern.

'50 feet!' Suddenly we could hear the roar of the sea as the bows crashed through the surface. The forward half of the submarine stood upright above the waves for a few seconds and then fell forwards into the sea with a thump. Compressed air began to hiss into the bow tanks: the boat was down by the head and Weber was attempting to compensate. Everything was complete confusion. Any second we expected to be rammed by a destroyer.

Boatswain Walter Gross grabbed his escape gear from a hook in the NCO's room and shouted, 'Get your Draeger[10] and life-jacket. The Captain's given the order to abandon ship. Pass it on!'

I was amazed to find Hein Jürgensen still asleep in his bunk. 'Come on, Hein,' I shouted, shaking his arm roughly, 'we're getting off.' Jürgensen sat up quickly, still drunk with sleep, and stared at me in bemusement.

'We're in Lorient already?'

'No, you ass, we're abandoning ship.'

He gripped my arm. 'What shall I wear, canvas shoes or boots?'

'What do you swim best in?' I tore myself free and found Schewe raiding the refrigerator; the Warrant Officer had found himself a large tongue of beef. 'You should have something to eat yourself, Hirschfeld,' he said, 'tomorrow we'll be behind barbed wire.' I closed the fridge door without speaking and pushed Schewe aside, then made my way quickly to the radio room and found Hagen bitterly complaining that thieves had stolen our escape gear and life-jackets.

Already the crew were leaving the boat. Alfred Winter was standing at the foot of the conning tower ladder urging the hands upwards. Meanwhile, in a corner of the control room, Otto Peters was expelling the compressed air from the system preparatory to initiating the scuttling procedure. Swathes of smoke from the electrical fire aft were drifting forwards from the stern.

Little Wüsteney was sitting at the hydroplanes crying, 'It's all over. Our lovely boat!' Winter grabbed him without ceremony and shoved him to the ladder. 'Get up and out! Quick, the destroyers! Before they ram us!'

Weber was also at the foot of the ladder, staring up through the open manhole. Winter had his arms across the Chief Engineer's chest. Above the hiss of the compressed air, I heard Winter shout at the Lieutenant, 'You get off last after you've opened all the vents! And I'll make sure you do!'

I felt a tug at my sleeve: it was Lt Keller, kitted out with his escape gear and life-jacket. 'Hirschfeld, we must destroy the secret papers,' he said. According to standing orders, all classified documents were supposed to be put into a weighted sack and fired out through a torpedo tube. After a quick glance forward, I told him, 'We can't fire them, all the torpedomen have left.'

44

'Well at least get the water-soluble papers out and tread them in the bilge water.' Only now did I realize that the coconut matting on the central corridor grating was almost awash. While I went to the radio room safes, Keller sacked the Captain's cabin, tossing out all the water-soluble documents he could find; as this was going on, Ferdinand Hagen came past sporting a life-jacket and gave me a grin.

'Where did you get that?' I asked.

'From the Officers' Mess,' he whispered. 'Look, there's the Captain's escape set on his bed!'

I checked the container and then said to Keller, 'Isn't the Captain wearing a Draeger and life-jacket?'

Keller answered without looking. 'No, he doesn't need one. He's not going to be picked up alive. Leave him in peace.'

There was some confused shouting in the control room; at first it was impossible to understand what was being said, and then Otto Peters dived across to the blow valves and shut off all the open taps. The hissing of the compressed air ceased abruptly. Winter started to pull men back from the ladder and bellowed upwards, 'What's going on up there?'

'There are no destroyers,' said the voice of Lt Schwartzkopff.

A sigh of relief swept through the boat; we could hardly believe it. All this for nothing? Lt Keller and I exchanged glances and then bent down to salvage what papers we could from the bilge water.

Fischer had come down into the control room. 'Winter, get that fire in the electric motor put out and tell Schewe to start up the diesels. We have got to get away from here quickly.' Then he came through the pressure doorway and saw Keller and myself each clutching two handfuls of sodden documents. He made no comment and sat down on his bed. His dark blond hair straggled in long strands across his face.

'Hirschfeld, we must have something to eat,' he said in a tired voice.

'Yes, sir, I'll have strong coffee made at once,' I replied, forgetting for the moment that there was no electric current for the galley. The cook came past and I said, 'Järschel, make us coffee, and try to save what bread you can. The loaves are all over the place.'

The cook nodded dubiously. 'Most of them are in the shit, Petty Officer. The shit bucket in the bow room tipped all its contents down here.' With that he made his way back to the galley, muttering.

This explained why it stank so much in the boat. There were more important matters to be attended to than coffee: no sooner had the electrical fire been dowsed than Schewe was having to tackle a fire

45

in the port diesel; when they trooped aft for the purpose of retrieving the bodies of the drowned crewmen in the stern torpedo room they passed through a snowy landscape of foam to get there.

It had been assumed that the stern room had been flooded, but when the watertight door was opened the two trapped torpedomen stumbled out, green in the gills, but, to judge by their language, very much alive. They had not been able to communicate by telephone because the cable had been torn out of its socket when one of them had grabbed it in an attempt to keep his balance during the sudden emergency at depth. Two of the bulkheads had buckled under the immense pressure – it was estimated that the stern was at about 900 feet – and the aft torpedo hatch cover had been slightly damaged, admitting a trickle of water.

I went up to the bridge with the Second Lieutenant. The crippled U-boat rose and fell lightly in the long swell. On the eastern horizon a number of columns of smoke smudged the skyline. Keller pushed a cigarette between my lips and, while lighting it, said quietly, 'If we don't get out of here soon we're dead ducks. I just made a hydrophone check. The destroyers haven't gone, they're over there. They only lost contact with us because we went so deep.'

The boat trembled and the starboard exhaust gasped. 'Starboard diesel can be run at low speed!' came a shout. On the one engine the boat was slowly driven forward into the waves, in a south-easterly direction.

The damage to the submarine was extensive: the heads of the two main engine room ventilation masts were fractured; the aft hydro-plane motor and batteries were shut down; the port electric motor was burnt out; the starboard propeller shaft was knocking so loudly that it could be heard at the bow; nearly half of the hydrophone microphones were out of commission, and the boat was trailing an oil slick.

The emergency at depth had been caused by the negligence of the Chief Engineer. Upon examination of the depth gauges, Otto Peters had established that all were functioning correctly, but that the master gauge in the control room had been shut off. Wüsteney was supposed to have closed down the depth gauge in the conning tower, but had turned off the one in the control room instead. The Chief Engineer had neglected to drain the tube of the control room gauge and so had failed to bring to light Wüsteney's error. Accordingly the boat had simply drifted slowly deeper while the Chief mistakenly believed that he had the boat trimmed at 300 feet. How much everything depended on each man doing his job properly! Possibly it was the intervention of Providence, for it was only our being at such

46

a tremendous depth that had saved us from the destroyers. The Captain would never have gone below 500 feet.

'Well, at least we know how deep we can go with this boat,' said Otto Peters with a grin, 'and that's something the yards could never have told us.'

The wind was north-westerly and gusting to Force 7, and *U-109* made good progress over the ground for the next 48 hours. On 23 May, 1941, the wind rose to gale force from the west and the boat began to roll violently in the high swell. Schewe's engineers cursed mightily as they struggled to repair the damage in the engine room.

U-boat Command ordered the *Westboote* to form a new patrol line and Fischer ordered the navigator to set a course to join it, even though he was aware that it would be impossible to submerge with safety, and this led to a heated discussion in the Officers' Mess. Schwartzkopff, Keller and Weber were all vehemently opposed to continuing the voyage. The main worry was the split in the ventilation masts: if either of these gave while the boat was submerged so much water would penetrate that the submarine would not be able to regain the surface. The Captain was virtually obliged to give way to his officers and eventually he told me to signal Lorient that he was abandoning the mission and heading for port.

The blustery dawn of 24 May revealed a huge swell rolling from the west, driven before severe gale force winds, the sea frequently swamping the bridge from astern. Fischer was steering a course to the south, after which he was proposing to run due east into Lorient.

U-109 made a trial dive to 60 feet, but Weber was soon reporting that the boat was out of control and had fallen to 180 feet: it was simply impossible to trim the boat using just one electric motor. Besides this, the stuffing boxes and one of the ventilation masts were now leaking severely and the Commander was finally convinced of the danger in submerging in this condition. When we surfaced, Telegraphist Hümpel took down and decoded the signal repeats, and I gasped when I read a message from U-boat Command which stated:

Battlecruiser *Hood* sunk this morning in Denmark Strait by *Bismarck*. Heavy cruisers shadowing *Bismarck* and *Prinz Eugen*. *Bismarck* attempting to draw shadowing forces across line of *Westboote*.

Westboote? The Commander read the signal aloud, roared out an exclamation, then announced the victory to the crew over the loudspeakers. It had been the dream of all U-boat men to sink this famous British warship. They had used to call to the shore, 'We're

47

off to get the *Hood!*' as they cast off on a fresh voyage. But now the *Bismarck* and the *Prinz Eugen* had beaten them to it.[12]

All through 25 May the crippled *U-109* kept on a course for Biscay through high seas while the *Bismarck*, which had taken a hit in the fore-peak and could only make 28 knots, was now heading across the Atlantic for Brest, trailed by numerous units of the Home Fleet; the British had sent out carriers and capital units from Canada, Britain and Gibraltar in an effort to cut off her escape. On 26 May radio reports indicated an increasing naval presence in the North Atlantic and that evening U-boat Command signalled that the *Bismarck* had been hit in the rudder and was temporarily unable to steer. The *Bismarck* was about 600 miles from Brest and *U-109* was 100 miles to the south-west of her. Shortly after, the BdU sent a supplementary signal:

> To all Biscay boats. Whoever has a torpedo, go to the protection of the *Bismarck*.

The Captain read this message thoughtfully and then, with a meaningful look at me, said, 'Yes, this also means us. He summoned the Chief Engineer and asked him if the boat could be run at top speed.

'No, Captain, the shafts would burn. And the stuffing boxes would leak even more.' The Captain nodded and the Chief was dismissed. A few moments later Fischer crept off to the stern room and slyly collared one of the engine room hands.

'Petty Officer Breuer, I'm sure you want to get back to port as quickly as possible, don't you? Then can we run at full speed?' Breuer scratched his head. 'Well, yes, I suppose so, sir, but only if you put a man with an oil can on each shaft all the time, then you could. But you'll ruin the shafts.' The Captain dismissed the cautionary remark with a wave of his hand. 'Unimportant. Put the men on the shafts. We'll run at top speed.'

Fischer went to the control room immediately and ordered the helmsman to telegraph for full speed ahead and then steer northwards for the *Bismarck*. The boat trembled as the diesels began to hammer hard; the bows rose into the oncoming sea and then toppled into the following trough with a thunderous concussion, to be struck by the next wave slamming against the tower mantle with tremendous force.

The Chief Engineer came storming into the control room. 'Who ordered that?' he screamed at the coxswain. Petersen stared at him for a few seconds and then returned his attention to his charts.

The Captain stepped out of the shadows. 'I ordered it.'

'But sir, I reported to you that the engines can't be run at high speed!' Weber was highly agitated; he was almost shouting at the Commander. 'I have also reported to you that this boat is not battleworthy!'

'Silence!' There was a dangerous undertone in the Captain's voice. 'A battleship is worth the sacrifice of a submarine. Today we have the chance to sink an enemy battleship, perhaps a carrier. We have torpedoes on board. The other boats have none. Tomorrow, if we should meet an enemy unit, we will go down fighting. We shall not allow ourselves to be taken.'

Aghast, the Chief looked around helplessly for support. As far as the Commander was concerned, Weber no longer existed. Together with the coxswain, Warrant Officer Petersen, Fischer contemplated the charts.

I went off to the NCO's Mess. When I told Otto Peters what had transpired, he struck the bulkhead with his fist.

'Damn stupidity! So close to port and now we're coming back out again! I could strangle that Breuer.'

'He couldn't help it, Otto. He still thinks we're on our way home.'

Otto Peters groaned in desperation. 'How could anyone be so gormless?' he said.

A deep depression lay over the North Atlantic; the wind howled over the greyish waste of foaming ridges and *U-109* wallowed heavily in the severe storm. Early on the morning of 27 May, at the change of the watches, Lt Schwartzkopff reported that the bridge was continuously awash while the night was black as pitch; he wanted a reduction in speed. The Captain shook his head.

'We have to press on, Number One, otherwise we'll never get there in time. I'll go up myself.'

The Captain dressed up in his long black oilskin coat, sou'wester and rubber sea boots, but as he was about to mount the ladder Keller shouted down, 'Both engines stop! Full speed astern!' Such an order could only be given in the most dire circumstances. The Captain scrambled up the ladder. The engine room responded like lightning. The diesels were thrown into reverse and the whole boat shuddered under the increased power. When the Chief Engineer appeared in the control room and asked what was wrong, he was met with a shrug of the shoulders. Otto Peters whispered to me, 'Have you got your lifejacket? I think you might be needing it in a minute.'

'Both engines stop!'

It was suddenly very quiet in the boat. The submarine began to slew round broadside to the high wind and a violent rolling motion began as the sea broke over the exposed hull. Anxiety reigned for long minutes.

'Both ahead slow.' The boat returned to the previous course and then Fischer telegraphed for full ahead. When he came below he said to the men in the conning tower, 'We were very lucky there. Six destroyers coming up from the south-east, so close they nearly ran us down.'

'They didn't see us, sir?' asked the coxswain.

'No,' Fischer laughed, 'otherwise they would have blown us out of the water. They were literally 150 feet before the bows. Honestly, you can't see a thing up there.'

'Perhaps we should reduce speed a little,' Petersen suggested. 'It seems pointless to run on so blindly with the lookouts more or less under water all the time.'

The Commander raised his eyebrows. 'My dear Petersen, since last evening, the *Bismarck* has been shadowed by superior enemy naval forces, trying to steer by her propellers. Surely you must know what that means in this sea?' His voice sounded hoarse as he continued, 'The *Bismarck* is lost!'

I went cold as I thought of the 2400 men now condemned to die aboard Germany's greatest battleship. Many of them were personal friends, and, but for an excess of alcohol and a ferry which sailed a minute early, I would have caught the evening train to Wilhelmshaven that evening, would have been a member of the radio crew of the *Karlsruhe* and would right now be with them on the *Bismarck*.

'Don't you see, Petersen, tonight is the chance to get a carrier. We must be there to try, no matter what the sacrifice we have to make.'

Petersen turned in resignation to his charts. When I went to the radio room I found my hands full taking down the huge volume of signals traffic on the U-boat frequencies. Wohlfahrt in *U-556* had been ordered to go alongside the *Bismarck* to retrieve the Fleet War Diary, but could not comply for lack of fuel. Kentrat in *U-74* had volunteered to attempt the mission, but had also reported that his boat had suffered depth-charge damage, was flooding and could not submerge for more than an hour at a time. It appeared he was very close to *Bismarck*. A message from the battleship was relayed to all U-boats.

We fight to the last shell. Long live the Führer! Long live Germany!

Thus the men of the *Bismarck* knew their fate: nothing could save them now. The nearest U-boats had no torpedoes and *U-109*, heading at full speed to her assistance, had all but two torpedoes of a full load but could not dive.[13]

Just before 0300 hrs the Commander went up to the bridge; the watch officer had reported seeing gun flashes against the night sky. Fischer and Keller spent several hours staring at the distant lightning of the artillery. The storm howled around the boat. The wind had freshened considerably in the last hour, and the seas were as high as a house. A terrible night.

Hagen relieved me at 0800 hrs. While I was putting on my leather jacket, the Captain summoned me. 'Are you going up? Then tell the officer of the watch that I'm turning in. If he sees any aircraft, he is to wake me immediately.'

I passed on the message to the coxswain. Petersen took the glasses from his eyes. 'Yes, everything is ready below for scuttling,' I told him. Petersen nodded, pressed the Zeiss into the sockets of his eyes and rested his elbows on the bridge coaming. It was dawning greyly. A huge sea rolled in from the north-west, driving the boat ever eastwards.

'Unwise of you to come up here without your lifejacket, isn't it?' Petersen asked me.

'But who would be flying in this weather?' Petersen gave me a sharp glance; we both knew that the Luftwaffe had been unable to assist the *Bismarck* for that very reason.

'Aircraft at 160°,' said one of the aft lookouts.

'Damn, five machines,' shouted Wenzel. Soon the aircraft could be seen abeam at a distance of five miles and with the naked eye; from the bridge they watched the flight through their binoculars until it disappeared.

'That was lucky,' said Wenzel. 'Perhaps they're making for their carrier and can't be bothered with us.'

The coxswain kicked the hatch lid shut. 'Right, listen. Keep your mouths shut about that. It never happened.' They all nodded. Then I went below; it definitely wasn't safe on the bridge without a lifejacket.

The 10,000-ton Fleet oiler *Ermland*, which had sailed early that morning from St Nazaire with 10-inch hawsers to tow the battleship home, had been recalled. Hagen told me that the BBC had announced the sinking of the *Bismarck*. At 1400 hrs Naval Command admitted the probability that the *Bismarck* had been sunk; all U-boats were ordered to look for survivors. *U-109* searched all day but found nothing, only white crests on the waves as far as the eye could see. At nightfall Fischer broke off the search and headed for Lorient at full speed.

Bismarck survivors later reported that the entire radio crew had locked themselves in the communications centre and to the last man had gone down with the ship.

By the morning of 29 May the storm had abated and the sea was calmer as *U-109* ran in the last hundred miles to the French Biscay port; we could even smell the land. The Captain allowed all off-watch men on the bridge, where appetizers were served by the cook.

The coxswain looked upon this with ill-concealed disapproval. 'We're not bloody well home yet!' he roared at the lookouts. 'You all keep a sharp watch!'

A few minutes later Boatswain Walter Gross shouted, 'Periscope to starboard!' The chatter stifled: all eyes searched the waves.

'Where?' asked the Captain.

'Gone, sir. It was about 300 feet away. A thick periscope.'

The Captain ordered a zig-zag. The wake came round in a curve as the diesels began a furious hammering. After a while the Captain shook his head. 'You were mistaken, Gross.'

'I saw it clearly, sir. It was a typical English periscope.'

'Gross knows something about English periscopes, sir,' said the Coxswain. Fischer made no response and I suggested that it should be reported at once by signal.

'No, leave it. It will only get them all stirred up in Lorient,' the Captain replied. Fischer did not believe in the periscope. I thought anxiously about *U-74*, following us some miles astern, outlined against the clouds, blithely unaware of the menace waiting for her beneath the waters of Biscay. *U-74* had three *Bismarck* survivors aboard.

'Land ahead,' reported Wenzel. It was Ile de Croix. A trawler equipped with anti-mine gear was drifting in wait; *U-109* fell in astern and followed. The sun smiled down on us.

'Well, Coxswain,' I said to Petersen with a sarcastic grin, 'and what can possibly happen to us now?' He gave me a long, hard look, placed a fatherly hand on my shoulder and said in his warm, sonorous voice, 'Have you never heard of ground mines? You can cross above them with perfect safety 24 times, but on the 25th occasion, they blow you up.'

Hümpel came to the foot of the conning tower ladder and shouted up,

'Petty Officer Hirschfeld to the radio room!' I went below.

'Message from *U-74*,' Hagen told me. 'Kentrat says, "Have just avoided fan of six torpedoes in grid square BF ..."'

I sent Hümpel to the bridge with a copy of the signal and the Commander came down directly. The Coxswain's mate, Hein Jürgensen, placed a small cross on the chart where Walter Gross had seen the periscope, then compared the Biscay chart with the grid square. The coordinates were the same. From that position six torpedoes had been shot off at Kentrat in *U-74*.

The Captain looked shaken.

'We ought to have reported it,' I told him. Fischer nodded grimly. His negligence would have cost the lives of the crew of *U-74* if the English commander had shot straight.

U-109 manoeuvred at slow speed through the Narrows between Kernevel and the fortress of Port Louis, past the rusting old cruiser *Strasbourg*, formerly the German Jutland veteran *Regensburg*, and then made fast alongside the rusting bulk of the old sailing ship *Isere*, where we were greeted by the Flotilla Chief and many officers and men of the Lorient base.[14]

The first war patrol of the German submarine *U-109* was completed.

* * *

The morning of 30 May, 1941, was gloriously sunny. The crew of *U-109* formed up in two ranks on the parade ground in front of the Prefecture.

'Attention! Eyes right!' Admiral Dönitz suddenly appeared with a few aides. Fischer stepped forward smartly and reported the safe return of *U-109* from her first mission. The Admiral thanked him and then slowly approached the front rank. He was slim, tall and serious looking. The Admiral greeted each of the officers with a handshake. Then we all heard his voice.

'Well, Weber, you always seem to be at the bottom of it when the shit starts flying.'

The Chief Engineer blushed bright red. 'I could do nothing about it, Admiral,' he protested.

'You said that the last time.' We all knew what Dönitz meant. Weber had been the Chief Engineer of a U-boat whose crew were interned after an unfortunate miscalculation of the trim had put the boat ashore on the Norwegian coast. Weber and the other crew members had eventually been freed when the German Army invaded Norway.

Dönitz walked slowly along the ranks, stopping here and there to exchange compliments. 'Ah, our old friend Petersen is also here. How are you?' He grasped the Coxswain's hand with a smile.

'Thank you, well, Admiral.'

'It pleases me to hear it. It's a better life on the bigger boats, isn't it?'

'Indeed, Admiral. At least I can stand upright in them.'

The BdU nodded and then slowly continued his inspection, looking from face to face. Then he placed himself about fifteen paces from the front rank and folded his arms across his chest. His lips were suddenly narrow.

'Your patrol was shit. You know that.' His voice was hard, sharp. 'And when you go deep, there's no need to break the world record.'

Otto Peters gave me a nudge and whispered, 'He's addressing the whole crew, but it's aimed at the Captain.'

'Your 7,000 tons wasn't much. You'll have to do better.' He let his gaze range over the officers, then stared hard at the Commander. Fischer saluted: he had understood. Dönitz smiled and his voice was now conciliatory as he continued, 'But at least you brought the boat back. I suppose that's worth something.'

The Admiral fished inside his jacket pocket and brought out an Iron Cross, Second Class, and pressed it into the hand of the Captain. Fischer smiled modestly and slipped the medal inside his tunic.

'He will be a shade more mad on the next voyage because of that,' Otto Peters whispered.

Admiral Dönitz said, 'Does anybody have anything they wish to say to me?' His question seemed to be directed at the officers. Weber stepped forward, and Fischer shot him a glance. The parade was dismissed; only Otto Peters was detailed to remain behind.

Some time later he reappeared. He was wearing the Iron Cross, First Class. Weber had reported that Otto Peters' action during the deep dive off Greenland had saved the boat and crew.

'But there's something very nasty being brewed in the Prefecture,' Peters said to me. 'Schwartzkopff and Keller both wanted to see the Admiral privately. I think they've denounced the Captain.'

- 4 -

BLEICHRODT ASSUMES COMMAND

The next day, 31 May, 1941, the shout went up that *U-556* was berthing and we ran down to the pier where the *Isere* was moored and watched Wohlfahrt's boat manoeuvring alongside, her bearded crew lining the deck and wreathed in smiles. A number of pennants, each representing a ship sunk and its tonnage, fluttered from the extended periscope tube. The pennants added up to 49,000 tons. A band played a stirring military march, the mooring lines flew across, *U-556* made fast and Admiral Dönitz strode briskly aboard to greet Wohlfahrt and present him with his Knight's Cross.

Afterwards, I took my old friend Schlupp, Wohlfahrt's senior telegraphist, to the barracks mess, where I learned that it was *U-556* which had torpedoed the tanker off Greenland ten days earlier and saved us from being rammed.[15] Schlupp was a heavy drinker and had sold most of his uniforms to finance his addiction. I asked him how much of his naval wardrobe he had kept. 'Ah, just one of everything. If I don't get drowned on the next trip, I'm listed for court-martial when I get back,' he said.

I laughed. 'If they find you guilty, they won't let you sail on U-boats any more.'

'I know, and that's the terrible thing about it,' he said, and meant it. However, Schlupp never stood his court-martial; Wohlfahrt and his crew were sunk twenty-eight days later.

That evening I was due to begin my furlough; when I collected my leave permit from the First Lieutenant I learned that Fischer had been relieved of command and banished from the U-boat Arm. Lt Schwartzkopff was grinning as he gave me the news, but I couldn't see why he was so pleased about it, for it was my personal view that Fischer was an outstanding commander, devoted to his duty and prepared to die for honour doing it, as he had proved during the

Bismarck affair. It was, as he had said at the time, worth the sacrifice of a submarine in order to destroy an enemy carrier or battleship.

According to the entry in the *U-109* War Diary, it was the opinion of U-boat Command that Fischer had not been fully in control of the situation which developed on 21 May, 1941. In particular, it was alleged that:

(1) he had failed to ensure that the boat was maintained in trim at depth,
(2) although the action taken by Petty Officer Peters was correct and essential, the Captain had not ordered it.
(3) the Captain had made no attempt to halt the fast ascent of the boat, and
(4) he had prematurely given the order to abandon the vessel.

Taking all this into account when considering the existing doubts concerning Fischer's competence, which had first arisen during the tactical exercises in the Baltic, the BdU had determined that the reservations expressed by the training officer were justified, and accordingly he found himself compelled to remove Fischer from command forthwith.[16]

I only saw this official entry much later. Irrespective of whether it was preferable for a boat to be saddled with a zealous commander or with an incompetent Chief Engineer, it appalled me that Schwartz-kopff and Keller, almost certainly with the connivance of the real culprit, Weber, appeared to have submitted a deliberately misleading account of the events with a view to securing the dismissal of the Commander, while Weber for his part escaped scot-free.

After my ten-day leave was over, I took the Paris express on the morning of 11 June, 1941. Otto Peters got in at Bremen: we shook hands but barely spoke until our arrival in the French capital. On the way we passed many troop transports clanking to the east. Panzers, artillery, and more panzers, all leaving France. When we stopped opposite a transport train I asked some of the infantrymen where they were heading, but they didn't seem to know.

The journey to the Gare du Nord from Hamburg took twenty-three hours. At Paris-Montparnasse, from where the connection for Brest departed, we spun a long story to the German station staff officer, and although he didn't believe a word of it, he cheerfully endorsed our passes for the 1800 hrs night express, leaving us free to spend the day touring Paris.

The sun laughed down from a clear blue sky and it was beautifully warm. At Napoleon's sarcophagus the superintendent told us that, since the German occupation a year previously, the total of German servicemen visiting the last resting place of the great Corsican was greater than the total of all French visitors over the last ten years.

The Eiffel Tower lift was out of order, so we climbed to the top by the stairs and looked across the city and into the countryside beyond. 'Just look down,' said Otto Peters, 'we were as deep as that. Difficult to imagine, isn't it?' I looked at the tiny people far beneath and shuddered as I thought of the tremendous pressure of water concentrated on the hull during the deep dive off Greenland.

We caught the 1800 hrs night express for Brest and, on arrival at Lorient, found the boat still undergoing an extensive overhaul in the yards. We spent the long summer days on the beach at Carnac. The sun beat down from a cloudless sky and a soft breeze fanned our tanning bodies. It seemed very much like peacetime, except that the only holidaymakers were U-boat crewmen. We stayed in the Grand Hotel, slept in wide French beds and ate like lords. From my room I had a view over sea and sand; when I opened the windows giving on to the balcony, I could hear the thunder of the surf.

The idyll was smashed on the morning of 22 June. German news bulletins were full of the invasion of the Soviet Union by the Wehrmacht that morning. With a sinking heart I realized that this would save Britain and prolong the war indefinitely. Now we would have to sail the seas against the British for years, perhaps for ever. Grimly, I thought of what had happened to the last army which had mounted a serious invasion of Russia and remembered Napoleon.

Next day, at Lorient, I went aboard *U-109* to make the last checks prior to the forthcoming second patrol. While I was in the radio room the new commander arrived. I reported myself as the senior telegraphist and Heinrich Bleichrodt, holder of the Knight's Cross, gave me a long, critical look before offering me his hand. 'Petty Officer, we must work closely together. Is that clear?'

'*Jawohl, Herr Kaleu!*'

After he had gone Schwartzkopff put his head into the radio room.

'Well, what do you reckon? Now we've got a real commander, haven't we?' I thought about the answer for some time before I replied, 'Yes, at least this one's already got his Knight's Cross,' and the Lieutenant laughed.

The new captain, known throughout the U-boat Arm as 'Ajax', had brought with him a number of crewmen from his previous command, *U-67*, including Boatswain Berthold Seidel, who had completed so many U-boat voyages that it was said of him that if he was on board a U-boat it couldn't be sunk. Seidel replaced Kuddel

Wenzel, who had been given a place on the next coxswain's training course. I wondered what Bruno Petersen would make of all these changes.

On the afternoon of 27 June we were served roast turkey and champagne, so the French serving girls knew that we would be leaving next day. Often we flirted with them, but it was supposed to go no further; ratings so inclined were under orders to visit brothels under Army supervision and to steer clear of casual liaisons. Many of the local girls had venereal diseases, which were widely suspected to be used by the British as a secret weapon, and we were to discover later just how seriously this could interfere with the efficient running of a U-boat at sea.

On Saturday 28 June we packed our belongings into a chest, made out a last will and testament and handed them all in for safe keeping to the Flotilla Admin Office. At 1900 hrs we paraded on the after-deck of the submarine, alongside the *Isere*. A band played, the Captain made a quick head count and then reported to the Flotilla Chief, who was accompanied by a large retinue, that *U-109* was ready to sail on patrol. The Senior Officer thanked him and made a mercifully brief speech. The lines were cast off and we motored out to the strains of *Wir fahren gegen England*. With pulsing diesels we passed through the Narrows of Kernevel and Port Louis, where, in the grounds of Admiral Dönitz's villa, three staff officers waved their caps in farewell. The long bows curtsied in the Biscay swell, we went to full revolutions and headed out to sea. The Commander announced that we would operate off the West African coast for four months, then we submerged to 550 feet to check the condition of the boat. We found there that the periscopes were leaking badly and, when proceeding at slow speed submerged, the starboard diesel coupling made a loud banging. Otherwise the boat seemed in a reasonable state of repair.

U-109 crossed Biscay on the surface under clear blue skies and in summer temperatures. The boat squatted low in the water with her load of twenty-five torpedoes. Once we were eighty miles to the west of Cape Ortegal we proceeded south-west on the electric motors to save fuel, and, south of the Azores, the lookouts wore tropical helmets to protect them against the fierce rays of the sun.

Lt Cdr Bleichrodt spent a lot of time listening to the news bulletins. They were always embellished with stories of victories against the Soviet forces on a massive scale, but the Captain always looked very pensive when he heard them. I think he was remembering 1812.

We cruised the usual steamer routes for a week and saw nothing but fleecy trade-wind clouds and a glassy sea with gentle swell. By

1045 hrs on 6 July we had reached a position some 300 miles west of Madeira, having ghosted through a belt of calms when the lookouts cried 'Mastheads in sight!' The Commander took his binoculars from their hook and went up to the conning tower. The diesels cut in and surged to full ahead. It was an independent ship heading south and the chase began.

U-109 raced in a wide semi-circle towards the interception point with the steamer, keeping only the tips of her masts in sight. We were not overhauling her very quickly even though she was making broad zig-zags from her mean course, and so we knew that this was a fast ship making at least 14 knots. The Commander wanted to make a submerged attack in daylight and by early afternoon he was in the ideal position on her bow.

The telegraphists, who had been tuned to the 600m and 36m international frequencies, now went to the hydrophones room and Hagen immediately got a good bearing on the target. Once the torpedo caps had been opened it fell quiet in the boat. Maureschat was at the attack computer and I heard the Captain say, 'He's coming straight for us, that's good.'

However, it was another hour before the submarine was in a shooting position. The depth rudders snarled occasionally; one of them was grazing against something; obviously the repairers hadn't done the job properly. In the tower the Captain was giving a stream of position and course corrections which Maureschat repeated in a monotone and fed into the computer. Suddenly Bleichrodt said, 'Damn, he's zig-zagged, what a nuisance.' The news spread through the boat like a forest fire. The sea was fairly calm; a good man on lookout would probably have spotted our periscope.

Now we had to wait until the steamer was beyond the horizon to begin the approach manoeuvre all over again. The bow caps were closed and the torpedo mate, Werner Borchardt, came down the central corridor and said to me with a laugh, 'These shitty subs. Much too slow under water, exactly the same as in the last war. And we're supposed to win this war with them. I can't see it, myself.'

It seemed an eternity before the steamer was out of sight. At 1630 Bleichrodt gave the order to surface and a gust of fresh air swept through the boat as the hatch cover was opened. The diesels roared into life: the Commander announced that we would try a surfaced attack that night. The international distress frequencies were silent. At 0130 Bleichrodt ordered action stations and had the torpedo tubes readied. The steamer was silhouetted in the silvery path of a large moon while we crept towards her from the darkness, trailing a gleaming wake. Schwartzkopff was at the range-finding optic on the bridge and the Commander conned the boat. At just under two miles we fired off the first eel, which was intended to bring the steamer to a standstill. In the hydrophones room I listened to it running.

The torpedo mate came down the corridor from the bow room with his stopwatch and I handed him the parallel hydrophones. The minutes passed: we waited for the explosion, then exchanged disappointed looks.

'Missed,' I said. Borchardt nodded. 'Can you tell whether it went ahead or astern of him?'

'No, you heard it for yourself. The propeller of the torpedo obscures everything.'

On the bridge they were yelling for Borchardt. He laughed. 'You see, now they'll say the eel didn't run properly,' he said and went off in indignation, prepared to defend his honour; he had the telegraphists as his witnesses that the torpedo had run its set course.

The steamer had not zig-zagged and it took only another hour to get ahead of her bow once more: the range was a mile and the second torpedo hissed away.

Borchardt came running down the gangway looking at his stopwatch. At the hydrophones I could hear that the torpedo was running true, but there was no hit. Borchardt looked at me in disbelief. On the bridge Bleichrodt had a grim expression on his face. Surely it must be possible to get this steamer.

The third attack began at 0400 from 800 yards. The torpedo ran and ran: another miss. The crew below decks were very restless and the muttering had begun. They wanted somebody other than Schwartzkopff to operate the aiming optic. Fortunately this couldn't be heard on the bridge.

Bleichrodt had had all the fire-control instruments checked over but hadn't been able to establish why we kept missing. Boatswain Walter Gross reported that the steamer had now stopped; her bow-wave had fallen away. She was behaving in a very cocky fashion. The Commander muttered to himself, 'The swine.' The fourth torpedo was loosed off immediately at the stationary freighter, but as soon as it had streaked away a large white ruffle of foam appeared either side of the ship's bow and Walter Gross reported that she was moving at full speed.

'Then this torpedo will miss as well,' Bleichrodt concluded.

'I think he adjusted his speed every time we fired,' said Schwartzkopff.

'Well, if that's the case, he must have hydrophones. And if he avoided every torpedo and never once wirelessed that he was under attack, then there's more to him than meets the eye.'

The officers stared in silence at the mysterious ship. The fourth torpedo ran for seven minutes and I used this unimportant fact as an excuse to come to the bridge; my real interest was in seeing the steamer.

'We will have to sink him with the cannon, sir,' Keller called out.

'I don't trust that ship. It could be a U-boat trap.'

'But we can't just let him go,' Keller insisted.

'It could be a waste of torpedoes simply to fire one after the other at him,' Schwartzkopff said.

Bleichrodt ignored them both and contemplated the enemy freighter through his binoculars.

'He's still going at full speed, sir!' Gross reported. Bleichrodt allowed his binoculars to drop to his chest. 'OK,' he said with a smile, 'if you won't have it any other way, we'll give it a try with the deck gun. Clear the decks to engage with gunfire.'

The Chief Engineer broadcast the order over the loudspeakers and the hands below looked up as if to say, 'At last!' The gun crew scrambled up to the foredeck: they wore lifejackets but did not need to dress up, for the night was warm. Floor plates in the control room above the ammunition chamber were taken up and the heavy shells conveyed to the bridge by human chain. The boat cruised at full ahead through the sea.

Maureschat reported the deck gun ready to fire and, once the range was right, Bleichrodt gave the order and the 10.5 cm cannon barked and recoiled. It was positioned directly above the radio room and the noise was almost intolerable for us as we maintained a watch on the distress frequencies. The receivers were suspended in individual cradles to protect them against the jarring. Shot after shot howled over towards the enemy ship.

'SSS SSS *City of Auckland* 33°14′N 31°21′W SSS,' she morsed.[17]

Feverishly we thumbed through Lloyds Register: '*City of Auckland*, 8000 BRT, built AG Weser, Bremen.' I raced to the foot of the tower ladder to report the information to the Commander, but I couldn't make myself heard above the din.

'Hit astern!' someone shouted. The gun roared again. I went to the bridge and informed Bleichrodt of the identity of the steamer. The Commander kept the binoculars to his eyes. 'So, 8000 tons, I thought she was about that. Damn, she's laying a smoke screen.'

'Or Maureschat hit the smoke-making apparatus,' Schwartzkopff said.

'Also possible, but what sort of merchant ship has got a smoke installation fitted?'

The gun spoke twice more and flames leapt up through the thick black fog.

'Another hit astern,' said Keller. Then the curtains of smoke hid the steamer completely.

'Cease fire, stop engines,' said Bleichrodt and the speed quickly fell off the boat.

'Let's go in and finish him off,' Keller called out. We all murmured in agreement.

'The steamer's gun on the poop must be out of action,' suggested Schwartzkopff. Bleichrodt merely smiled. 'I'm going to look after our own skins first,' he said calmly. 'I still think that's a Q-ship. He's not finished yet, not by a long chalk. We'll wait a bit.'

The boat lay stopped while the figures on our bridge gazed in silence at the billowing cloud of smoke. The wavelets slapped lazily against our hull and the movement of the boat rolled the empty cartridge cases noisily back and forth across the foredeck. Thirty-five shots had been fired. The gun crew stood ready; nobody could understand the Commander's unreasonable caution; surely we should attack? Suddenly Schwartzkopff shouted, 'He's coming out of it, sir!' The steamer emerged from his smoke cloud with a creaming bow-wave, and Bleichrodt muttered, 'I thought as much. He's going to try to ram us,' and with that he ordered full ahead and hard a' starboard.

I thought that this was an over-reaction, for the enemy ship was still a good distance away. The Commander called for maximum speed and the diesels seemed to go mad, kicking up a huge wake as we showed our stern to the pursuer. The gun crew was still on the fore-casing but couldn't fire the weapon because the target was masked by the conning tower.

'He's turning away,' Schwartzkopff said. The ship's outline was becoming longer; suddenly there was a belch of lightning flashes from the steamer's side and a moment later we ducked involuntarily as a salvo screamed overhead. 'That was a broadside with medium calibre guns!' Keller shouted.

Bleichrodt nagged at his lip. 'I told you it could be a trap. That is a Q-ship.' He pressed his binoculars to his eyes, then told the quartermaster to steer east. I was still on the bridge: I should have been below but my presence had been forgotten in the excitement. There was another ripple of flashes from the steamer: it was damned dangerous; this salvo was long; we were in her range.

62

'Secure the gun. Gun crew inside the boat!' Bleichrodt shouted to Maureschat.

'What about the shell-cases, sir?'

'Throw them overboard!' While the cases were splashing into the wash on either flank of the boat, Schwartzkopff remarked, 'He seems to have given up shooting. We must make a very difficult target for him.'

Keller shook his head. 'No, it's just that he can't fire over his bow. As long as we can't see his broadside we're probably safe.'

An hour passed with ourselves as the hunted. The steamer had only squawked once, and this was so unusual that it led Bleichrodt to conclude that the *City of Auckland* was acting under naval direction. I went to the control room where the coxswain was hunched over the chart table. 'What are we going to do when it gets light?' I asked him.

'Keep on running. We mustn't dive.'

'And where will we finish up if we keep on running?'

Petersen showed me our position on the chart. 'On the beach at Agadir. Or we could make a run for it through the Canaries.'

'Well, that's all very nice. But what will we really do?'

Petersen rested his head on his hand and reflected. 'There's still a chance for us. One hour before it gets light the moon will disappear. That will be the darkest hour of the night. We must use it.'

Through the early hours the chase continued. We had a speed advantage of about 4 knots and gradually the distance between the two vessels widened. Towards dawn it became darker; the moon was low on the horizon and shrouded in mist. The lookouts silently observed their allotted quadrants through binoculars; the captain was propped against the periscope housing, staring astern. The steamer was no longer visible to the naked eye and only the low white ripple of her bow-wave confirmed that she was still very much intent on the pursuit.

When I next visited the bridge Bleichrodt grasped my arm and asked if she had wirelessed. 'It's all quiet, sir,' I replied.

'Good. Now go below and tell Borchardt to prepare the stern tubes. When it's completely dark we'll turn to starboard and perhaps we can bump her off as she passes by.' I relayed the Commander's order and the news of what was to be attempted spread quickly through the boat. The excitement grew as they contemplated this crafty manoeuvre to send the Q-ship to the bottom.

When it had become completely dark the engines were reduced to slow ahead to reduce the wake and the boat's head came round 90° to starboard. Then we switched to the electric motors for silent running at half speed. The men crept to battle stations. Stern tubes 5 and 6 were reported ready. Hümpel and I kept the radio watch and Ferdinand Hagen was in the sound room. We waited and waited. The *City of Auckland* did not appear, did not signal and Ferdinand could not find her propeller sounds in the hydrophones.

After an hour of complete silence Bleichrodt gave the order to stand down and then settled in his bunk with a sigh.

'That skunk probably stopped as soon as he lost sight of us,' he said with a laugh. 'His bow-wave simply fell away as we watched. He's a very refined character. He's probably somewhere out there right now listening for our diesels.'

Shortly before dawn we dived and reloaded the four forward torpedo tubes and then set off in search of the steamer. At noon Bleichrodt gave it up. It irked him that she had escaped and the incident disturbed him to a much greater extent than was really warranted.

On a trial dive it was found that air bubbles were rising from the conning tower. Schewe thought that the acetylene bottles stored there might be the source, but, after soaping and tightening the seals, it was clear that these were not responsible.

We cruised south-east of the Azores in glorious summer weather, but, with the exception of a few dolphins and a school of six whales which escorted the boat for about an hour, the ocean was deserted.

The BdU signalled to all boats:

For the duration of the Russian campaign the Führer wishes to avoid all possible sources of conflict with the United States. U-boat commanders must exercise prudence in this respect. US merchant vessels must not be attacked irrespective of whether found within or outside the blockade zone, in convoy or independently. Warships of the rank of cruiser or above identified as enemy may be attacked either within or outside the blockade zone. But no warship is necessarily enemy merely because it is sailing by night without lights, even in the blockade zone.

This was all much easier said than done. By Sunday 13 July, 1941, *U-109* was off Tenerife and had been out two weeks from Lorient. We motored slowly through acres of cotton bales which must have been adrift for weeks, since no ship had been sunk here recently. Besides ourselves in the Central Atlantic were *U-66* (Zapp), *U-123* (Hardegen) and *U-A* (Eckermann), which were all off Freetown, but none had reported a success. Because of the sinkings achieved in the area a few months earlier by U-boats, the British had decided to steer clear of it, at any rate temporarily.

On *U-109* our periscopes were leaking abysmally, even on shallow dives; the stuffing boxes had been fitted askew and couldn't be put straight. It was bad workmanship – or worse – by the dockyard.

Schewe told me that, with thirty-one torpedoes still aboard, we couldn't allow the fuel bunkers to fall below 50 cubic metres, otherwise the boat would become top heavy. That evening the BdU informed Bleichrodt, who had earlier requested some essential spare parts and more fuel:

> Supply envisaged *Moro* night of 21 July. Report by short signal Yes if arrival possible on stated date. Otherwise give preferred date.

Bleichrodt showed the signal to the First Lieutenant and said, 'What a load of crap.'

'Where's *Moro?*' asked Schwartzkopff.

With a sly grin I suggested, 'Could it be southern Spain?'

The Commander asked the coxswain. 'Yes, gentlemen, let's set course for Cadiz!'

Shortly after midnight on 17 July Bleichrodt signalled U-boat Command that he would prefer to rendezvous with a supply ship in the Equator area, but they informed him that none was available: even the secret bases in the harbours of Dakar and Las Palmas could no longer be used. Temporarily, we would have to use Cadiz.

On 18 July the Wireless Observation Service reported a convoy of fifteen ships escorted by four destroyers departing from Gibraltar on a bearing to the west-north-west, and we headed for it at top speed. There was a long swell from the north-east and we shipped a lot of sea green over the bridge. *U-109* was the only submarine in this vicinity and there was no air reconnaissance. As soon as we began to approach the Bay of Cadiz Bleichrodt gave up interest in the convoy.

Early on the morning of 21 July, 1941, we stood towards the neutral coast: it was illegal under the conventions of neutrality for vessels of war to refit and re-arm in a neutral harbour and it was important that the British did not come into possession of good proof of the activity.[19]

The Cape St Vincent light was sighted at 0100 at a distance of sixty miles: by dawn we were under the coat of Spain and we dived once Petersen had calculated that Cadiz could be reached submerged by nightfall.

Towards 1400 the Commander examined the horizons with the periscope and shortly afterwards called me into the control room.

'Can you hear anything in the hydrophones?'

'No, sir.'

'I can see a fishing vessel about two and a half miles away. Looks like a Portuguese. You should have reported it some time ago.'

'Yes, Captain, I will examine the equipment immediately.'

I felt uneasy as I returned to the hydrophones room, for this was something beyond my experience. The wireless crew examined the exterior pressure boxes for moisture and broke down the assembly into its component parts, but everything appeared to be in order. When the Commander retracted the periscope and came forward for a report I told him that the equipment was definitely in working order but that there seemed to be no reception. Bleichrodt's voice had a dangerous edge to it as he said, 'That vessel's heading straight for us and you can't hear it. How can you report that your equipment is functioning properly?'

I cleaned the set and replaced all ninety-six tubes. The result was the same; I could hear the sea, but not machinery or propeller noise. Keller arrived and asked me what was wrong.

'I don't know, Lieutenant. Either the Captain's hallucinating or that's a sailing ship. There are no propeller noises to be heard.' Keller peered around cautiously and saw that the Captain was in the control room but out of earshot. 'Perhaps it's the Flying Dutchman,' he said softly and we both laughed.

A few hours later, when Hümpel had the radio watch, I hurried to the hydrophones room when the Captain shouted that he could see another ship through the periscope. When the vessel was about two miles off I picked out the faintest propeller sound. Keller came to join me and had just sat down when Bleichrodt asked me what type of ship I thought it was.

The Lieutenant and I looked at each other and shrugged, and then Keller took the voice pipe and said quietly, 'It's a fishing boat. Her bottom has been recently painted with red lead. The Captain's on the bridge smoking a fat cigar which I'm fairly sure is in the left-hand corner of his mouth.'

We listened with bated breath as the helmsman in the conning tower repeated the message word for word in a monotone, and for a moment there was a deathly silence in the tower.

'Telegraphist petty officer to the tower hatch!'

I took off the headphones and stood up. 'Tell him straight away that it was me,' Keller said with a laugh. As I came through the circular pressure doorway into the control room I saw that all the men there were grinning. At the foot of the tower ladder I reported myself to the Commander and, before I could speak, Bleichrodt gave me a rocket. It was some time before I had the chance to inform the Captain that it had been Keller who had made the report through the voice-pipe, and after this sank in, Bleichrodt told me to summon the Second Lieutenant.

While the Commander was screaming at Keller the whole crew could barely conceal their delight; even the Chief Engineer wasn't able to hide a broad grin. But for me the affair was not so funny. Why was the underwater audibility here so poor? At dusk the Commander saw the shadows of three vessels without lights dead ahead and these could only be British naval vessels. When I told the Captain that I was unable to detect sound through the hydrophone equipment he told me to smash it up. He was in a boiling rage, unreasoning and unreasonable, and it was possibly the first serious manifestation of the neurosis he was developing.

As there was no time to go round the patrol boats, Bleichrodt decided to sail through beneath them at 180 feet, at 90 revolutions. I continued to use the hydrophones for some time without success when suddenly I heard the British ships. I leant forward and reported the fact to the Captain.

'What are they doing?'

'They're moving very slowly, probably trying to hear us. We're right under the middle patrol vessel.' The captain took Hümpel's headset and listened with a frown. Above us the screws were slowly grinding through the water.

'They can hear as poorly as we did just now,' I explained. 'It must be to do with the water layers.' Bleichrodt returned the hydrophones and gave me a pitying look. 'Smash the bloody thing up, I told you. But I'll have more to say about this when we're back in port,' he promised, and went away muttering.

'In his eyes, we've really shit ourselves,' said Hümpel.

'Just keep quiet and wait,' I told him.' There's nothing wrong with the equipment. At this depth we should definitely be able to hear something. You'll have to get used to the fact that officers of the Seaman Branch all mistrust telegraphy simply because they don't understand it.'

Hümpel scratched his head. 'If that's the case, I have no wish to be a boat's senior telegraphist,' he said.

At 2200 we surfaced. The coxswain had brought us precisely to the approaches to the harbour of Cadiz; as usual his navigation had been immaculate. The U-boat glided into the port just after midnight and all three watchkeeping officers and the Captain were on the bridge. It was a wonderful summer night and the bright lights of the quay installations glittered in the still waters of the harbour. According to information supplied by U-boat Command, the German supply ship *Thalia* was at anchor in the middle of the bay.

'There, ahead to port,' Schwartzkopff reported softly. The figures on the bridge levelled their binoculars towards the shadowy outline.

'I can make out three steamers there,' said Petersen.

'Yes, dammit. Now all we have to do is pick out the right one,' Bleichrodt told them, 'and one of the others is bound to be a Tommy ship, keeping a kindly watch over ours.'

Schwartzkopff had a sketch of the *Thalia* and was comparing her lines with the silhouettes of the three moored merchantmen. 'It's the first one,' he said at length.

Bleichrodt was sceptical. 'Ask them for the recognition signal,' the Commander ordered Walter Gross, who was holding a large lamp with a blue filter. The boatswain flashed across the coded request. When the reply came back, it was gibberish.

'There's something wrong here,' Walter Gross said loudly.

'The swine are trying to take us in,' Bleichrodt remarked.

We motored slowly past the second ship, which by her superstructure could not be the *Thalia* and, when Walter Gross signalled the third ship, the correct response came back immediately from her wheelhouse. Bleichrodt ordered hand weapons to be distributed amongst the bridge personnel as a precautionary measure and instructions were given that if an attempt should be made to board the boat we were to open fire immediately. Even I was issued with a machine pistol.

We manoeuvred round the harbour basin in a wide curve, came alongside the German supply ship from astern and stopped. High above us dark figures silently watched our arrival before lowering a Jacob's ladder. Schwartzkopff climbed up and a few moments later shouted his confirmation that all was well; safety catches were applied to the hand weapons and the crew swarmed up on deck to begin the feverish work of replenishment in the darkness.

By 0500 we had topped up the bunkers and shipped aboard the spare parts we required, plus three torpedoes and fresh provisions, including vegetables and fruit. When the off-watch men returned from a visit to the *Thalia* Ferdinand Hagen was so drunk that he had to be carried back aboard. The lines were thrown clear and we made for the open sea at full speed on the electric motors.

Not long after clearing the port of Cadiz we had to dive hurriedly when we saw that the three British patrol vessels had closed in and were waiting for us just outside the Spanish 3-mile limit.

'They knew we were coming,' Bleichrodt told me. 'The first steamer that gave us the garbled response was a Britisher. He's been there several days. He probably signalled to the destroyers about us.'

However we eluded the British warships without difficulty in the poor acoustic conditions underwater and Bleichrodt headed the boat for the Atlantic. During a sweep with the periscope he noticed that the boat was still leaving a trail of large bubbles in her wake.

On 24 July an Italian submarine reported a Gibraltar-bound convoy south-west of Cape St Vincent, but the position was vague and there was no homing signal. We sailed west through the oily swell to the south of Madeira, sighting only three neutrals. Schewe was cursing the poor quality of the fuel that the *Thalia* had given us and the trail of bubbles that could not be stopped. The mood in the boat was rock-bottom: there were no ships to be found because the British had called a halt to their Freetown sailings.

On 30 July, when our fruitless wanderings had brought us to a point north of the Cape Verde Islands, the BdU ordered Bleichrodt to proceed northwards in zig-zags at 180 miles of longitude per day with the possibility of action soon against a convoy leaving Gibraltar. Three other boats in the south, *U-93*, *U-94* and *U-124*, were also instructed to make their way in that direction; only Hardegen in *U-123* was to remain off Freetown.

A large whale decided to accompany us, taking up station sometimes as close as nine feet from the hull. When Bleichrodt inspected the great animal from the bridge, he said, 'I only hope he doesn't rub alongside, he could damage one of the depth rudders.' The Chief Engineer put his head up and, after one look, exclaimed, 'Man, if he gives us a swipe with his tail he could knock off the steering gear. I suggest we dive, sir.' A few moments later *U-109* slid into the depths.

The whale made a welcome change from the monotonous U-boat routine of watches, meals and sleep, the incessant drone of the diesels and the slow thrashing of the screws. The commander was nervous and easily irritated. He was a famous name and a Knight's Cross holder and much was expected of him by the BdU, but so far he had achieved nothing. The whale seemed happy in company with *U-109*, for when the boat surfaced again we found it was still with us and spouting so heavily that the officer of the watch had to send below for four sets of oilskins and sou'westers.

On 2 August we had been at sea five weeks. It was uncomfortably warm in our long steel cylinder: drinking water had to be rationed to one glass per day per man because the desalinating machine was broken. We washed in seawater, no longer shaved, and when we became thirsty we drank the red wine of the *Thalia*. The periscope stuffing boxes were leaking severely and there was a lot of water sloshing around in the boat.

Three days later, when we were close to Madeira again, Bleichrodt put us on a course for the Moroccan coast at Casablanca. We sailed through warm rain showers in poor visibility in a high swell which occasionally sent a green mass of water rolling above the bridge to surprise the lookouts. A man was stationed permanently in the tower to dry their binoculars and the quartermaster, who steered in the tower, had to wear oilskins because so much water crashed in through the open hatch. It was a fairly pointless exercise scouting for shipping in the conditions and we spent a lot more time submerged than usual.

However, one day, after several hours pitching and rolling on the surface, Otto Peters came into the NCO's mess wiping his face with the kerchief which he habitually wore round his throat. 'I don't know why he keeps four men on the bridge,' he said, 'one's enough. There's no ships left in the Atlantic.' The control room petty officer liked to be provocative; nothing pleased him more than to upset everybody. We sipped our coffee, ignoring him. He poured himself a cup and sat opposite us with a sly grin. 'Boys, boys,' he said to nobody in particular, 'we've been out nearly six weeks and we've still got 24 torpedoes aboard. I think that's something of a record for the U-boat Arm. I wonder if we'll still have them with us by Christmas?' We looked at the smirking face in stony silence. He gave me a nudge. 'This is going to be a long, long voyage. So long without a woman, too. I'll be getting off this boat soon.'

Suddenly there was a roll of thunder in the distance and two sharp underwater explosions. We looked at each other in consternation. 'Oh God,' said Otto, 'when I think about our trail of bubbles . . .'

'Petty Officer Hirschfeld to the control room!' Schewe was standing behind the chart table near the retractable radio aerial, illuminating it with a flashlamp. 'The aerial is leaking, take a look at the stuffing boxes,' Schewe told me. There was a fine trickle of water running down the exterior of the tube and into the bilge. 'We want to seal off the tower boxes to stop the leak, but that will mean that you won't be able to raise the aerial.'

'OK, do it. We won't be wanting to transmit from periscope depth anyway,' I replied. As I was making my way forward, I had to pass through the Officers' Mess; Keller grasped my arm and said in a whisper, 'I can't decode the Officers Only signal we received last night. Give me a hand with it, but don't tell anyone, OK?'

'But of course, Lieutenant!' I quickly found his error and decoded the message.

Achtung! Suspicion of sabotage on U-boat torpedoes. In two torpedoes returned from a mission a quantity of foreign matter had been introduced into the outer ring of the direction-keeping apparatus to impart a sheer, and setting angles had been altered so that torpedoes would run in a circle. Check all torpedoes and report similar discoveries with torpedo number. BdU.

'The swine,' said Keller, 'we could sink ourselves with our own eels,' and he hurried off to show the signal to the Commander. Werner Borchardt and his mechanics had to spend the whole day checking all twenty-four torpedoes, but found nothing of note to report.

As we neared Casablanca the seas were very high and confused and the boat rolled wildly. One could only sleep securely by thrusting a leg through the guard-rails along the side of the bunk. I placed a signal from the BdU before the Captain:

0938/7/178 Departure Gibraltar convoy expected 8 August. Remain unseen at all costs. Maintain radio silence unless important tactically.

Otto Peters stuck his unshaven pirate's face into the radio room. 'What's the whisper, Hirschfeld? Another accursed convoy?'

'Yes it is, Otto, and I only hope we're not the contact boat.'

The following day was 8 August and Korth in *U-93* reported a naval group consisting of a battleship, a troop transport and two destroyers on a westerly course, but the Gibraltar convoy was considered to be such a high priority that U-boats were instructed to proceed no more than sixteen hours' sailing time from their specified waiting positions.

The small Spanish town of Tarifa lies on a promontory facing the Moroccan coast which is no more than eight miles distant, and from here German agents were easily able to keep all Straits shipping under the closest observation through binoculars. On 9 August they reported that the convoy had emerged into the Gulf of Cadiz and was proceeding south-west close in along the Moroccan shore. If it held to this course *U-109* would be the contact boat, I realized – something we were all most keen to avoid. The convoy consisted of about seventy ships, many of which were small, in the 1500–2500 tons range. Bleichrodt swore softly as he read the signal telling him this and, when I confided to him my fears that *U-109* would be the homing boat, he said, 'Don't worry about it, Petty Officer. If we are, we'll make one report and then attack, going through the middle of the convoy firing off all our tubes to right and left, as I once did with

Teddy Suhren in *U-48*. But seventy ships! My God, what a convoy!' He shook his head and returned the signal log. The reports made no mention of escort vessels, which seemed a bit odd.

Bleichrodt had been ordered to make at high speed for grid square DJ2215 about twenty miles off Casablanca; as the boat responded, the bows burrowed deeply into the heavy seas and huge waves slammed against the tower. The bridge watch was regularly buried for up to ten seconds at a time under the great liquid hills and the Chief had to keep the bilge pump running constantly because the lookouts were more concerned with remaining aboard then kicking the manhole lid shut every time a breaker climbed up and swamped the bridge.

Early on the morning of 10 August the BdU notified the pack, which was strung out in a line from Casablanca to the Azores, that the convoy was now proceeding through the Gulf of Cadiz in a westerly direction, and the nearest boats were ordered to patrol up and down north and south across the anticipated track of the convoy. *U-109* pounded up and down in the high seas under low hanging cloud all morning and, just as the crew were settling down to the afternoon meal, the alarm bells rang, the bridge watch came tumbling down into the control room and the vents banged open. Within 35 seconds we were under. Schwartzkopff told me that a destroyer with three funnels had been spotted at a distance of four miles, despite the poor visibility.

'Why are we at periscope depth?' I enquired.

'The Commander is going to sink this one if we can get close enough.'

I reported that I was unable to hear the destroyer's propellers through the hydrophones, and Bleichrodt, who was at the attack periscope in the conning tower and who had just lost the destroyer from sight, started to rant in the most bellicose manner about the hydrophone equipment. As we were preparing to surface the enemy warship was seen in the periscope approaching from astern. I leant forward and through the voice-pipe eavesdropped the conversation in the control room.

'He's coming directly for us,' the Commander was saying. 'That's odd. He can't have seen us. Petersen, write this down. "Tall narrow bridge, three funnels, with a larger gap between the rear two. A tall, thin foremast with a large crows' nest. Astern, only a short signal mast."' There was a long silence, broken only by the occasional purr of the periscope motor. The Chief was evidently having great difficulty holding the boat at periscope depth in the heavy seaway.

'Battle stations,' said the Captain. Maureschat went to the attack computer in the tower and the torpedo mechanics readied the forward tubes. Suddenly the propellers became audible in the hydrophones. 'So there's nothing wrong with the equipment then?' Schwartzkopff said to me in a tone of surprise. 'Of course not, Lieutenant, it's all to do with the water and the fact that at the moment we're crossing some shallows here.'

At last we had one of the destroyers at our mercy and we were crossing our fingers that the torpedoes didn't let us down.

'Chief! Keep the boat down!' the Captain shouted suddenly, and the periscope was quickly lowered.

'Request an increase in speed, sir. I can't hold her like this!' Weber cried.

I went cold: if we broke surface now the destroyer would see us for sure. The Chief Engineer managed to keep the boat submerged, but now we went so deep that even with the periscope at maximum extension, all the Captain could see through it was water. While Weber was juggling with the taps and controls in the effort to return the boat to the required depth, the destroyer had made herself scarce.

'Shit,' said Bleichrodt, 'now he's turned away. We've lost him.' Everywhere there was a disappointed silence, and a cold, lingering stare fell upon the Chief Engineer.

We surfaced at 1500. Kaufmann in *U-79* had reported the convoy in sight in grid square CG8661, a position south of the Algarve on the parallel of Cadiz. The convoy had therefore changed course, but *U-79* had been driven off by the escorts and had now lost contact. Bleichrodt headed north-west to intercept.

The long-drawn-out gale persisted overnight, but the cloud cover began to thin and break up shortly after dawn, dangerous conditions so close to Gibraltar. Just after 0900 the port diesel cooling pump failed. We had to continue on one engine and at 1100 hrs we made a steep emergency dive to 180 feet when an aircraft attacked us from cloud. After a few moments there were two deafening explosions.

'Those went off ahead of us,' said Keller. 'He's a crafty dog, this one, he didn't drop them into the spot where we dived like most of them do.'

There were no damage reports. 'Keller, you'll have to take an extra lookout with you on the bridge just to watch the sky. At least while we're in the Bay of Gibraltar, anyway,' said Bleichrodt.

'Yes, sir. And how long will we be staying down?'

'We'll remain at 180 feet for an hour. He won't stay around that long.' In the distance there was a growl of underwater thunder, depth charges; that was where the convoy probably was.

When I went into the control room to examine the radio aerial and direction finder I found that the former was dry and the latter leaking a steady spray. Schewe was leaning on the periscope well, a doubtful expression on his features. 'And that's only at 180 feet. At 300 feet the depth rudder operators will have to wear their oilskins,' he said.

'What's that noise in the stern?' I asked. Schewe gave me a worried nod.

'The diesel couplings are knocking. It can probably be heard some way off. But we can't do anything about it.'

More thunderclaps rent the ocean, much closer than before. The coxswain commented from the chart table, 'Someone's going to get sunk out there.' We counted off whole patterns of explosions, and it was methodical, not a few depth charges scattered in the deep at random. When there was a pause in the closer bombardment we could still hear a backdrop of distant thundering. Peters shook his head. 'This noise all the time,' he said, 'I wonder what the fish think of it.'

Bleichrodt was curious to see what was going on and surfaced with caution, but sea and sky were empty, and when I showed him the signal reports at midday it was clear that the situation was confused; many boats had reported seeing the convoy, or at least *a* convoy, but at widely diverse locations. The BdU considered that boats should concentrate on *U-93*'s sighting at 0800 when the convoy was seen in grid square CG8226, close to Cape St Vincent and heading north towards Lisbon. On the way we spoke to Schulz (*U-124*) and von Tiesenhausen(*U-331*), who were both operating in reliance on the report of an FW200 aircraft that the convoy was well to the south-west of Cape St Vincent, but for some reason the Commander discounted this and continued the pursuit northwards. More and more signals were piling up about single columns of ships steering the most unlikely courses: three steamers and four destroyers here, eight steamers with seven sloops or corvettes there. There were as many warships as freighters. At 1545 Kuppisch in *U-94* announced that he had the convoy in sight, heading west at slow speed in grid square 5876. This was off Silves, on the Portuguese coast below Lisbon.

At 1600 we submerged to allow the engineers to work on the port diesel. During the wait I heard Schwartzkopff and the Commander discussing the convoy.

'This piece of theatre is a naval diversion to keep as many U-boats in this corner of the Atlantic as possible. Meanwhile the important convoys sail undisturbed from Canada to England,' Bleichrodt said.

But this was not the view of the BdU who, in a signal to all boats that afternoon exhorted us:

> This convoy must not be allowed to reach England under any circumstances!

We surfaced towards midnight. Parts of the compressed air piping system and three of the vents were damaged and the tanks could only be blown slowly and cautiously. The diesel exhaust valves were leaking. Bleichrodt continued the search throughout the early hours of 12 August. There was a stiff north-west breeze which was piling up an uncomfortably high swell and the night was as dark as pitch with very poor visibility. The convoy had definitely split into a number of smaller groups which seemed to be merely sailing back and forth; some U-boats had reported that, when they sighted one of these smaller convoys, they had been detected by a destroyer or corvette which bore down on them with unerring accuracy even in the darkness. This had never happened before.

At 0425 von Tiesenhausen signalled that he had the convoy in sight west of Lisbon and heading north west at 7 knots, so Bleichrodt decided to link up with him. At daybreak we actually got a glimpse of some activity on the horizon, but were driven off by a Sunderland flying boat. At 1600 we had to make an emergency dive when a Liberator bomber came for us at low level and dropped a bomb, and another astern an hour later, and this despite the irregular zig-zags we had been making while submerged.

'Chief, we must be leaving an oil slick,' Bleichrodt said, 'or was that last bomb coincidence?'

'That's something we can only find out when we surface, sir.'

When we did surface the bridge watch immediately spotted the slick.

Bleichrodt looked very pensive as he contemplated attacking a well-defended convoy while trailing an oil slick and a stream of large bubbles.

Among the most recent signals was a report from Hardegen in *U-123*, who had last been heard from near the Gulf of Guinea, and I thought that he must have a very fast U-boat to have got here so soon. Hardegen was the only commander to have actually seen the main convoy, which he had allowed to pass overhead of him. He described it as having at its centre a heavy cruiser with a steel mattress on the mainmast which he suspected to be a locating device. The cruiser had a close escort of four destroyers. There was a ring of corvettes and destroyers loosely placed around this central group, and another ring of assorted small warships surrounding that. This looked very bad; it seemed as if the convoy might really be the field trials of a new anti-U-boat system and, if so, would be little more than a lure and a death trap for us. It was heading nonchalantly this way and that and at a speed so slow that there was no prospect that it would be anywhere near England even in a fortnight. Bleichrodt was now concentrating on Hardegen's information and, at about 1900, the lookouts reported mastheads. Bleichrodt, keeping his distance, announced he would attack after dark. The weather was favourable, with thick cloud and occasional heavy showers reducing visibility. The Commander had just stretched out on his bunk for a few hours' sleep when the alarm bells rang and *U-109* dived steeply. Schwartzkopff came to the Captain's nook, his oilskins and sou'wester still dripping.

'Destroyer, sir, came bows-on, port side, out of a squall.'

'Did he see us?'

'Definitely, the distance was less than four miles.'

Hümpel gave me the reserve headphones; already we could clearly hear the twitter of the destroyer's propellers. The captain asked me if I had a clear fix on the British vessel.

'Yes, sir, at 270°.'

'Good. Chief, go to 300 feet.' The Commander gave the coxswain a new course to steer. The enemy's screws were grinding ever nearer, ever louder. Suddenly the boat was shaken as if by a giant's fist; there were three tremendous explosions, fairly near, but fortunately dead astern. A water-level glass cracked in the control room. I clutched the hydrophones installation. Hümpel stared at me. 'Is it going to be like Greenland again?' he asked.

'Of course not. It's only a single destroyer. There, the dog's turning.' I passed this information to the Commander, and shortly the boat curved round on a new course and sank to 450 feet. The depth rudder operators cursed at the heavy drizzle from the leaking direction finder above them.

Above us the destroyer was still turning, and then he cut our course.

We held our breath; the noise of the destroyer's propellers seemed to fill the boat. We heard the depth charges splash into the sea. I felt weak as the fear constricted my chest; I listened to the screws dwindling as the destroyer ran off at speed to keep from being blown apart by the explosion from her own depth charges. I counted off the seconds: there was no explosion. Just as we breathed a sigh of relief the inferno broke loose and a series of massive hammer blows struck the hull on the port side. In the middle of the enduring

It screamed above the din,

rgency generator cut in. I
ssure from the explosions
bling. There was damage
f the external seals were
d on again.

time,' Keller remarked. I
ap with each attack. That

sea at full speed, but her
's manoeuvre and crossed
f the next pattern rumbled
e British warship pounded
oil slick, again cut across
rges inaccurately and then

r we headed west, towards
to be; at 2140 Hardegen
quare CG4551, about 200
south of our boat.
leichrodt said he had found
and the sea running high,
en there would be an escort
e had no choice but to turn
patrol vessel always seemed
estimated the convoy to be;
ntinued on what seemed a
odt deduced that the escorts
e cruiser.
th, Bleichrodt believing that
other U-boats participating
possible to get through the
ne reported the convoy at
ly discounted, since we had
othing; then von Tiesenhau-
CG4153, 100 miles north of
hour earlier. Bruno Petersen
he tiny crosses on his charts

ng homing signals, but we
irection finder was flooded;
Sunderland had been circling

above the convoy all night. At dawn a number of mastheads were seen, but a destroyer promptly came towards us at high speed and, although reluctant to do so on account of the long oil slick, Bleichrodt was forced to dive in order to escape. He selected a heading to the north; the British vessel was approaching from the east.

'Do you have him?' the Captain asked me at the hydrophones.

'Yes, sir, and he's getting louder pretty quickly.'

'Good. Notice whether he follows us round or heads straight for the spot where we dived. We'll stay at 90 feet.' I felt a cold shiver run up my spine. If the destroyer kept to the original course Bleichrodt would attempt to nail him with the stern tubes; that was why we were so close to periscope depth.

The destroyer maintained its course and the anticipation of the Captain seemed about to be rewarded, when suddenly the twittering of the propeller blades died away.

'Destroyer has stopped,' I called into the control room. The Captain ordered slow ahead, 90 revolutions. Above, the enemy ship was hove-to, listening down. It fell quiet in the boat.

'What's he doing now, Hirschfeld?'

'I can't hear him any more.'

'But you must surely be able to hear the auxiliary machinery or something.'

'Nothing! Nothing at all.' The Commander frowned. 'I told you to boil that equipment in acid,' he said and went back through the circular doorway into the control room.

Keller sidled up to me. 'What's up then?'

'He still thinks there's something wrong with the hydrophones,' I told him. Keller nodded. 'He doesn't trust anything in any part of the boat. We're making an awful lot of water in the stern. I don't think we can survive a depth-charging. That's what's making him so nervous.' Keller put his head into the control room and then padded back. 'We're going deeper. Perhaps you'll be able to hear better.'

It helped; after a while I could hear the destroyer's screws softly revolving.

'Destroyer is at slow ahead,' I informed the control room.

Keller was still standing at my side. 'If he spots our oil slick . . .' he muttered grimly.

There was a long period of waiting. Water could be heard trickling into the boat, particularly in the area of the galley. Then the destroyer's propellers began to grind again.

'Destroyer approaching.'

'Go to 450 feet.' The electric motors were at full ahead to get us as quickly as possible to the lower depth. The Chief trimmed the boat at 480 feet and then the British vessel ejected another group of depth charges which tumbled down for thirty seconds before exploding. It was almost incredible that after such a close pattern of detonations the boat could still be afloat, but it didn't seem that the flooding had got any worse.

The destroyer was making off at high speed. 'If he's really departing,' Keller remarked to the Commander, 'then he couldn't get a fix on us. I think he definitely couldn't hear us, since we couldn't hear him.'

'Well in that case he must have seen our oil slick, otherwise how did he manage to get that last series so close? Or do you have another opinion?'

'No, sir, but why is he leaving then?'

The Commander shrugged. 'They probably called him back. Just listen to the depth charges in the distance. There are other boats closer to the convoy that have to be dealt with.'

The destroyer *was* leaving. It was fortunate that he had no Asdic and that the engineers had managed to silence the banging of the diesel coupling. We crept away underwater and surfaced much later that morning. In the signal repeats an Italian submarine reported the midday position of the convoy to be grid square CG4172, heading due west, which was precisely where von Tiesenhausen had seen it twelve hours earlier. We slunk off to the north-west to repair with a view to an attack later that night. There seemed to be little point in trying to do much in daylight.

At 1547 we had to dive to 300 feet when a low-flying Sunderland approached. We were not attacked immediately, but after fifteen minutes three huge thunderclaps rolled through the depths. We stared at each other in astonishment. These were not bombs but depth charges, dropped from an aircraft, and a little later, when the boat came to periscope depth, the Sunderland banked round in a curve and let us have three more.

At 1730, when Bleichrodt was searching for the aircraft with the sky-scope, Schwartzkopff discovered the trail of bubbles through the attack periscope. A steady flow, some of the bubbles being as large as the palm of a hand, was rising to the surface from the interior of the tower.

The signals traffic showed that three other boats had been savaged and were returning to port: the afternoon's depth-charging had been directed against Hardegen in *U-123* and the Italian boat *Marconi*. Nobody had a success to report.

Now there was a conference in the Officers' Mess. Weber stated that the damage to the boat could not be repaired with the tools on board and at 2200 Bleichrodt decided to return to Lorient; there was no point in going on with the boat in this state. We were glad that he had come to this conclusion, although we knew that it had been a difficult one for him to take. For the first time in his career as a U-boat commander, he was bringing a boat home with a full load of torpedoes.

The next morning Kuppisch in *U-94* and Schulz in *U-124* both signalled to U-boat Command that they were on their way to base with serious damage. Six boats had been forced to retire and the convoy would reach England. It was the first really significant battlefield defeat for the U-boat Arm.

U-109 crept along the Spanish coast and off Cape Finisterre turned north-east for Lorient. The previous day *U-124* had seen an FW200 going down into the sea trailing a long ribbon of smoke: returning U-boats were requested to look out for the crew.

At 0200 on 16 August we turned to investigate a white star-shell, but were forced away as a corvette came straight for us; we had nearly stumbled into an anti-submarine group.

'I can't shake off the impression that they can locate us even from their small corvettes,' Keller told me later. 'What do you think? Is it possible?'

'It's obvious to me, Lieutenant,' I replied, 'they've developed small aerials and don't need a big mattress on the masthead.'

In the NCO's mess that morning Werner Borchardt said, 'Imagine this, Wolfgang. We're running into port and the mood is absolutely rock-bottom. Can you understand it?' I looked round at all the hangdog faces: only Otto Peters wore a carefree smirk. Berthold Seidel came from his bunk to pour himself a cup of coffee. He had sailed on every voyage with Bleichrodt. 'Yes,' he said, 'no ships sunk and coming home without a single pennant on the periscope. It's never happened to me before.' There was a long pause and then a thought seemed to strike him. 'Oh my God,' he said, 'What if the Führer knew?' We all laughed: it was our newest catch-phrase, taken from BBC propaganda broadcasts.

On the last evening before docking we had to avoid numerous fishing smacks near the Ile de Croix and, submerged to 90 feet, to spend the night on the bottom. Bleichrodt deemed it safer there than waiting offshore at anchor. The current was powerful and the keel rolled and crunched across the shingle and shell of the sea bed.

'Can't you get the boat to rest a bit quieter than this?' the Commander snapped at the Chief, as the latter wandered past on his way to his bunk. An extra ten tons of water ballast was admitted to

WOLFGANG HIRSCHFELD
(Left) Telegraphist, Stralsund, January 1936
(Right) Junior Petty Officer, U-Boat Training Flotilla, Pillau, 1940

Oslo 1938. German and Italian ratings on the quay in front of the Italian sail-training ship *Amerigo Vespucci.* (Hirschfeld fourth from right)

WOLFGANG HIRSCHFELD

Senior Petty Officer, *U-109*.
Lorient, October, 1942

Warrant Officer, 1943

Lieutenant Commander (later Commander) Hans Georg Fischer.
Training and first Atlantic Patrol, Spring, 1941

Lieutenant Commander (later Commander) Heinrich Bleichrodt ('AJAX')
Commanded *U-109* on six war voyages between June, 1941, and January, 1943. Seen here in 1943, wearing the Oak Leaves to his Knight's Cross, awarded in September, 1942

Warrant Officer Petersen taking a sun sight. Atlantic cruise July-August, 1941. On U-boats navigation was the responsibility of the Coxswain. Petersen was outstanding in this respect

On the bridge – Summer cruise, 1941. Bleichrodt with Paul Pötter (nearest the camera). Pötter would later be one of the few survivors of *U-859*, sunk by the Royal Navy off Penang in the closing days of the war

In the Atlantic, 1941.
A view of *U-109*, looking forward.
Note the 105mm gun and (fore-
ground) part of the torpedo loading
cradle

**Lookout duty off Labrador,
Winter, 1941.**
Leading Seaman Alois Wagenhofer
(left) and Cdr Eberhard Hoffmann,
Commander-Aspirant, later lost in
command of *U-165*

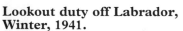

Bleichrodt in bridge attire. Behind, Helmsman Paul
Pötter

Off Bermuda, 16 April, 1942. Bleichrodt and the First Mate of the Swiss
steamer *Calanda* go through the ship's papers, closely watched by Lt Witte

the tanks, but no improvement was noticed, and so we spent a restless night listening to the scraping of the keel over the gravel.

At 1100 *U-109* surfaced into the sunshine and followed the waiting minesweeper escort towards the coast. At slow speed the boat passed through the Narrows between Kernevel and Port Louis. Beneath the trees on the banks of the River Skorf staff officers waved their caps from the grounds of the BdU's mansion. Then the minesweeper bore away, revealing the crowded hulk of the *Isere* dead ahead. A band played, the lines flew across and *U-109* returned safely from her second war patrol.[20]

*   *   *

Washed and shaved, we stood in our No. 1 blue uniforms in the courtyard of the Salzwedel Barracks awaiting the arrival of the BdU. Punctually at ten the black Mercedes limousine rolled between the wrought iron gates and stopped. Lt Cdr Bleichrodt brought the crew of *U-109* to attention and saluted. Dönitz returned the greeting and thanked Bleichrodt curtly. Then he came slowly towards the men and stood facing the front rank.

'At ease,' he said. The Admiral folded his arms and stood silently, his lips and eyes narrow. The tension was electric. Slightly behind the Admiral lurked the Commander. At last the Admiral broke the silence. 'Men of the *U-109*! You were off the coast of Africa and you achieved nothing.' He paused. 'But you cannot be faulted for that.' He spoke slowly and quietly, yet his voice was sharpening as he went on, 'Off the coast of Spain, you found a convoy and sank nothing.' He paused again, and then resumed with a deeper, harsher tone, 'I have the impression that you didn't even try.'

He turned his head slowly to the Commander, who stood like a pillar of stone, his right hand raised to the peak of his cap in salute. The Admiral looked long and hard at the crew once more. 'I never want to have to say that about *U-109* again.' With that he made his way slowly back to his limousine. Bleichrodt called the crew to attention, but the Admiral did not look back. Without another word he got into his Mercedes and was driven away.

'Oh, he's *really* wild at us,' Otto Peters said.

Bleilchrodt see-sawed on his toes for a moment and then said, 'Gather round.' We formed a semi-circle around him, and he gave a mischievous smile. 'Men, we shouldn't take the Admiral's words too much to heart. They weren't meant as seriously as they sounded. You all know that the boat wasn't battleworthy. With the boat in that state, we could never have got embroiled in a convoy battle and

81

expected to come out of it alive. I brought both yourselves and the boat safely back home and I believe that must be worth something.'

The coxswain nodded and the men grinned; even the Captain found the grinning infectious. 'Now don't let anything get you down. The Senior NCOs will supply the yard with their indents for repair and tomorrow the first watch will take their furlough. Lieutenant Seidel of the Signals Office is waiting to speak to Petty Officer Hirschfeld today in connection with my report about the hydrophones.'

After the parade had been dismissed Berthold Seidel said to me, 'See, that's the real Ajax. He doesn't shit his trousers no matter what the BdU says.' I nodded. 'Yes, but he's not forgiven me for the hydrophones.'

Warrant Officer Bleihauer said, 'Come with me, I'll take you to Lt Seidel.'

'Fair enough, but I'd like to bring Petty Officer Hagen along as a witness,' I replied.

'As you please,' said Bleihauer, and the three of us went off to the Signals Office of the 2nd U-Flotilla where Lt Seidel received us warmly and said in his very pleasant manner, 'Yes, my dear Hirschfeld, the Commander says here in his report on the question as to why he broke off the patrol that the hydrophones were frequently out of service or gave unsatisfactory results. Is that the case?'

'I never reported the hydrophones out of service,' I said. 'Lieutenant, may I speak off the record?'

'Of course,' Seidel replied, 'we're all telegraphists here.'

I explained to him what had transpired off Cadiz and subsequently. Seidel frowned. 'I have had reports from other boats that audibility near Gibraltar is very poor. That can only be due to the fast currents and water layers in that area. Even the affair with the destroyer must be put down to the underwater conditions, because you heard him clearly afterwards.'

'Yes,' I retorted, 'but you just trying telling that to an officer of the Seaman Branch. In the circumstances both of us have decided to request a transfer to another boat. We cannot sail with a Commander who has no faith in us.'

Seidel gave a laugh. 'But gentlemen, Bleichrodt won't let you go. Now don't be hasty. First have your leave, and in the meantime we'll have the hydrophones looked at. Then we'll see. So for now, adios!'

When we were outside Bleihauer clapped me on the shoulder. 'What a load of nonsense, another boat! I'll check the hydrophones myself for you. So, off you go.'

I went to the Yard and handed in my request for repairs. Then, still smarting, I packed my suitcase, went to Lorient railway station and took the Brest-Paris night express for my furlough.

– 5 –

A WELL CONDUCTED SPECIAL MISSION

On return from leave following a voyage all Lorient crews had to attend a one-week health cure under the supervision of the Institute of U-boat Diseases at Carnac, and when we weren't in the clinic, we were lodged in the Grand Hotel on the sea front. On the evening of 17 September, 1941, I returned to the barracks mess with Hagen. A trial run had been scheduled for the submarine the following morning, which meant that the third war patrol was in the offing. The shipyard telecommunications technicians had examined the hydrophones, but, as expected, had been unable to find any fault.

In the bar we were soon joined by Warrant Officer Bleihauer and, over drinks, our party indignantly debated the thorny question of the hydrophones and the manner in which Bleichrodt had impugned our honour as telegraphy specialists. Lt Waldemar Seidel watched us in amusement from a corner of the room. At another table behind us a number of Knight's Cross holders were loudly discussing their voyages. Bleihauer turned round and said, 'Rather a lot of throat specialists here today.'[21] At this, Ferdinand Hagen looked round too and then whispered, 'Oh shit, don't look now, here comes the Old Man.' I heard Bleichrodt approach the other table and greet his fellow Commanders with a loud hoo-hah.

'Hallo Ajax! Is Torpedo Carrier *U-109* ready again?' someone shouted, and at this there was an echo of laughter around the room. At our table we could now only catch fragments of the conversation ('... and what did Dönitz say to that? ...'), and so we carried on quietly drinking, our tokens quickly accumulating. Payment was only made on leaving.

Suddenly I felt a hand fall on my shoulders. Bleichrodt was standing directly behind me.

83

'Hagen, make room for me,' he said and, squeezing himself between us, scooped our chips into the pocket of his reefer jacket and ordered a fresh round. He made a toast and we quickly drank our glasses with dour expressions. Bleichrodt jabbed his elbow into my ribs. 'Telegraphy is shit, right?' I stared doggedly ahead as I replied, 'On your boat, big shit.'

'So we're agreed on it! Cheers!'

Bleichrodt pointed at the warrant officer and said, 'From now on we'll call him "Leadarse"'.[22] Bleihauer smiled and replied, 'It's an honour, sir. Tomorrow we receive the boat back from the repairers and I shall be aboard, sir.'

'Yes, Leadarse, and I'm over the moon about it.' Then, affably directing his question to me, he enquired, 'Is the radio equipment functional?'

'Yes,' Ferdinand intervened grimly, 'and there was nothing wrong with the hydrophones.'

Bleichrodt nodded. 'Children, children, let's leave the old hydrophones out of this. I'm afraid it's all a bit too technical for me.'

At that moment the air-raid alarm sounded and we had to vacate the barracks. A senior boatswain, who knew Bleichrodt from his school sailing ship days, invited our group to follow him to the vaults of a nearby small château where we could safely imbibe. We teetered drunkenly behind the boatswain through the darkness while flak guns of all calibres fired up at the bombers. When we got to the cellars we found that Lt Seidel had added himself to our number, having decided to keep an eye on us telegraphists in our own best interests.

The underground room was furnished with thick carpets and a number of plush armchairs, into which we all sprawled. The senior boatswain had a good supply of Sekt but no glasses, so we had to drink directly from the bottle. Bleichrodt kept making a toast which we had to answer each time by taking a large swig and I soon realized that the captain's motive was to drink us all under the table.

Ferdinand nudged me and said, 'Have you noticed?'

'Of course, he wants to get us paralytic so that he can say that the telegraphists always drop out of commission first.' Lt Seidel, who was sitting close to me, kicked my foot unobtrusively to stop me saying anything more.

'But Hirschfeld,' said Bleichrodt with a smile, 'we all want to continue sailing together. It's just that you've got to understand that when things go wrong it's always going to be blamed on the telegraphists.'

Although my senses were very hazy, I noticed that the Commander's words were slightly jumbled; even Bleichrodt wasn't in full control of his faculties.

'Did you hear that?' Ferdinand shouted. His speech was slurred and he was having difficulty in remaining aboard his armchair. I jumped up suddenly. 'No!' I shouted, 'we're not standing for it! We are getting off your boat. This is . . .' My mind searched frantically for the word I wanted. '. . . DISCRIMINATION!' I finished triumphantly. I was very drunk and I knew it.

Bleichrodt smirked calmly. 'Hirschfeld, this won't do. I think you should go outside.'

'Yes,' I replied and staggered towards the armoured door. Bleihauer and Seidel rose to assist me. The doorway appeared so narrow that I had to ask Seidel to lead the way so that I could follow him through it, and, once this obstacle had been negotiated, the alcohol at last won the day and I collapsed unconscious.

When the air-raid was over Ferdinand and I were loaded aboard the Flotilla armoured car and driven to the barracks. The Flotilla drivers were former Russian officers of the Czar who between the wars had found employment in Paris driving taxis. Bleihauer said that, after depositing us in our quarters, they returned to Keroman for Bleichrodt, who by then was in much the same condition as myself and had to be dragged to his room in the Prefecture.

I slept like the dead for four hours and Telegraphist Leibling shook me awake shortly before 0800. I had only time to put my head under the cold tap for a few moments before running down to the harbour where the boat was ready to cast off. Bleichrodt was leaning against the periscope housing, grinning at us as we climbed the ladder to the bridge. Twelve bottles of beer stood on the rim of the tower coaming. The Commander had confiscated them from Midshipman Hengen as he attempted to smuggle them aboard. Bleichrodt beckoned to us and pressed a bottle into the hands of the four of us, Hagen, Leibling, Hümpel and me. 'It's for your afterthirst,' he explained, and then put a half-empty bottle to his lips and upended it.

We set out for the Bay of Biscay punctually at 0800. There were a number of shipyard engineers on board, plus Bleihauer and Engineer Captain Charly Scheel, whose purpose it was to see whether the trail of bubbles had been fully eradicated.

Walter Gross had to get the dinghy ready for Captain Scheel. It was a small metal boat with sealed air chambers which provided it with sufficient buoyancy not to sink even when swamped and had a socket for a screw plug under the duckboards. Walter Gross neglected to observe that the plug was absent and that the socket had been stuffed with a cloth.

Captain Scheel sat contentedly in the dinghy with his hands on its two short oars and, after he had been cautioned by the officers to keep a sharp watch for torpedoes, since British submarines were known to be active in the area, *U-109* submerged. Bleichrodt sat in the tower watching the Flotilla Engineer through the attack periscope. I was in the control room checking the direction finder and radio aerial for water-tightness when I heard the Captain give a roar of laughter. 'Keller and Weber, come and have a look at this quickly! The dinghy's flooded, and Charly Scheel is clinging to the sky-scope!' The two officers sprinted into the control room and climbed up while Petersen, Otto Peters and I stood under the tower hatch and listened.

'Oh dear, he's shaking his fist at us,' said Keller, 'I think we'd better surface.' The story went rapidly through the boat, and there was loud laughter through all the rooms. Only Walter Gross didn't see the funny side of it, for he was responsible for the seaworthiness of the dinghy.

Lt Weber blew the tanks, but the Captain couldn't fully open the bridge hatch cover because the dinghy had wedged across it. Through the gap he shouted that the submarine would have to submerge again so that the Flotilla Engineer could pull the dinghy clear and float it across to the Winter-garden. Therefore Captain Scheel had to have another swim. When he eventually came aboard, his anger was manifest for all to see. Walter Gross accepted his rocket with bowed head and then offered the outraged officer a new set of overalls, underwear and U-boat leathers from the boat's inventory.

'And we'll never see them again,' said the boatswain.

As we dieseled back to Lorient Leibling said to me, 'What's wrong with Hagen? He's hardly spoken to me.'

'Don't worry about it,' I told him. 'He was upset by what happened last night with the Captain.'

Soon after we tied up at the pier Ferdinand said he was going to the infirmary. 'Man, are you really unwell?' I asked, and Ferdinand merely nodded and went off. A short while later he reappeared and drew me into the radio room. With tears in his eyes, he confessed that he had gonorrhoea. This meant that he would have to stay ashore for the next voyage, and I went with Bleihauer to Kernevel to obtain a replacement petty officer from the Personnel reserve.

Lt Schwartzkopff had been transferred at his own request to Commander Hessler's boat *U-107* and had sailed ten days earlier on a patrol; on his return, he would attend the U-boat Commander's training course. We had a guest aboard *U-109*, Commander Eberhard Hoffmann, who was sailing on a pre-command voyage for experience. He had previously only seen service with the Naval command in Berlin as a planner, but wore the Iron Cross, First Class.

The coxswain nodded soberly as I explained Hagen's departure. 'So many people leaving the boat. I wouldn't be surprised if there wasn't something significant in that.'

Boatswain Berthold Seidel clapped Petersen on the shoulder. 'Coxswain, as long as I'm aboard this U-boat, no harm can come to her. You know that the Captain believes in that. That's why he drags me with him from boat to boat.' Petersen nodded. 'That means you'll remain a boatswain for as long as Bleichrodt remains at sea.' Berthold laughed. 'I don't care. Main thing is, we all carry on living.'

Siegfried Keller had been promoted to full lieutenant but remained second watchkeeping officer. Schwartzkopff had been replaced by Lt Friedrich Wilhelm Wissmann as First Lieutenant.

Maureschat had been called to the staff office to face an inquiry chaired by Lt (Admin) Hoffmann into the shortage of thirty-five shell cases upon the return of the boat from the recent patrol. He recounted bitterly how he had been subjected to the ignominy of having to listen to a lecture on the correct manner of bringing the empty cartridge cases down into the boat after an action given by men who had never once heard a shot fired in anger.

U-109 prepared to sail on her third war patrol on the evening of Sunday, 21 September, 1941. The crew paraded on the foredeck, the Commander at our head. Bleichrodt wore his oldest reefer jacket, its elbows reinforced with patches of Grade O sail canvas, his trousers bulging out of salt-stained sea boots. He was drunk but stood as straight as a marble column. The officers lining the rail of the *Isere* waved Sekt bottles at him and called, 'Look, Ajax, look!', but Ajax Bleichrodt ignored them. For him the patrol had already begun.

The new Flotilla Chief came aboard. Viktor Schütze wore the Knight's Cross with Oak Leaves and had previously commanded several U-boats. The lower deck called him Fatty and with some justification.

Bleichrodt ordered 'Attention! Eyes right!' and reported *U-109* ready to sail. Schütze thanked him shortly, having noticed the drunken state of the Commander, and then the small, penetrating eyes of the Flotilla Chief wandered along the swaying ranks. He addressed us robustly about Germany's destiny upon the Great Ocean. We groaned inwardly and, when Schütze began to speak of the Music of the Depth Charges, we nudged each other and only restrained ourselves with difficulty from laughing out loud. Berthold Seidel whispered to me, 'Isn't he dear little fat thing? If it wasn't for the Oak Leaves around his throat, you'd think he's never been on a U-boat, wouldn't you?'

From the loudspeakers the U-boat song *Wir fahren gegen England* blared out. The Flotilla Chief went ashore, the mooring lines were cast off and *U-109* glided into the Channel. The third war patrol had begun.

By midnight of the second day we had reached the 600-foot depth contour of the Bay of Biscay where Bleichrodt decided to make a deep dive to 550 feet in order to test the state of the boat. He still seemed very sceptical about both the submarine and the repairers.

We made a slow descent, trimming first at 120 feet to check the external seals and instruments, and then went deeper to 300 feet. There was a warning shout as powerful jets of water began to spray in all directions from the direction finder; the depth rudder operators, seated beneath it, were already dressed in their oilskins. I greased around the socket and bound the stuffing boxes to stop the leak, but this meant that we wouldn't be able to raise the direction finder aerial. Bleichrodt leaned on the chart table and silently listed the reports being submitted from each division. There was a telephone call from the bow room requesting the attendance of a telegraphist. Bleichrodt merely looked at me and I took a screwdriver and went forward with some apprehension.

The torpedo mate, Werner Borchardt, pointed to the distributor boxes for the hydrophones; from where the cable came through the pressure hull on the starboard side there was a fine spray drizzling over the boxes. I gasped: if the cable to the radio room was flooded the repairers would have to open up the whole of the forecasing. I squeezed myself between the torpedo tubes and the pressure hull, unscrewed the starboard distributor box and, as I removed the cover, I released a small deluge which poured down over my face. When I did the same to the box on the port side I was drenched even before I had lifted the cover free. Meanwhile, the length of cable between the entry point from the pressure hull and the distributor box had now split and a jet of water as thick as a finger was playing powerfully against a torpedo tube door.

'Shit,' said Borchardt, 'come away from the tubes and make sure that jet of water doesn't touch you. If it's coming in at exterior pressure, it'll put a hole in your head.' I withdrew hurriedly and returned to the control room. Passing through the galley, I noticed there was a fine spray showering the refrigerator. 'Yes, I have reported it,' Järschel assured me. In the control room the Commander was still at the chart table, wearing a wrathful expression; when I told him that the hydrophone distributor boxes were flooded and the system wasn't working, Bleichrodt bit his lower lip and said, 'Listen to your aerial'.

I placed an ear against the tube; it sounded like a water cistern. When I turned on the drainage tap, a steady flow hissed into the bilges. Bleichrodt gave me a nod. 'You see, I was right. Telegraphy is shit. Prepare a signal, Hirschfeld, we're turning back. There's also a lot wrong in the engine room and the external seals aren't watertight.' The Commander announced to the crew that he was abandoning the mission and then gave me the full text of the signal, requesting an escort for 0600 the next morning.

While Leibling was encoding this signal I warmed up the transmitter and receivers ready to send as soon as the boat surfaced. The hydrophones were out of commission and the night was black, so we came up blind and set off for Lorient at full speed. A few minutes after tuning in the short wave receiver the set went dead. I sent Hümpel into the hydrophones room with instructions to tune the All-Frequency receiver to the short wave band and plug it through to the radio room. This was done successfully, but after a few minutes this receiver also failed. I slammed the headphones down and glanced at the instruments on the display panel, which showed the output of the transformers in the engine room, and I could hardly believe my eyes when I looked at the voltmeter for the radio receivers.

'Look, Hümpel, they're at 350 Volts. How is that possible?' Hümpel stared at the instrument panel. 'The voltmeter must be reading false. The transformers were properly calibrated. I checked them over with Petty Officer Hagen.'

'No, Hümpel, I think the reading is correct. Both receivers went down because of the voltage. Go astern straightaway and check the resistances.'

The Captain appeared in the doorway. 'What's up, Hirschfeld? Have you sent that signal yet?' I explained the situation to him and Bleichrodt gave a resigned shake of the head. 'Include in the signal, "Both short wave receivers out of commission". But what are you going to do now?'

'I will just have to transmit blind across the traffic. The transmitter's in the search mode for a vacant frequency.' When I was ready to send, Hümpel returned from the stern. 'I don't understand it,' he said, 'the resistances hadn't been fixed and had changed themselves, probably through the diesel vibrations. but they *were* fixed when we had the trial voyage though.'

A most unpleasant explanation now presented itself to me. On the acceptance voyage all the communications equipment had been functioning properly. Then the boat had returned to the repairers for a few minor engine room adjustments. Could all this have been done then? It seemed difficult to believe. We had such a good relationship with the repair workers and had supplied the supervisor and his four men with alcohol, cigarettes and coffee. Had they tried to repay our small kindness with the gift of death? It couldn't have been the French, for there was always an armed guard on each boat to prevent them coming aboard: only German shipyard workers had access to U-boats.

The escort was punctual; *U-109* glided into the harbour basin, passed the deserted hulk of the *Isere* and headed for the shipyard. A group of engineers waiting on the wharf came aboard as soon as we had made fast.

'Before we have a shipyard meeting, I must inspect your reported faults for myself,' the radio engineer informed me.

'OK, we'll start at the front,' I said. Maureschat opened up the foredeck and we all clambered through the dripping rods and pipework until we reached the hydrophone pressure cans. 'The whole starboard side is probably flooded,' I said.

'I find that hard to believe,' the engineer replied, and, grasping the edge of one of the supposedly screwed-down covers, lifted it off. He stared at me in amazement. The next cover was loose, and the next, and the next. We exchanged glances. 'It's no wonder they're all flooded, Hirschfeld, the pressure cans are all open'.

'Yes, someone must have unscrewed them after the trial voyage. On the acceptance trip everything was OK.'

The engineer gave me a dark look. 'Do you think this could be sabotage?'

'Well, if you can think of some other word to describe it . . .'

'I will personally conduct the investigation. Were there any French workers on board?'

I reflected for a moment. 'Previously, yes. But not after the acceptance trial. It must have been the German shipyard workers.' I went cold at the enormity of the accusation. Saboteurs in our own ranks! From now on we would have to be watchful even in port.

The new repairs were estimated for fourteen days.

Warrant Officer Bleihauer arrived with the latest news, which included the copy of an order issued by the US Navy Minister, Knox, on 15 September, 1941: All commerce raiders, irrespective of

90

whether they be surface or submarine pirates, were to be captured or destroyed by all available means.

A strange neutrality!

'And what do we do about it?' I asked.

'Well, nothing whatever, of course,' Bleihauer replied. 'You know your *Führerbefehl* don't you?'

We spent some time in the Grand Hotel at Carnac and then Leibling and I were summoned to Lorient by Lt Seidel. 'Hirschfeld, I'm sorry to drag you away, but there's no other boat or radio crew available at the moment and the BdU wants to try out a Coded Morse Conversation. Do you think you can do it?' I shrugged my shoulders: First, I had to understand what it entailed.

Two radio operators morsing messages *en clair* between their two stations was engaged in a 'conversation'. But when one of these two stations was the radio room of a German U-boat and the other was the Signals Headquarters of the BdU, the fact that each signal had to be encoded before sending and then decoded upon receipt introduced into the proceedings a delay factor which might sometimes be several hours. What the BdU was proposing was the elimination of the delay by feeding messages through an Enigma cipher machine at each end. It seemed a cinch.

'Hirschfeld,' Lt Seidel said with a smile, 'at 1500 hrs, tune in your receiver and transmitter to Kernevel. At 1600 hrs, we will start the conversations with Dönitz. Pray God we don't let ourselves down.' I did as instructed, and also checked all the circuits and the resistances. They were in order.

When Seidel reappeared, Leibling and I informed him that all was ready and he said, 'Gentlemen, this is an historical moment. The first Coded Morse Conversation between the BdU and *U-109* will go down in history!'

'Does the Führer know that?' I asked, and we all laughed.

At 1600 the Kernevel transmitter began sending at about a quarter the usual speed. Hümpel tapped the incoming morse characters into the Enigma machine and I wrote down the decoded message after each deciphered character had been illuminated. Admiral Dönitz sent greetings to Lt Seidel, asked if the tempo wasn't too fast, what Seidel thought of the new idea and if he thought it could be used between Kernevel and the Atlantic boats as an urgent means of communicating.

Now it was Seidel's turn. He dictated quite slowly, Hümpel tapped the message into the machine, and I morsed out each illuminated character as it appeared. 'Here is *U-109*. We understand you well. Under good conditions of reception . . .'

'Stop!' I shouted. I could no longer hear my own transmission, and when I pressed down on the key it was silent. All the dials of the instrumentation had fallen to zero. Even the receiver was dead.

'What's wrong?' asked Seidel.

'No more juice!' I cast the headphones aside and went quickly to the display panel in the hydrophones room. All instruments were at zero. None of the transformers was working.

'Damn,' I shouted out, 'that was the shipyard workers!'

Lt Seidel had gone red in the face. 'So, Hirschfeld, if anything can possibly go wrong with a project, it will definitely fail if it's tried out aboard *U-109*, won't it?'

'Just a moment, I'll be back soon,' I promised and swung my way through the circular doorways to the engine room in the stern. Somewhere the current had been clamped off – but where? I went back to the diesel room and up through the open hatch to the after-casing, and asked the sentry on duty there if he had seen the workers who had been in the electric motor room.

'They've all gone,' the sentry replied. 'They work by German Summer Time.' I went back to the radio room to inform Seidel that there would be no more electric current for the day.

'Hirschfeld, we have made eternal fools of ourselves. Now I'll have to phone the Admiral to explain.'

'Lieutenant, don't take it so badly,' I replied. 'We are simply once again the victims of the dockyard grandees.' Seidel gave me a sad wave and made his departure. Leibling closed up the cipher machine and said, 'After that, I think we need a drink.' No sooner said than done. Warrant Officer Bleihauer was in the barracks mess waiting for us.

'Leadarse, do you think the BdU will ever be able to forgive us?' I asked.

Bleihauer shook his head sorrowfully. 'No, never.' He gave the matter some thought and then added, 'Possibly when you've all been drowned. Then he will say, "Oh yes, *U-109*; wasn't that the boat with those two telegraphists who let me down so badly that day?".' We laughed so loud at this that everyone in the mess turned round and stared at us.

On 30 September the experiment was repeated successfully. Both Admiral Dönitz and Lt Seidel expressed their satisfaction and the honour of the *U-109* telegraphists was restored.

Three days later, while we were taking on board munitions and provisions, I was standing with Lt Seidel on the foredeck when Ferdinand Hagen returned from the infirmary armed with his certificate of health. 'Just tell them that you want to sail again on this rustbucket,' laughed Seidel.

'If I have to go to sea again, then it's only with this boat,' he replied.

I was happy to welcome him back, and his replacement was returned to the Kernevel bunker consoled only with the promise that the war would last many years yet and that it wouldn't be long before he could volunteer for death on another boat.

That afternoon, at the Telegraphy Conference, Lt Seidel told us that with immediate effect U-boats would keep a log record of the conditions of radio and hydrophone reception in each sea area. This would be for the information of future crews, partly with a view to avoiding the unpleasantness and suspicion such as that which had soured the relations with Lt Cdr Bleichrodt on the last voyage.

On 5 October, 1941, we vacated our rooms in the Salzwedel Barracks and at 1900 *U-109* sailed without ceremony. Radio engineer Brechelt, Warrant Officer Bleihauer and a number of civilians were on the Winter-garden; they were to accompany the boat to the 600-feet contour and check the boat over on the trial deep dive. An armed trawler was the escort. At midnight the next day the trial dive passed off without incident and the escort vessel was called alongside to take off the passengers. Once the transfer had been accomplished Bleichrodt cupped his hands around his mouth and shouted across, 'Hey, Leadarse! Make sure you get home safely! Don't you get knocked off on the way!'

'Thank you, and the same to you, Commander!' the reply came back. Then the trawler disappeared into the darkness. Bleichrodt laughed. 'They're happy we let them go,' he said. Everybody was scared of the Bay of Biscay. On the surface, *U-109* headed westwards on her third war patrol thirteen days late.

For the next five days we travelled on a westerly heading into a heavy swell. 420 sea miles ahead, other boats had reported two convoys steering north and south respectively, but our progress was limited by the sea state, and it was clear that we would be unable to reach either.

On 8 October Bleichrodt joined me in the radio room to listen to an important speech by the Führer. The Captain glanced at me frequently with the most pained expression: he said nothing but I could guess what he was thinking. How could the *Führerhauptquartier* already be talking about a final victory over the Russians when German troops were not yet even in Moscow, let alone on the Volga? And what might await us behind the Urals? And why did the Japanese not join us?

The following day the BdU began to make repeated requests to Kleinschmidt in *U-111* to report his position, but there was no reply. His boat was around the Canaries, where we had met the *City of Auckland* on the last voyage.

U-109 surged onward under leaden skies and into a head sea which continually swept over the bridge lookouts: you had to weave through their dripping clothing whenever you went through the electric motor room. The lookouts cursed the North Atlantic. Last voyage it had been so pleasantly warm.

'Just wait till we get to Greenland,' Maureschat told them, 'you're all going to get your very arses frostbitten up there this time. Remember, it'll be winter in Labrador now.'

We had orders to join a scouting line of boats south of Cape Farewell; it came as part of a long signal which included a warning to boats to beware of a U-boat trap operating south of Madeira.

When the storm abated on 12 October it left the legacy of a monstrous swell and the boat rolled so heavily in the seas that we had to strap ourselves into our cots when attempting to sleep. The Commander had even arranged to carry out the daily trial dive around midday so as to give the cook the opportunity to prepare the meal and for us to eat it in reasonable comfort: we went to 250 feet, for the swell was so powerful that its effects could still be felt at 180 feet.

At the chart table Bruno Petersen asked me, 'What's up with Kleinschmidt?'

'I think a U-boat trap got him. Whatever the reason, he's had it.' Petersen nodded and tapped the chart with his pencil. 'You see, Hirschfeld, you can just as easily get sunk in the south.'

'I know, but it's much nicer to die in warm water.'

Petersen smiled. 'And all those sweet little sharks to help you.'

As we progressed towards Cape Farewell it was calmer, but now the air began to smell of winter. We were 250 miles south-east of the Cape, the most northerly boat of a north-south scouting line of submarines searching for the eastbound British convoys which frequently sailed the most devious courses in their efforts to evade us. 400 miles astern five boats had reported that they were about to attack a strongly defended convoy in high seas; we must have passed very close to it in the storm. If we had been submerged, we would have detected it by use of hydrophones.

Lt Keller put his head into the radio room when he saw the signal log.

'It's strange, you know,' he said with a grin, 'this boat seems to be avoiding contact with convoys almost as though it had a mind of its own.'

'I know, Lieutenant, it probably has something to do with the last time it was in these parts,' I said, and he laughed.

On 16 October Bleichrodt was ordered to make for Cape St Charles at the head of the Belle Isle Strait. This was because the BdU wanted to find out whether convoys were proceeding north through this strait between Labrador and Newfoundland and then following the Great Circle route to England, and thus eluding the usual U-boat scouting lines by coming round the northern flank. Already we were feeling the iciness of the Labrador wind and so humid was it in the boat that clothes in lockers were damp, and all the loaves in the hammocks and potatoes stored in sacks in the control room were showing mould. At night the sea was as black as coal and the Northern Lights flared in the heavens. The aurora borealis wrought havoc with radio reception and, because we could not pick up German broadcasts, Cdr Hoffmann and Lt Wissmann joined me in the radio room to listen in to the medium wave American radio news programmes and it was from that source that we heard of the attack on the destroyer *Kearney* by a German U-boat. The neutral American vessel, which had formed part of a convoy escort, had been disabled with many casualties, but was making for Iceland and was expected to arrive.

Next day U-boat Command asked the twenty or so boats in the area who had hit the American destroyer, but, to judge by the answers, nobody had done it. How could one distinguish between British and American destroyers in a convoy battle at night? When the American station reported that a Bill had been approved to arm the mercantile marine, this seemed to clarify why the BdU was making such a fuss about the *Kearney*.

It was bitterly cold but visibility was excellent in the Belle Isle Strait: there were few clouds and the horizons were empty. The bows rose and fell in the swell as if the boat was breathing, and the diesels hummed like two contented workhorses. Well to the east U-boats had discovered four fast steamers escorted by two destroyers, which they were pursuing at from 15 to 18 knots: a slower convoy of twenty-two ships had been located south of Newfoundland, and Flachsenberg was transmitting a signal from a convoy he had found to the south of us, but none of them were in striking distance.

Early on 21 October I was awoken by breakers crashing against the tower; outside it was gusting to force 11 with accompanying snowstorms. When the lookouts came down into the control room on being relieved their beards were frozen to the collars of their oilskins and long icicles hung down from the rim of their sou'westers; their clothing was frozen as hard as armour.

Two days later we reached the ordered position at 53°N 55°W sixty miles off Labrador: the bridge watch now wore thick sheep-skins in addition to everything else and were so bulky that it took an age for them to re-enter the boat through the bridge manhole. They could never have had so much clothing on if there had been any sort of aerial activity. But there were no aircraft, and also no ships: nothing but gulls as far as the eye could see, all strangely silent, wheeling and gliding along the coast of this eerie wasteland, whose only redeeming feature was the glorious Northern Lights.

On 24 October we began to pound up and down the Belle Isle Strait. We had a thick coating of ice on the net cutter and deck cannon. During the afternoon dark clouds appeared on the western horizon and a series of howling squalls swept in with astonishing force, spattering out hailstones jagged enough to lacerate the faces of the lookouts. The winds were so strong that it was no longer possible to hold binoculars to the eyes. The watchkeeper shouted down for the harnesses, and no sooner had the snap-hooks been fastened to the bridge coaming than the first mountainous seas, whipped to a fury by the winds, began to sweep over the boat. We rolled so far over that it sometimes seemed that we would capsize, although with our lead keel we knew that could never happen.

We remained surfaced, the Commander keeping the speed down to a few knots. During a period of relative calm I went up to the bridge where the coxswain had the watch.

'Glad you're not Seaman Branch?' He had to shout above the howling of the wind and the crash of the breakers for me to hear him. I nodded.

'In my next life I think I'll be a telegraphist,' he bellowed into my ear. I laughed. 'But when we were in the south, you were sunning yourselves up here while below we were being lightly braised!' I shouted back.

We sailed on through mist, rain, ice and snow storm, and in the boat it was always damp. We had jettisoned the mouldy loaves and potatoes, and the eight-hour respite between watches for the look-outs was no longer sufficient time to dry their clothing in the engine room. On the night of 26 October the boat began to roll with a strange, stiff movement even though there was no heavy swell. At dawn the watchkeeper reported that the forecasing was heavily iced over. The deck cannon was encased in a gigantic block of ice: the glistening white mantles around the tower and Winter-garden had made the boat top-heavy.

'If we use the axes on it, we'll damage the forecasing,' Walter Gross told the Captain when Bleichrodt arrived on the bridge to survey the situation.

'Nobody would be able to stand and work there anyway,' the Captain said. 'If anyone fell in, we'd never be able to get him out in time.'

'I suggest we dive,' said Lt Wissmann from his collar of ice. The Captain nodded. 'Yes, it's the only solution to get rid of it. I only hope the vents open.'

We went below to our diving stations but at the command 'Flood!' nothing happened because the vents were frozen shut. It took considerable effort to get them open and so submerge to 120 feet. After four hours we surfaced. The water temperature had been warmer than the air temperature and we found that the ice had thawed, but a new ice crust began to form immediately, and so we settled into a regime of four hours up and four hours down. The mood in the boat was dismal.

'Just think of the boats that operate in the polar seas all the time,' I said in the NCO's mess. 'At least we know we'll be going somewhere warmer eventually.'

'Christmas maybe,' said Otto Peters, 'we'll never find a convoy round here.'

It was so cold in the boat that I was wearing my entire seaboard wardrobe: thick winter underwear, dark blue woollen combinations, grey moleskin suit and then U-boat leathers with a sheepskin. Type IX U-boats had a diesel-exhaust heating system which generated the most warmth for the boat when we ran at full speed. Our surface speed was very slow, producing little heat, and the Chief had forbidden the use of the 2000 Watt electric fires because of the drain on the boat's batteries. In the NCO's room we had two of these heaters, one under the drop table and the other near my bunk. We were huddled together looking at them in the bestial cold when Otto Peters came in from the control room.

'Damn, it's no warmer in here,' he growled. 'Why don't you put the heater on?'

'Now Otto, you know very well that Weber would go mad if we did that,' I said.

'The batteries are fully charged. Weber wouldn't notice.' He came to the heater by my bunk and switched it on full. It slowly began to glow and we formed a tight semi-circle and held our hands above it.

'That's it,' said Otto, 'and next we'll each have a little spell with

97

our stomach over it so that we all get nicely warmed through.' We did this, but already the heater had begun to smell.

'Look Otto, someone's put the ventilation on,' I exclaimed. Otto peered down the corridor. 'Oh God,' he said, 'what a nose that dog's got. Here he comes.' We turned the heater off and threw a quantity of blankets over it to conceal it from sight. The Chief Engineer came into the mess sniffing the air and looking about him suspiciously.

'Have you had the electric heater on in here?' he demanded. Otto reclined on his bunk and shook his head sadly. 'There's our heater under the drop table. Have a feel. It's as cold as we are.' The chief touched it just to make sure and then glanced forward and shook his head. 'But there *was* a heater on somewhere,' he insisted, 'I definitely smelt it.'

'It's probably them in the stern room,' Otto said. Weber gave us one final mistrusting look and then went.

We began to spend much more time submerged each day. Hydrophone reception in this area was abnormally good and we could hear very much further than the lookouts could see.

On 28 October Bleichrodt received orders to proceed to the Grand Newfoundland Bank and the bows turned to course 130°. The hydrophone operator could soon hear the thunder of distant depth-charging from hundreds of miles ahead of us: the audibility in these waters was astounding. The BdU had given one of the other groups, *Reisswolf* ('Shredding machine'), orders to start shredding the convoy: within forty-eight hours U-109 should be able to join in the carnage.

The coxswain showed me our destination on the chart: when we got there we would be in the track of a convoy being shadowed by Kentrat in U-74.

When Cdr Hoffmann visited the radio room to watch us at work I asked him how he had won his Iron Cross, First Class. 'At Naval Command for planning the surface fleet strategy against the British merchant routes,' he said. 'I volunteered for the U-boat Arm in order to earn it.' I was lost for words. He had surrendered a safe Admiralty job to volunteer for death as a U-boat commander.

At 2200 on 29 October we received the signal *Mordbrenner ran!*, which was the order for our group of fire-raisers to go for the convoy. With diesels at full speed and with a following sea we headed for the British ships in a violent snowstorm and with heavy icing on our deck fittings and superstructure. Five hours later the BdU signalled:

Bleichrodt. Do not operate against Kentrat convoy.
Take up position 8 miles off south cape Newfoundland.

The Commander read the signal, pressed his lips together and went to the chart table, handing the message to the coxswain without comment. Then they both bent over the chart, calculated the ETA to the ordered position and examined the latest convoy position reported by Kentrat. The Commander stood up. 'We will attack the convoy,' he said.

The diesels continued to hammer the boat southwards to an interception point with the convoy at 0400 the next morning. Soon we were in the Gulf Stream and we cast aside our furs and thick combinations.

Shortly before 0400 Kentrat signalled that he had lost contact with the convoy. It was a bitter blow, but then at dawn our lookouts spotted two smudges of smoke on the eastern horizon, and when the mastheads came in sight they were recognized as escort vessels. We ran off to the south at high speed and then headed back northwards in broad zigzags across the assumed course of the convoy. We saw nothing. Keller said to me with a grin, 'I told you, when *U-109* comes along, everything around makes itself scarce.'

'Just wait, Lieutenant, something will be along very shortly.'

'You're an optimist,' he told me.

At 1445 the bridge watch reported mastheads; a tanker and a passenger freighter, but no sooner had we finished rubbing our hands together than the alarm bells rang and the vents banged open even before the tower hatch cover was secure. We went down at a very steep incline and the Chief began to scream hysterically for the stern vent to be opened; it had jammed, and so then he shouted for it to be opened manually.

I opened the voice-pipe to the tower and heard the Commander, who was seated at the main periscope, shout, 'Damn! The plane's heading straight for us! Chief, our arse is still sticking up out of the water!' Another few seconds passed and then he called out again, 'Chief! Why isn't the stern coming under? Get it under, quick!'

The Chief replied, 'Vent One is jammed, sir. Shall I blow the tanks?'

'No!' roared Bleichrodt, 'clear the tower. Close all pressure doors!' First I heard the slam and clank as the doors were shut and dogged, then the boat trembled.

'Bow's hit the bottom!' shouted the ratings in the forward room. We were on the Newfoundland Bank, our bows in the mud and sand, and the stern projecting above the surface. The Captain was sitting astride the pressure doorway forward of the control room.

'Everyone quiet, we're going to get clouted now,' he said with composure. I felt my spine go cold. So this is how we would die, bombed by an aircraft on the Grand Banks. But it was only 150 feet here, I thought. If the bulkheads held, perhaps some of us might make it to the surface with a breathing set. And then I thought of the freezing water and realized that there was no prospect of survival at all. The boat was deathly quiet. We were all waiting for the explosions to finish our mortal span, but nothing happened. It was a feeling almost akin to disappointment. We raised our heads in astonishment. What, no bombs? and our stern sticking up out of the water? It was impossible to believe it.

The Commander rose slowly, climbed the ladder to the tower and opened the lower hatch. After a quick check with the sky-scope, he said, 'Machine is flying off. Strange. Open pressure doors. Chief, if you'd finally like to bring the stern under would you do so?'

Warrant Officer Winter climbed up the central corridor to the stern and after a while succeeded in opening Vent One. Water gurgled into the tank, the stern of the boat sank and settled horizontally on the ground. The electric motors began to hum and U-109 began to bump along the sandy bottom in a series of jerks.

'Forward depth rudder to rise,' the Chief hissed.

The keel of the boat continued to slide along the bottom.

'Rise! Rise I said,' the Chief screamed.

In an ironic tone, Otto Peters remarked, 'You haven't blown the interior ballast tanks yet, Lieutenant.' I couldn't see the Chief's face, but I could imagine it, and at once I recalled the words Admiral Dönitz had said to him: 'Ah, Weber, you always seem to be at the bottom of it when the shit starts flying.'

Grimly, the Chief gave the order to blow the tanks and the boat rose. Järschel had been in the stern after the emergency watching three men vainly trying to open the vent; it spoke volumes for the cook's strength that when he took the iron crowbar and attempted to open it himself, the bar bent. The Commander's anger dissolved when he saw Järschel's muscular arms and the misshapen crowbar.

'Chief, I want you to find out for me how the vent jammed like that. It certainly couldn't have been iced up.' I detected a certain menace in his voice as he said this. The Chief had the vents repeatedly opened and shut but failed to find any fault; this disturbed him because a defect that occurs only sometimes is a dangerous one.

We surfaced, hoping to find the two fat merchant vessels again but after an hour we were forced to dive when a destroyer approached us fast from astern, and later that evening we played cat and mouse with another destroyer for a few hours and after this the Commander abandoned all hope of finding his prizes.

We wasted a few more days off the Cabot Strait searching for stragglers from Kentrat's convoy, and at midday on 2 November U-boat Command told Bleichrodt that he was free to manoeuvre. We headed south at once to overhaul the diesels and were soon sweltering in the unaccustomed warmth as we entered the Gulf Stream on the latitude of New York.

We received an Officers-Only signal. This was a message which when decoded revealed another code, which then had to be given, together with the Enigma cipher machine, to the Signals Officer, who would put in a new setting for the cogs and obtain the clear text. After a while Lt Keller returned it to me and requested my assistance, 'but keep quiet about it, won't you?'

'Of course, Lieutenant!'

The signal ordered *U-109* to undertake a special task – to proceed to a position east of Bermuda and on 10 November rendezvous with the 4793-ton Norwegian motor ship *Silvaplana*. She had been captured by the German raider *Atlantis* in the Kermadec Islands on 10 September and was a modern ship belonging to Tschudi and Eitzen Co., an important prize for the 2000 tons of crude rubber, 5000 tons of sago, hides, spices, coffee and tea she carried. She had a German prize crew of fifteen and all the original Norwegian complement. Her destination was now Bordeaux. So we would be arriving home for the second time running without a single pennant on the periscope, I thought.

We headed south-east: only the officers, the coxswain and the telegraphists knew the mission. Maureschat could hardly restrain his curiosity and fed me a string of well-thought-out and seemingly innocuous questions, which much amused Otto Peters. 'For heaven's sake, Eduard, just wait. The main thing is we're not heading north. Just be satisfied with that,' the control room mate told him.

The sun shone down from a blue sky and the off-watch crewmen were allowed to spend time basking on the Winter-garden, since enemy aircraft overflew this area only very rarely. It was very warm and even the torpedo mate was lured up from the farthest recesses of the boat. 'I've got a horrible feeling that we're going to take the torpedoes home again,' Werner Borchardt said to me, 'or have you got an inkling about where we might get rid of some of them?' Another fisherman. I laughed. 'Why don't you just wait and see? Just four more days and it will be crystal clear to you.' On 7 November the Commander announced the mission to the men: *U-109* was to meet the *Silvaplana* at a point close to the Anton Corridor, an internationally agreed sea lane for neutral ships, and there protect her against attacks from both sea and air.

Otto Peters scratched his head. 'Did you hear that? Protect her against attack from the air? What do they think we are, a flak-cruiser?' Cdr Hoffmann, who heard this as he was passing, laughed. 'Yes, that wording was definitely dreamed up in Berlin,' he said.

The heavy swell lifted the boat and drove us eastwards, sparing the bunkers. On the day prior to the rendezvous Keller and I were perching on the iron rails of the Winter-garden. 'Do you realize why this is the only boat which the BdU could possibly select for this mission?' he asked me. Keller grinned as I shook my head. 'Well, the BdU has at last tumbled to the fact that *U-109* is the only boat capable of crossing the Atlantic without meeting an enemy ship.'

'I only hope we meet our own ship,' I responded, 'there's a big leeway to allow for.'

Keller nodded. 'I know. Just look at these waves. Twenty to fifty feet in height and 200 yards between the crests, yet we're sitting here in the dry.' No sooner had he spoken than a large wave reared up from astern over the Winter-garden and we both got our feet wet.

The torpedo men had been quietly running a book that we would never meet up with the freighter, but at 1145 the next day the watchkeeper reported mastheads and we dived to periscope depth to inspect the ship, which had arrived very suddenly. The lookouts said that she had left no smoke trail. From the hydrophones, I confirmed that it was a merchantman and not a destroyer, but Bleichrodt seemed dubious and spent some time at the periscope.

The periscope motor hummed sporadically to maintain a position just above the sea surface: the Chief couldn't keep the trim effectively in the heavy seaway.

Eventually the Commander said, 'Now I can see her full length. The superstructure looks right. Thin high masts, gun on poop, hatches, all as advised, washing hanging out to dry on foredeck. This must be her. Surface!' Identifications signals were exchanged and the prize crew, who had been at sea since March, 1940, confirmed that the Norwegians had given no trouble. Bleichrodt explained to the prize captain of the *Silvaplana* that, if challenged by a warship, he would dive immediately and the freighter should then attempt to draw the enemy vessel across our path. Then, with the *Silvaplana* following half a mile astern, we steered east-north-east at ten knots. At some time soon we expected to see some of the four Fw200 aircraft which were supposed to be flying reconnaissance for us along the Spanish coast.

On the next day, 11 November, the captain of the prize mentioned during an exchange of semaphore that he had been a U-boat officer in the First World War. As *U-109* would make a trial dive at midday, Bleichrodt invited him to observe an emergency dive and time it.

Bleichrodt would hold up a signal flag and when it fell that would indicate the alarm. On the ship they confirmed that they had understood. At 1200 we were ready. Naturally there had been some sharp practice by Bleichrodt. All stations had been informed and were at preparedness, the exhaust masts had been closed and there were to be only three men on the bridge. In the freighter's wheelhouse, all binoculars were focused on the U-boat. The Commander raised his arm, cried 'Alarm' and let the flag fall. The vents banged open and the bridge watch jumped down the manhole and even before the lid had clicked shut the sea was sweeping across the tower. The boat began to sink steeply into the depths. I was just thinking that this must be the fastest dive ever recorded by a Type IX submarine when I heard the voice of the Chief Engineer shouting excitedly, 'Depth rudders hard rise forward! Blow internal ballast tanks! Blow them I tell you!'

I had the unpleasant feeling that something was seriously amiss and, as I reached the hydrophones room, I saw with alarm the enormous angle of inclination reading. Hümpel had braced himself against the hydrophone equipment. 'It's damned steep, isn't it?' he asked, 'what do you think?' I was gripping the doorframe for support. I thought that, as a demonstration, this was going a bit far.

'Blow them! Blow them!' Weber was screaming.

Through the pressure doorway I could see two of the hands vainly struggling to turn the large valve wheel which would blow the internal ballast tanks.

Otto Peters shouted, 'Valve wheel's jammed!'

'Get the valve-wheel bar!' the Chief cried. This was an iron bar with a claw head which fitted a spoke of the wheel and had a lever long enough for several men to exert pressure on it together in order to prise open the wheel.

'The bar's fallen behind the potato crates!' someone shouted. It was now very dangerous, because it would take time to retrieve it. We were at 180 feet; the two internal ballast tanks were located inside the pressure hull and held up to ten tons of seawater which was admitted at submergence in order to increase the weight of the boat, but this water had to be blown out at 90 feet or else there was a danger that the tanks would burst and flood the hull.

'Captain, I can't hold her! We must blow all tanks!' the Chief pleaded.

'Well blow them then,' said Bleichrodt.

Otto Peters was standing ready by the 'Christmas Tree', a triangular arrangement of small valve wheels which controlled the supply of compressed air to the dive tanks and was the means of expelling the seawater ballast. At a glance from the Chief, he opened all the valves and this halted the steep descent, but the bow heaviness could not be corrected.

I had tuned in the hydrophones to establish the position of the *Silvaplana*, and at the same time I heard the Captain say, 'Weber, the only thing you haven't done wrong so far is to ram the steamer's keel from below.'

U-109 began to rise quickly stern first; it was similar to the deep dive off Cape Farewell but facing in the opposite direction. After a few seconds we heard the roar of the sea and surfaced rudder first. The Commander opened the tower hatch and mounted the bridge as though nothing untoward had occurred. 'Bridge watch dress up,' he called down calmly. The lookouts appeared and took up their respective sectors.

'Steamer is signalling, sir,' said one of the after lookouts.

'Don't take any notice,' Bleichrodt told him. After a while the lookout said, 'He keeps calling us, sir. Perhaps it's important.'

'All right,' the Captain muttered, 'ask him what he wants.'

The boatswain called out each word as it was flagged over. 'That-was-a-smart-dive-stop-I-timed-it-at-25-seconds-stop-question-do-you-always-surface-stern-first-stop.'

Bleichrodt glared in annoyance at the *Silvaplana*.

'Signal, "Only when we want a bit of a diversion"' he said. 'No, on second thoughts, send, "It's my Chief Engineer. He always insists on reversing up."'

But privately Bleichrodt was furious with Weber and again I remembered Admiral Dönitz' remark: 'Ah Weber, you always seem to be at the bottom of it when the shit starts flying.'

For four days we headed towards northern Spain along the Anton Corridor. The Commander never looked happy: he was not convinced that nobody would ever shoot there. Late on the evening of 15 November when I asked the coxswain for our position, he tapped the chart with a pencil and said with a smile, 'My dear Petty Officer, in five hours we will be off Cape Ortegal.' As ever, his chartwork was immaculate; at midnight we had Cape Estaca in sight and the Commander ordered the *Silvaplana* to complete her voyage inside Spanish territorial waters while we escorted her on her port beam from just outside the three-mile limit. Early next morning, when I went to the bridge to watch the first streak of dawn, I gazed at the wonderful sight of the white freighter in the early redness of the sun. She was outlined against a backdrop of the dark, rocky coast behind which soared the snowy peaks of the Cantabrian Mountains. I longed to experience the peace that the Spaniards, or at least some of them, were enjoying.

In the radio room Hümpel showed me a copy signal in which we were promised Luftwaffe protection for the portion of the run along the coast from Gijon to Bilbao. At midday in the NCO's mess Otto Peters said, 'Well boys, this is the last Sunday at sea. Soon we'll all be back home with Mummy.' Werner Borchardt gave him an ironic look. 'Don't get too excited just yet, Otto.' At that moment there was a shout from the bridge that an aircraft was approaching. The Captain climbed up and the lookout confirmed that it was a Heinkel 115. This was the air escort: we had been told it would be a Heinkel 115 seaplane. Suddenly the alarm bells rang and we dived; before we reached 120 feet there were three deafening explosions astern. The watchkeeper told me that the Heinkel had come in from the north, the Captain had fired off the agreed recognition signal and the aircraft fired off three coloured flares which we did not understand and then dived down towards us like a hawk.

When we trimmed at 180 feet the Commander said to me in a voice barely disguising his wrath, 'Hirschfeld, you gave me an incorrect recognition signal. That could have cost us all our lives. Check for your error.' I went pale. It had been Leibling who decoded the signal from the BdU; previously either Ferdinand Hagen or I had always done it. Nevertheless, as senior telegraphist, I carried the ultimate responsibility. I said nothing and just stared at Leibling. The Commander was in a terrible rage and had thrown himself on his bunk. With trembling fingers, Leibling riffled through the rough work book for the signal decrypt and compared it with the written note of the recognition group he had given to the coxswain. They were similar; it was not here that the error lay.

'And the original signal?' I asked. Leibling looked at the date. 'We destroyed it. It came two days ago,' he said with resignation. Standing Orders prescribed that signals on which the decoded text had been written were to be destroyed within 48 hours of receipt when the boat was operating in shallow waters or close to land.

On the off-chance I leafed through all the signals we still had and could hardly believe our luck when I found the one we wanted. Leibling had written the decoded text directly into the log, and so the original message had not been destroyed. Now we could finally establish who was at fault. I set up the Enigma machine for the date in question and decoded the signal again. For 16 November it was definitely Recognition Signal Five. Leibling and I both breathed a huge sigh of relief.

When I reported that our Recognition Signal had been the correct one, Bleichrodt propped himself up on his elbows and said slowly, 'That is very interesting. So the airfield gave their pilot the wrong signal, did they? Well, just wait until we're home. Then they're really going to hear a few home truths.'

An hour later, when we surfaced, the aircraft had gone and we chased after the *Silvaplana* at full speed. From some distance they enquired by lamp if we needed any assistance, but Bleichrodt merely signalled back that they should remain in Spanish waters no matter what should happen.

The BdU morsed:

Bleichrodt. If damaged by own aircraft bombs re *Silvaplana* report in.

'They've already realized then,' the Commander said to me. 'OK, we won't log it.' At 2300 we were off Santander: it was a very warm night, black as pitch: the *Silvaplana* had even set her navigation lights. Four minesweepers were waiting in the darkness; by Aldis lamp the Commander transferred the prize into their custody and the convoy now headed towards Biarritz.

It was very much like summer. The off-watch men were disporting themselves on bridge and Winter-garden; I stood beside Lt Keller leaning on the tower coaming, staring into the coal black water. The bow-wave and wake of each of the vessels stirred up phosphorescent plankton and it looked as if they were ploughing the sea. The minesweeping boats maintained a constant chatter between themselves with their large searchlights.

'Just look at all these lights,' I said to Keller. 'And all Biscay has been warned of British submarines operating here. If there's a Tommy boat in the area, he'll bag the lot of us.' Keller nodded. 'Yes, they're stupid, but these minesweeping thickheads are all the same. I'll be interested to find out if they manage to get the steamer to Bordeaux.'

Suddenly he seized my arm violently and pointed to starboard. My blood froze. Three gleaming torpedo tracks were racing swiftly towards us perfectly parallel: the middle one would strike us under the conning tower.

'Torpedoes!' Walter Gross shouted.

'We've had it,' another voice groaned quietly. No evasive manoeuvre was possible. The Captain stared in fascination at Death approaching us. Now it *was* our turn. And then, no more than six feet away from the hull, the three dolphins changed course and sped off ahead of the boat.

'My God, that was a fright,' said Bleichrodt. We all breathed again in relief. 'That's a warning for us,' Lt Wissmann told the Captain and Bleichrodt nodded. 'We'll take our leave here, we can't be of any more assistance to that ship. Let's just hope these floating neon signs get her to port in one piece.'

Just after midnight on 17 November U-boat Command acknowledged our request for an escort at the Ile de Croix at 0600 the next morning. Because a German anti-submarine group was operating between Biarritz and Lorient we had to sail a diversionary course which took us out into the Bay again in order to proceed to Lorient by Route Green, the approved U-boat approach alley to the port.

Already there was a relaxed atmosphere in the boat as we prepared for putting in. Järschel had shared out the remaining provisions among the crew. 'It would be a shame to hand it in so that the Flotilla studs can get fat on it,' he explained. I merely shut my eyes to these goings-on.

At 2000 that evening, when Lt Keller and his three lookouts trooped up to the bridge, there was no more than a light swell. In the darkness we had nothing to fear from patrolling aircraft here in Biscay but Keller had not been up there very long before he cried out, 'Battle stations!'

I went cold. The Commander jumped up from his bunk and grabbed his leather jacket. 'That Keller must have finally flipped,' he said to me as he went off to the bridge. The whole boat was in uproar as the hands went to their duty stations.

I followed the Captain through into the control room where the Chief asked me what was up. 'I'm just going to see,' I told him from the ladder. I could hear every word above me.

'Let me fire, Captain,' Keller shouted. 'He's dead ahead!'

'No! I can't see anything yet,' Bleichrodt roared back. It was very black in the open and the Commander's eyes were still night-blind and had not yet become accustomed to the darkness.

'Captain, I can see him very clearly. Range 800 yards!' I heard Keller tell him. 'We must either shoot now or turn away.'

For a few moments it fell silent. Then Bleichrodt said, 'Bear away to port. Full ahead both, zig-zag course!' Maureschat was at the attack computer in the tower; he had been there all the time, but I had only just noticed him.

'What's going on, Ede?' I asked.

'A big submarine ahead. It just surfaced. Keller says it's a Tommy.'

'Why don't we fire then?'

'No idea. The Old Man won't do it. You heard that yourself.'

'Well that's a fine thing,' I murmured.

'You can say that again,' Maureschat answered.

U-109 hammered through the calm black sea as if whipped by the Furies. The crew had remained at battle stations; in the control room I explained to the Chief what had happened. The men listened and then looked away in exasperation. After a couple of hours the boat came round to the east on Route Green and we stood down from the alert. When the Captain came down into the control room he couldn't help noticing all the dark looks, sensing the simmering resentment and perhaps hearing some of the murmurings of discontent. After hanging up his reefer jacket he came to the radio room.

'What's the matter with them all?' Bleichrodt said. After some thought I replied, 'They're all moaning because you didn't sink that submarine.'

The Captain stroked his beard. 'The blockheads, what do they know about it?' Then with a smile he said, 'Give me the microphone and plug me through to all rooms.' I did this at once and he announced, 'This is the Commander. Listen men. There is a Standing Order for Commanders that we must not shoot at any submarine in this grid square because it might be an Italian. You will understand why I did not wish to take a gamble. That's all.' The loudspeakers clicked off. We hadn't thought of that, of course: the Italians had very large submarines and it was easy to confuse the outline of British and Italian boats in the darkness.

At 0600 hrs on 18 November we anchored off the Ile de Croix and waited for our minesweeper escort under the protection of the huge flak batteries on the island, of which we had a somewhat misty view.

By 0900 the escort had still not put in an appearance and on two occasions, when we enquired of passing patrol vessels if they knew of its whereabouts, they replied that they had no idea. Bleichrodt looked extremely angry. The second of these vessels was a converted merchant ship bristling with flak guns of all calibres; it steamed past us almost nonchalantly and this so enraged the Commander that he ordered the anchor raised: now he would sail into Lorient without an escort, irrespective of whether it was against standing orders or not.

The anchor windlass was started up and Walter Gross stood at the bow and made hand signals. The chain rattled and clanked slowly through the hawse pipe into its locker. The diesels were started and the boat moved slowly ahead. I was idly watching the converted merchant vessel; suddenly a giant column of water arose close to its bow and completely obscured the forward part of the ship. We stared for long seconds and then the column collapsed and the ship steamed on unconcernedly. She was sweeping with a remote detection gear. This explained everything: we were in a minefield, probably laid the previous evening by the RAF.

The anchor chain rattled and the anchor dropped like lightning. 500 yards away the mine destructor vessel detonated another mine and the shock wave rocked the boat. We were surrounded by mines and we had blithely selected the centre of the minefield to anchor, completely unaware of the danger.

'Boys, we're in exactly the right spot here,' the coxswain said grimly.

'Yes, we're not home yet,' I replied, without the faintest trace of irony.

Petersen nodded. 'Don't I always tell you that?'

We swung around our anchor for three hours and at midday an old grey minesweeper came slowly out and circled us before signalling that we should follow her. She was equipped with a remote detection gear and towed two otters for cutting the wires of moored mines. We took up station directly astern of the otters, the figures on our bridge staring ahead, glasses at their eyes, giving as they hoped ample sea room to any mine that happened to be adrift in the vicinity.

U-109 passed slowly between Kernevel and the Fortress: the trees were bare, but on the bulk of the *Isere* the band of the 317th Infantry Regiment welcomed us home with a rousing march, and both on the hulk and the quayside there was a large turn-out to cheer us in. When we tied up alongside the *Isere* we knew we were safe.

'Don't forget the torpedoes are glad to be home again too,' said Werner Borchardt.

On the following day we finished cleaning out the boat and took her to the Lorient yards. Then, after a bath, a shave and a haircut we paraded in the courtyard of the Salzwedel Barracks. Lt Cdr Bleichrodt reported to the BdU the return of *U-109* from patrol. Admiral Dönitz walked slowly along our right flank and greeted the officers. Then he addressed the coxswain. 'Ah, Petersen . . .' The BdU smiled. 'After the next voyage, I'm taking you off. I've got a job for you.' He said something else that I couldn't hear. He walked along the rank and looked each of us in the eye. Then he stood and faced us all. He seemed content with us this time and congratulated us on a well-conducted special mission. The safe arrival of the *Silvaplana* with her valuable cargo had been important for the Reich. But now we should get the boat ready as soon as possible. Results in the last two months had been unsatisfactory and it was essential that we were at sea again before Christmas.

'Well I'll drink to that,' Otto Peters said.

A number of awards were made and I received the Iron Cross, Second Class. I was also promoted to Senior Petty Officer (*Oberfunkmaat*) which was usual after two years in the rank of *Funkmaat*.

When we were dismissed I said to Bruno Petersen, 'That's a bit of luck for you, Coxswain!' He gazed at me for some time. 'He shouldn't have told me,' he said gravely.

'But you should be pleased.' Petersen clapped me on the shoulder. 'It's not a good thing to know in advance that you will be getting off after the next voyage, for then on that voyage there's usually a disaster.' Once again I had to laugh at his superstitious nature.

'But Seidel will still be aboard,' I reminded him, 'and as long as he's on board *U-109*, we can't be sunk. You know that.'

'Well yes,' he said with a laugh, as he realized that he was confronted with a conflict of superstitions, 'let's hope that's the case.'

Leading Telegraphist Hümpel had been selected for the next *Funkmaat's* course; at least half the crew of *U-109* should have been remustered to other boats by now to provide these submarines with their backbone of experienced NCOs, but Bleichrodt hung on to his men with an iron grasp. On a U-boat experience was everything.

On 3 December, when I returned from leave, I attended the newly renamed *Marineärztliches Forschungsinstitut für U-boot-Medizin* at Carnac, and at Kernevel we found out that the submarine Keller had wanted to torpedo was definitely not Italian. I wondered if the British submariners had any idea of how slender had been the thread that ensured their survival that night, for, if Bleichrodt had seen them clearly, he would have recognized them as British and fired.[23]

On 11 December, 1941, we were at last at war with the United States; it was only a surprise that the Japanese had set it in train rather than ourselves. But now we could treat our enemies as such and finally dispense with the artificiality of the *Führerbefehl* which had hitherto denied the *ipso facto* naval war that had existed between Germany and the United States since at least September, 1941.

– 6 –

'THE OUTCOME OF THE WAR DEPENDS ON YOUR SUCCESS'

On the afternoon of Saturday 27 December, 1941, two U-boats were moored abreast of the hulk *Isere*: the Torpedo Carrier *U-109* and *U-130*, the latter commanded by Cdr Ernst Kals, a dashing captain who, on the voyage round from Kiel, had attacked a convoy and sunk two steamers. His crew were smart in new U-boat leathers and polished shoes.

The crew of *U-109* paraded on the forecasing in their pirate outfits – hooped shirts from impounded French Navy stock and grey-dyed RAF battledress, while Bleichrodt, at our head, wore his oldest patched reefer jacket and trousers tucked into salt-streaked sea-boots. There had been a time once when we had been as elegant as the men of *U-130*, but it was long ago.

'They won't look like that a year from now,' a petty officer said, 'not if they're still alive, that is.'

'He's a very smart commander, that Kals,' Maureschat remarked. His voice was so loud that Bleichrodt couldn't help hearing him, but the Captain didn't seem to care. The Flotilla Chief, Schütze, was addressing the crew of *U-130* and talking about the Music of the Depth Charges. I wondered if he would subject us to this drivel again, but when he crossed our decks on the way back to the *Isere*, he merely cast an eye over our seedy-looking crew, muttered a brief blessing and departed.

The band played, the springs were cleared fore and aft and, using the electric motor, we drifted clear of the hulk. The diesels came to life and we headed for Biscay. We didn't look back: even Bleichrodt stared rigidly out to sea as we swept past Kernevel. The off-watch men threw their cigarette ends overboard and went down into the boat. *U-130* was ahead of us as we negotiated the Narrows at Port

Louis, but, once the fortress was astern, *U-109* surged to full ahead and overtook her.

'You seem to have a lot of fuel!' Kals shouted across with a laugh. Bleichrodt took up the bridge megaphone and replied, 'We just want to get out of Biscay. Then we'll take it easy.'

When we were standing well to the west of the Ile de Croix the commander summoned the off-watch men to the tower. This was something he had never done before at the start of a voyage. Deliberately he unfolded the paper bearing the operational orders and read them aloud. We were one of the boats of the first wave to attack American shipping close in to their coast; the other boats were *U-66* (Zapp), *U-123* (Hardegen) and Kals in *U-130*.

'It's difficult to believe, isn't it,' Otto Peters said to me afterwards, 'that we should send four U-boats to attack the United Sates. I had hoped we might have started with a few more.'

The diesels hammered us ever westward in the path of the setting sun and not until dusk did we finally lose sight of *U-130*. We made our trial deep dive on the 600-feet contour: there was a terrible screeching in the compressed air system, the cause of which could not be established.

By the evening of 30 December we had reached the longitude of 15°W and were already trailing behind the other three boats. Our orders as part of Operation *Paukenschlag* ('Drum Beat') were to approach the American coast unseen and, at the word of command, savage merchant ships over 10,000 tons measure. Keller grinned when he read this; he was sure we would go across and then come back without actually achieving anything.

On New Year's Eve, 1941, we lay on our bunks and dreamed of home. At 2000 hrs I relayed a radio broadcast by Joseph Goebbels through to all rooms. He spoke of victory after victory in the Soviet Union, but here on the Western Ocean we knew it was not so rosy. Our few obsolescent U-boats were pitted against an ever-improving anti-submarine defence and Dönitz had repeatedly promised that the war would be decided in the Atlantic. When the speech was finished, the bells of the Homeland pealed and found their echo in our hearts. We drank our punch, ate our bread and sausage and remembered the men on the Eastern Front fighting in the insufferable cold of a Russian winter. Bleichrodt went through the boat clinking glasses and shaking the hand of every man. Precisely at midnight U-boat Command signalled:

Men of the U-boat Arm! In the New Year we will be steelier, harder and more combative yet. Long live the Führer! BdU.

In Lorient, 6 October, 1942. Bleichrodt with Lt Joachim Schramm, who would later be lost with *U-109*, as her last Commander, on 7 May, 1943.

Bosun Berthold Seidel and Senior Bosun Eduard Maureschat, October, 1942. Berthold Seidel is wearing his recently awarded German Cross in Gold

Petty Officer Otto Peters talking to British prisoners aboard _U-109_, September, 1942. (Left) Gordon Gill, Second Radio Operator _Tuscan Star_, (right) Captain Caird of the _Vimiera_ and, with his back to the camera, the Captain of the _Peterton_

Midshipman Dieter Wex, Hirschfeld and Warrant Officer (Eng) Willi Schewe. Dieter Wex would later command _U-2354_ and, after the war, become a Captain in the Federal German Navy

U-109 returns from her sixth war mission. Bleichrodt, who had recently been awarded the Oak Leaves to his Knight's Cross, exchanges salutes with Cdr Viktor Schütze, Commander 2nd U-Boat Flotilla. The onlookers are on the deck of the hulk of the sailing ship *Isere*

Looking down on U-109 from the deck of the *Isere*. Behind Bleichrodt (wearing white topped cap) are Lts Helmut Bruns and Joachim Schramm. Like Schramm, Bruns too would be lost with *U-109* in May, 1943

Lieutenant Commander Johann Heinrich Fehler (1907-1993). Explosives Officer on the German raider *Atlantis* March, 1940 - November, 1941. Commander *U-234*, September, 1943 - May, 1945

U-234. **Commissioning ceremony, Kiel, 3 March, 1944.** The crew paraded in front of the former passenger liner, *St Louis.* Lt Karl Ernst Pfaff, extreme left, Hirschfeld, in his Warrant Officer's uniform, third man in the front rank

After the Commissioning ceremony. Lt Cdr Fehler and his wife

U-234. **The surrender, 16 May, 1945.** Seen from the bridge of the USS *Sutton*. On the foredeck, some of the converted mineshafts, used as cargo containers, can be seen. The container for the uranium is out of the picture

Wilhelmshaven, May, 1945. Commander 'AJAX' Bleichrodt surrenders U-Boat Flotilla No. 22 to the Royal Navy

There was also a longer signal from Grand Admiral Raeder in Berlin, but Bleichrodt did not bother to let the crew have the text.

At 0200 hrs I went to the bridge for a quiet smoke and heard Maureschat report the first sighting of 1942, a ketch on the starboard bow which had suddenly appeared from a squall, and without lights. We altered course to avoid contact while Maureschat debated with the Captain at length why we should sink the sailing vessel with a few rounds from the deck gun. Bleichrodt shook his head, looked at me and winked: Maureschat had not seen the signal advising us of a German anti-submarine decoy disguised as a ketch and operating in this vicinity.

In a signal the following day the BdU ordered U-109 to take up a position on the south coast of Newfoundland. Bleichrodt snapped the signal log shut in annoyance and lay back on his bunk. I knew what he was thinking – Newfoundland again; why not direct to New York or Cape Hatteras where the coastal shipping was undefended? Why Canada again?

We had two young midshipmen aboard, Wex and Hengen, and a Senior Midshipman, Helmut Bruns, who would take over as third watchkeeping officer following Bruno Petersen's departure at the end of the current voyage. Bruns was an arrogant type with a tired expression and was not liked.

Torpedo Mate Werner Borchardt said to the two youngsters, 'You're both nice, harmless chaps as long as you keep your traps shut. But Bruns will be very dangerous when he takes over the watch.'

'Why?' asked Dieter Wex, 'we've all got to start somewhere.'

'Yes,' said Borchardt, 'but we would rather that you break out of your egg-shells first before we trust you with our lives.'

How true this was. The Senior Midshipman was given his first turn as Watchkeeping Officer on 3 January. The Commander ordered an emergency trial dive which started well, but as soon as we were fully submerged there was an alarmed shout in the control room and the boat began to plunge downwards very heavily; the midshipman had dogged the upper hatch cover before it was shut and the sea was now filling the tower. Otto Peters managed to shut the control room hatch lid and the Chief trimmed the boat at 120 feet; then Otto stood beside the Commander. He was dripping with water and reminded me of a wet cat.

'Blow tanks,' said Bleichrodt. 'Curse our luck if the tower sinks us.'

Otto operated the blow valves and with some relief we heard the

Chief report that the boat was rising. 'It's sheer stupidity having these kids on board,' Otto said. 'All they do is cause us problems.'

Helmut Bruns appeared before the Commander with bowed head. 'You crazy idiot, haven't you even learnt to close the hatch yet? If you've flooded the periscopes, God help you,' Bleichrodt told him, but, fortunately for the midshipman, the flooding of the tower had caused no damage.

That same evening two of the engine room ratings reported that they had pubic lice and crabs, a condition which I confirmed with a magnifying glass. This was a serious matter for the boat and the Captain called the offenders 'shitbags'.

'Hirschfeld, have you enough Kuprex?' I nodded. 'Treat our two heroes. Clear out the forward toilet, which will be set aside for their own special use, and the rest of us will all have to share the stern head.' In the likely event that the infestation would spread, I could see several problems ahead for us.

The lower deck had got wind of our destination and there were some very glum faces about. A meteorological depression had also set in and the great Atlantic combers were soon welling up and pushing the boat a little backward at every rise. When the wind increased to hurricane force the waves attained immense size, and the waste of heaving water rolled the boat so far over that the lookouts could smack the wavetops with the palm of the hand. After one particular four-hour buffeting on the bridge, Maureschat appeared at the doorway to the radio room, his eyes inflamed and an encrustation of salt on his beard.

'Wolfgang, you've never seen anything like it up there. All hell's been let loose. If it carries on like this, we still won't be near Canada in a month.' Wiping his face he continued, 'Why does he keep us on this northerly course?'

'The orders say the most economical speed on the northern Great Circle,' I told him.

'Well, shit on the orders. Dönitz has no idea what the weather's like out here,' he replied.

For days we made little progress as the hurricane raged and we were frequently driven to seek refuge in the depths for many hours. One morning we were accompanied by a school of whales while submerged and we got a fright when one of them ventured too close and rubbed himself against the hull; with a simple flick of the tail a whale could dislodge the rudders or a propeller and then we would have been at the mercy of the elements.

On 10 January Bleichrodt was ordered by the BdU to operate off Nova Scotia between Halifax and Boston when we got to the

American coast. When that might be we had no means of knowing, for we were still painfully struggling against the weather in mid-Atlantic and in addition had problems with the starboard diesel cooling pump and the gyro-compass.

Two days later the steamer *Cyclops* reported that she had been torpedoed off Halifax. Bleichrodt swore loudly. Operation *Paukenschlag* was not supposed to begin until U-boat Command gave the order and now somebody had not only jumped the gun but had done it in our allotted area.

As we neared Canada we felt the first blasts of the icy winds. The sea was still running very high, although not breaking over the tower, and the lookouts were reasonably warm packed in furs beneath their oilskins. On 13 January, 1942, the official start date of Operation *Paukenschlag*, Kals in U-130 signalled his presence in the St Lawrence.

Bleichrodt shook his head. 'How could he possibly have got there so soon if he was obeying the sailing directions?' he said. The next day Hardegen in *U-123* claimed the *Cyclops*. We also heard from Topp in *U-552*; he had the smaller Type VII boat and it was a surprise that he could operate as far west as this.

Finally, on 18 January, we were under the coast of Nova Scotia steering for Cape Sable, the decks coated with ice; I tuned in the echo-sounder and called out when we had reached the 450-feet contour. This came at precisely the moment predicted by Bruno Petersen, a feat his navigation had achieved despite the defective gyro-compass. In the hydrophones we heard the occasional rumble of distant depth charges.

Late that night the lookouts reported a light; the coastal traffic had navigation lights set, presumably because of the danger of collision. We went to full speed, the bow carving two gleaming trails through the sea. It was an easy target: we aimed and fired one torpedo. After several minutes there was some terrible cursing on the bridge: we had missed. Then, long minutes after we had given up timing it, the torpedo exploded in the distance. I was carefully monitoring the international frequencies. After some time a vessel with the call sign *MSAD* broadcast a message giving only her position at 43°26′N 65°40′W and Halifax acknowledged. This would be the ship we had taken a pot at. Another vessel was transmitting at a low volume 'SSS *Empire Kingfisher* . . . sinking quickly . . .' but the message was garbled since a number of other stations were all morsing at the same time.

We fired off two more single torpedo shots at *MSAD* and missed with both; the cursing and mutterings had started again among the lower deck and the young midshipmen listened to it with appalled expressions.

On the bridge the officers checked their calculations, but were unable to find any error. We fired the fourth torpedo; the diesels were stopped and I listened through the hydrophones to the speeding missile and heard it veer away and miss. When I reported my observation to the Captain there was an icy silence. The fault lay either in the torpedoes or the aiming device. It was bitterly disappointing. We were off the American mainland, had encountered the first of numerous sitting ducks in the area and the torpedoes had let us down.

Bleichrodt was determined to sink *MSAD*. He closed the bow caps and Werner Borchardt went astern to try with tubes five and six. Within a short while we were nicely off the steamer's bow at 500 yards range. We fired the fifth torpedo; it set off and then sheered off course. The men stared at each other in rage and despair. It was unbelievable. Five torpedoes fired at one ship and all had failed to hit. Was this what we had crossed the Atlantic for?

The lookouts reported the Cape Sable light to starboard and Bleichrodt turned away to the south-east. We made our way between two steamers to the open sea. There were plenty of potential victims and no defences, but our weapons were blunt. There was nothing for it but to check all our remaining torpedoes.

The Commander came down from the bridge and lay on his bunk in a state of abject depression. The First Lieutenant followed him through. They looked like the losing players at a Cup Final. The dimunitive Keller said to Wissmann, 'We should have followed that steamer into Halifax. When he tied up at the pier, I bet we could have got him then.' The First Lieutenant pursed his lips and nodded. 'Yes, I think you've right. But we would have needed to fire the torpedo from about 50 yards to be sure of a hit.'

I told Bleichrodt about the message sent by the *Empire Kingfisher*. The Captain shook his head. 'I don't think it was one of our torpedoes. It was probably Kals.'

The next day the torpedoes were all checked over and the tubes reloaded. A defect was discovered in the direction-setting gear of the aiming device.

On the evening of 21 January we ran in towards Cape Sable again. Leibling had been decoding the most recent signals and had underlined three of them in red. 'Have sunk 53,360 tons off New York. *U-123* Hardegen'; from Zapp in *U-66* '18,000 tons sunk', and from the BdU to *U-109*, 'Bleichrodt report your successes'. As the Commander read the log his eyes narrowed momentarily and then he returned it without comment before going up to the bridge.

Towards dawn we were drifting in the shallows off the Cape when a freighter came up at high speed showing navigation lights. As he passed in front of our tubes we fired one torpedo. This time it was straight and true but suddenly the steamer made an abrupt change of course.

'Shit!' roared Borchardt. I nodded. 'It will pass him astern.'

'They're a washout on the bridge,' said one of the crew loudly. Through the voice-pipe I could hear that Maureschat was beside himself with rage. The boat went to maximum speed ahead as we gave chase, but the merchant vessel was always widening the gap. I went to the control room doorway and glanced in. Otto Peters raised his eyebrows, snaked past the Chief and came to my side. 'This is a fine Drum Beat, don't you think?' he said. 'If they carry on like this, we'll soon have no torpedoes left.' He checked to ensure that Weber wasn't listening. 'Still, at least we'd be able to go home then.'

'Yes, and just imagine what Dönitz would say when we got there.'

The steamer, the only ship we saw that night, showed us a clean pair of heels. Despondently we slunk down to the Gulf of Maine to try our luck at the intersection of the steamer routes between Boston, Portsmouth and Cape Sable.

We sighted a ship without lights, probably British, but were forced to dive at the approach of an aircraft and later a destroyer on routine patrol. Both of these showed navigation lights. We were not detected, but the quarry escaped. When, later, the Americans began to drop random depth-charge patterns as a deterrent we headed back to Cape Sable, where early on 23 January the watchkeeping officer spotted an unlit steamer of 6000 tons. We showed her our stern and, as she passed by at a range of 400 yards, one torpedo was fired which struck her after a short run. 'A hit!' roared the men.

'SSS *Andreas* 43°20'N 66°15'W SSS,' she morsed.

Lloyds Register said she was Greek, 6566 BRT.[23]

'Steamer sinking quickly by the stern,' the bridge men shouted down.

'I'm not surprised, an old tub like that. Half these Greek ships are rotten,' Otto Peters smirked.

The small and wiry figure of Assistant Coxswain Arnetzberger, understudying Bruno Petersen for the next voyage, appeared at the radio room door and asked me how the coastal stations were reacting.

'Halifax has repeated the distress message and now the whole coast is up in arms,' I told him. It sounded as though we had stirred up a hornets' nest and we wasted no time in making for the open sea where we would spend the daylight hours.

On 24 January Zapp, Kals and Hardegen all wirelessed home that they had no torpedoes left and were returning to Lorient having sunk over 130,000 tons between them; Hardegen had even sunk a steamer with his deck gun because he had no torpedoes. It was shattering for Bleichrodt. We had crabbed all round Nova Scotia for a week and had only one rustbucket to show for it while the fuel bunkers grew gradually less. That night we spent the lonely hours cruising off Yarmouth.

The BdU signalled:

Bleichrodt, you are at the hotspot of their traffic.

We all smiled when we saw this. Dönitz should come here and see the hotspot for himself, we said. Two more days we lurked around Cape Sable searching for Allied traffic, but we saw little else but a gradually increasing anti-submarine presence and numerous fishing boats. Bleichrodt, who had had quite enough of Nova Scotia, finally lost his patience and ordered the coxswain to set a course to the south over the Nantucket Bank.

'Captain,' the Chief Engineer interjected, 'I must inform you that we have only 85 cubic metres of fuel left.' Bleichrodt nagged at his lower lip as he thought about this problem, and then said, 'All the same, I'd like to make a little detour around New York. I'm not going back yet.'

We headed slowly south, chased on one occasion by a destroyer which dropped four depth charges close behind us as if to usher us off the premises; the patrol boats all seemed very edgy.

I was thinking about the fuel problem the next morning. Schewe had 5 cubic metres in reserve which the Chief didn't know about and this was a small margin which might get us across Biscay but not the Atlantic. Then I remembered a signal in which Kals in *U-130* had reported that he had no torpedoes and was returning to Lorient with 120 cubic metres. I reminded the Captain of this message and he came into the radio room to read it again.

'Yes,' he said slowly stroking his beard, 'we could try it. Signal the BdU, "Request 20 cubic metres fuel from Kals". Give our course and position – get them from the coxswain. Then we'll see. That would really help us.'

On 28 January we waited in the vicinity of the Nantucket light vessel for our answer. The storm which had helped to push us quickly to the south had abated; it was suddenly much warmer,

19°C, and scarcely credible that only two hours' voyage to the north from the Gulf Stream it was still deepest winter.

The BdU ordered us to rendezvous with Kals the next day. If we hadn't met up by 2100 hrs Bleichrodt was to send a homing signal consisting of a string of 'V's on 852 metres. I didn't like the sound of this, but early the next morning Kals advised the BdU that his direction finder was out of commission and that, if necessary, his boat would do the transmitting.

During the night the wind strengthened and the barometer plunged. By midday a hurricane had set in from the south with winds of Force 12 and a very high and confused sea state, which forced us to heave-to. The sky had a pale, yellowish look about it and it was so warm that the lookouts were on the bridge in their shirt-sleeves. We spent most of the afternoon submerged, but at 1900 hrs Bleichrodt decided to surface for a while for two reasons: he wasn't too sure of his position and he wanted to postpone the refuelling meet. One of the control room hands shouted along the corridor, 'Bridge watch dress up warm. The wind is north-west with snow and hail.' I looked at the astonished, disbelieving faces of the lookouts. It was still blowing a hurricane, but the wind had veered and was now blasting from the mainland, driving before it a heavy sea from the north-west.

On 31 January the hurricane had blown itself out sufficiently for Arnetzberger to establish our position accurately: we were 32 miles north of the rendezvous point. As previously agreed, *U-130* began to send homing signals and we met up with her at 38°06′N 66°44′W at midday. There was a long swell running which looked likely to make the oil transfer difficult. The preparations for this were still being undertaken four hours later when lookouts on both boats reported a smudge of smoke on the horizon. Our two submarines approached very closely and the captains conducted a megaphone conversation. Kals said he had no more torpedoes but wanted to trade oil for torpedoes with Bleichrodt. The Commander smiled mischievously and replied, 'I'm sorry Captain, I have to go after that steamer. I didn't mean to delay you so long.' Kals must have read Bleichrodt's selfish intention in this reply and merely laughed, 'Go and sink him first. I'll wait until you do.'

We turned off to pursue the steamer. It was a fast ship and we were slow to gain on her even though we were pursuing at top speed and the steamer for her part was hampered by having to zig-zag across her mean course.

Over a period of six and a half hours we worked ourselves into a moon-favourable position on her bow on four occasions, only to be frustrated each time by her wild and irregular zig-zags which showed that she might have suspected our presence. Possibly the volume of a signal which I had sent during the evening might have alerted her. At 0330 on 1 February Bleichrodt fired three torpedoes and obtained two hits, one forward and the other amidships. At once the stricken vessel reported:

SSS *Tacoma Star* torpedoed position 37°33′N 69°21′W

and then began to sink quickly by the head. Within minutes the giant shadow in the night was gone. We motored over to the scene of the sinking. The lookouts saw nothing, although they heard the noise of a small motor boat leaving the area: Ferdinand Hagen also heard it in the hydrophones. It would have taken a well-trained crew to have got a motor boat away so quickly. We turned back towards the rendezvous point at slow speed. The *Tacoma Star* had transmitted an incorrect position; she was sunk at 38°46′N 64°17′W. The stern lookout reported five lifeboats with riding lights, but that was the last that was ever seen of the steamer's crew.[25]

The barometer fell again that morning and the wind freshened from the south. A powerful swell began to develop and by midday the hurricane had returned. We hove-to; there was no prospect of refuelling in these heaving seas.

The BdU asked all boats:

Who torpedoed a steamer in grid square BE78? Report now.

I showed the signal to Bruno Petersen, who consulted his chart in the control room and indicated the place, north of the Azores. 'That's in the Anton Corridor,' he said, 'where nobody is allowed to shoot.' I recalled the *Silvaplana* on the last voyage: it was actually an internationally agreed route for the use of true neutrals voyaging to and from Europe.

'Has anyone reported in yet?' the coxswain asked.

'No, they're all keeping quiet. Perhaps it was a Tommy.'

Bruno Petersen smiled. 'I doubt it. The Tommies hang around the Biscay ports waiting for us. No, that was a German U-boat.'

I had just returned to the radio room when Leibling slid a fresh message across the table to me.

To everyone from BdU: German steamer *Spreewald* sending SOS at 45°15′N 24°45′W. Torpedoed at 1700 German Legal Time. On fire and sinking.

A number of U-boats had been ordered to the spot to search for survivors. At 1900 hrs Lt Erich Cremer in *U-333* reported:

Have sunk in BE78 in the Anton Corridor a definitely enemy steamer.

There followed a long description of both the freighter and the manner in which the attack had been carried out. All the U-boat frequencies fell silent. I remembered Bleichrodt's face while we were escorting the *Silvaplana* and how he wasn't convinced that nobody would shoot in the Anton Corridor. You only needed someone like Cremer . . .

Cremer. You have sunk the German steamer *Spreewald*.

That was all. Poor Cremer, he would be able to explain his side of the matter at his court martial when he got back to France.

On 2 February the storm howled and shrieked all day: we were uncertain of our position and of the whereabouts of Kals. At 1800 hrs Bleichrodt requested him to start sending the homing signal. When I transmitted this, as usual I used the forward net deflector cable as the aerial, and on handing over the radio watch to Ferdinand Hagen I drew his attention to Kals' D/F transmissions. On relieving Hagen at 2200 he gave me his most recent fix on Kals. 'You know, I've got the feeling that the direction finder is flooded,' he said dubiously, 'I can't seem to get an accurate bearing on him.' Automatically I glanced at the aerial socket board. 'Ferdinand, have you being doing it without the auxiliary aerial?' I asked. He stood up and paled. 'Oh shit! Of course, I didn't change the forward net deflector.'

'Go and eat,' I told him, 'and then have a sleep. I'll see whether your bearings are correct when he makes his next transmission.' Ferdinand bit his lip. 'Yes, but we've been sailing for four hours on my bearing. Bruno Petersen was already here cursing the direction finding and saying that it couldn't be right. He said that, if my heading was correct, we had been driven 90 miles off our estimated position, and he doesn't think that's possible. No, I think I made a mess of it.' I did too. The coxswain's navigation could rarely be faulted. And all the time the boat was guzzling fuel. Thirty minutes later, when I took a bearing on Kals' homing signal using the forward net deflector as auxiliary aerial, I got a definite bearing. Ferdinand had been feeding the coxswain the reciprocal; every turn of the screws took us further away from our milch cow.

With my heart thumping I made my way to the control room to

confess. Bruno Petersen was leaning over his charts and looked at me with his honest eyes. 'Yes, Coxswain,' I began, 'we've got to turn the boat round. The bearings were incorrect from the beginning.'

For a moment he was speechless. Then he threw down his pencil angrily on the chart table. 'This is a nice mess, Hirschfeld. I told Hagen he couldn't be right. And what are we supposed to do now?'

I listened to the diesels, driving us ever further away from *U-130*. 'We've got to turn back at once. Every minute on this course loses us more fuel,' I said quietly. Petersen nodded. 'I think that the Captain is going to be delighted with your direction finding.' Then he went below the tower hatch and called up the change of course to the watch officer. While he was doing this, Peters gave me a smirk. 'I wouldn't want to be in your shoes,' he said. 'The Old Man's sleeping at the moment, but when we turn he'll wake up.' I nodded. From the corner where the compass repeater was positioned, I saw two large frightened eyes staring at me. It was Wüsteney.

The bows came round and I stared through the circular bulkhead doorway to where the green curtain concealing the Captain's bunk swung gently to and fro. Then Bleichrodt called out, 'Control room!'

Wüsteney jumped up. 'Sir?' 'Why have we turned?' With a gesture of helplessness to us, Wüsteney said, 'The boat has turned 180°, sir.' There was a moment's silence, then Bleichrodt roared, 'Coxswain to me!' Petersen gave me a meaningful glance. 'You'd better come along too,' he said. I felt ill as I went forward. We stood outside the green curtain until ordered to enter.

Petersen immediately started to explain that during the night radio conditions had been very poor, but Bleichrodt interrupted him almost at once. 'Damned Telegraphy again! And another load of shit you've caused us. Even when you're asleep, Hirschfeld, you're responsible for your section,' he bellowed.

I tried to make him understand how the error had occurred, and that one of the stern net deflector aerials had been flooded in the hurricane, which had led ... He wasn't listening. He merely gave me a devastating look and said to himself, 'Our precious fuel!' and then I was dismissed.

Five hours to nowhere and five back, ten hours altogether; we wouldn't be able to meet up with Kals today either. Bleichrodt sent him a message requesting that he should run towards us on course 140°. Leibling laughed as he processed the signal through the encoding machine. 'The Captain's sending messages to people without involving the BdU any more,' he said. 'Nobody ever did that previously!'

Schewe, who had been listening to all these proceedings with some amusement, clapped me sympathetically on the shoulder. 'Don't worry about it,' he assured me. 'They've wasted plenty of fuel on this voyage unnecessarily. Your few hours don't matter. And we've still got enough to make it to the Azores.' It was the same old nonsense: scuttle the boat off the volcanic shore, take a fishing cutter to Lisbon, and then, in the Homeland, there'd always be another boat.

I had a conference with the coxswain and the cook about the provisions. We were very low on potatoes and had only tinned bread. Tinned meats were almost finished, but semolina, rice and macaroni was still plentiful. It was decided to start rationing in case we had to go back to the American coast.

We met up with *U-130* on the afternoon of 3 February; we were north of Bermuda, tossing in the great seas, and, although the wind was not much more than a strong breeze, it was obvious that we could not yet refuel; even a megaphone conversation was out of the question for fear of collision and the two captains communicated by flags. I thought that Kals was demonstrating the most remarkable patience; he had even agreed to go south with us to get clear of this unreliable meteorological area. I could imagine the whingeing from Bleichrodt if the roles had been reversed.

Our two U-boats pounded and rolled southwards in incessant rain and poor visibility, but during a break in the downpour on the evening of 4 February *U-130* reported mastheads in sight. Bleichrodt obtained Kals' agreement to leave and give chase and then *U-109* turned to the west and reeled buoyantly through the long green slopes after the enemy merchant vessel. It was a tanker. The pursuit was difficult in the conditions, but just after dark we got ahead of her bow and let her approach through the rain. We fired two torpedoes with a 15-second gap and after 90 seconds there were two explosions, one after the other and the ship began to belch smoke and flame. She began transmitting almost immediately on the international frequencies:

SSS SSS VGCY SSS 35°61′W SSS

In the Register of Callsigns (*Indicative d'Appel*) VGCY was the tanker *Montrolite* of 11,309 BRT. I shouted this information to the coxswain and the men slapped their thighs with delight. At last a fat tanker! It was glorious, it was war, but over there the poor sods would be running for their lives.

She didn't sink at once, but slewed round until she was broadside to the swell. We rolled in the heaving waste and watched the lifeboats being lowered. Bleichrodt asked where the tanker had been built. Lloyds Register stated Krupp, Germania Werft; this meant that she wouldn't sink easily, the bulkheads would have been too well designed. Once her boats were clear, we motored closer to the wounded ship and fired a third torpedo to finish her off. There was a second massive explosion and then the *Montrolite* began a vertical descent by the stern. Her last resting place was at 35°38′N 60°20′W. We turned south and Bleichrodt notified the BdU:

> Because of fuel situation, operation at coast no longer possible. Since 3 February together with Kals but fuel transfer not yet effected by reason weather. 58 cubic metres left. To Kals: please send homing signal as from 0700 hrs. Bleichrodt.

We met up with Kals again during the morning. He was most congratulatory about our success which of course could not have been achieved without his assistance. The wind had begun to increase to storm force from the west and, because of the advantageous stern sea which would help push us toward our destination, the two commanders agreed to travel eastwards in company with a view to carrying out the fuel transfer perhaps during the night.

Just after dusk a smoke trail was reported by the lookouts and, waving aside Bleichrodt's apology, Kals shouted, 'Don't worry, I'll wait!'

Schewe put his red beard into the radio room. 'If we run across any more steamers after this, we'll all be going home on *U-130*,' he said.

'We've only got two torpedoes left,' I told him.

'Well, that's a comfort,' he replied.

The steamer had two masts and a tall, fat smoke stack: she was making about ten knots with a lot of effort. There was a sizeable swell and Weber found it difficult to keep the trim at periscope depth. Keller came to join me with his stop-watch and three times over we counted the steamer's propeller revolutions. We agreed she was probably only making 8 knots; the Captain had estimated her size as 6,000 BRT.

Once the data was collated, Bleichrodt got the boat into position and fired the penultimate torpedo at a range of 2,000 yards. It ran straight and true. I lined up the ship and torpedo in the hydrophones. The bearing was the same. 'That must hit,' I said. The stop-watches ticked away, but there was no explosion when the moment arrived. Ten minutes later the torpedo was still drilling a track through the rollers. The steamer continued her progress unawares. 'Went under him,' I said. 'But it was only set for 10 feet,' Keller protested. 'Damn, now we've only got one eel left.'

The Captain retracted the periscope with a curse and called a conference of the three watchkeeping officers in the Officers' Mess. After a discussion it was agreed to wait for nightfall and then attack on the surface. We ran a parallel course to the target on her port side and calculated her speed now at 8.5 knots. The firing data was fed into the torpedo mechanism and the last eel was loosed off. Keller sat staring at his stop-watch. Torpedo Mate Werner Borchardt came down the central gangway from the bows and said 'That's my job done, I'm ready to go on leave.'

'Get off now if you want to,' Keller told him. The Lieutenant looked worried; time was up and there was still no hit. The distress frequencies were all silent. We had fired two torpedoes and missed with both, and the steamer didn't even know we were there. Bleichrodt descended from the bridge as if in a daze. He stood at the doorway to the radio room and stared at the brightly coloured table top. He looked very tired. Stroking his beard, he asked, 'Did she wireless?'

'No, sir, it's all quiet on the international frequencies.' With a nod he turned away and drew the green curtain behind him as he sought seclusion in his tiny compartment. Then I heard him settle on his bed.

Maureschat came to the radio room and said, 'Dammit, Wolfgang! They fired beneath him. Either that ship has a flat bottom or they set the torpedoes too deep.' I shrugged my shoulders, pointed to the green curtain and said, 'What are we going to do now?'

Maureschat whispered, 'He's going to let him go. I told him I would sink the freighter by gunfire.'

'And?'

'He told me to remember the *City of Auckland*.'

I nodded. 'There's a lot of U-boat traps operating round here, Ede.'

'So what? The night's pitch black. We only need to go so close.' He turned away in resignation. 'Ah well, I think I'll turn in.'

A short while later the tall blond figure of Lt Wissmann appeared at the doorway. 'Where is the Commander?' he demanded. I pointed to the green curtain and said quietly, 'He's lying on his bunk.' Wissmann nodded, turned to face the curtain and drew a deep breath, steeling himself for the confrontation. 'Captain, we can't just let this steamer go. The BdU would never forgive us!'

A second later Bleichrodt tore the curtain aside. 'You're all mad!' he screamed. The two officers were standing eyeball to eyeball and Wissmann was giving no ground.

'Very well,' the Commander roared after a few moments' silence, 'if that's what you want. Control room! Prepare for gun engagement!'

Then he turned to Wissmann and said quietly, 'Our blood be on your head, First Lieutenant.' Wissmann smiled. 'If I might suggest, sir, we could also use the flak guns.'

The Captain was already dressing up. 'For all I care, you can use every barrel aboard. Take the machine guns up there as well.' The Lieutenant nodded and went to the control room to make the necessary preparations. As the gun crew stampeded past the radio room I grabbed Maureschat's arm. 'Ede, don't forget to unscrew the muzzle plug!'

He laughed. 'You can count on it, Wolfgang!'

They went up as, in the control room, the floor plates were being lifted to give access to the ammunition chamber.

Berthold Seidel was manning the 3.7-cm flak gun on the after deck with two men; Walter Gross and an ordinary seaman were handling the two 20cm guns on the Winter-garden. Maureschat reported the 10.5-cm gun ready to fire. Even the double-barrelled machine guns had been fitted up on the tower coaming.

We cruised towards the labouring steamer through the darkness, waiting for moonrise.

Ferdinand was very nervous, stroking his beard and scratching behind his ear and saying, 'I'd just like to know now if it's going to be OK or whether the Old Man is right about that ship.'

I nodded. 'We'll know the answer to that as soon as we fire the first few salvoes. If it is a Q-ship they'll mow down our men at the guns and on the bridge. Then the telegraphists and the engineers can sail the boat home.'

Ferdinand ran his hands through his hair. 'If there's anything left to sail that is. Think of Kleinschmidt in *U-111*. They finished him off on the surface.'

It was exactly 0130 when the Commander gave the order to fire. The boat trembled as the first 10.5-cm shell howled away. The machine guns were hammering too. Ferdinand nudged me. The ship was sending on the 600 metre frequency: the radio operator was hitting the key at a frenetic pace.

RRR RRR halcyon RRR RRR

'What's this?' I exclaimed. 'It's not SSS he's sending, it's RRR!' We both laughed aloud; RRR meant 'I am being attacked by a regular warship.'

'He thinks we're a cruiser,' I called out as I raced for the bridge. I reported the fact to the Commander. The steamer was already on fire. In the light of the flames I could make out her unmanned gun on the poop.

'Is he still using his wireless?'

'Yes, sir, continuously.'

Bleichrodt cupped his hands round his mouth and leant over the bridge wind deflector. 'Maureschat!'

'Commander?' His voice was so loud it carried above the clatter of the machine guns.

'You've got to destroy the radio shack as soon as possible. It's just behind the wheelhouse.'

'Will do,' Maureschat roared.

With his next shot the bridge split open and the machine guns raked the wreckage. When I returned below Ferdinand said, 'He kept sending "RRR-bombarded in position 34°20′N 59°16′W RRR *Halcyon* bombarded" . . .'

I asked Arnetzberger to compare this position with the chart. We were very close to Bermuda.

'How does it look with the coastal stations?' I asked Ferdinand.

'They've all taken up the cry. The whole coast is up in arms. They keep repeating the RRR. They've gone crazy to think that a German warship is operating round here.' Above us the 10.5-cm gun was still remorselessly pounding the burning wreck. An hour after we had opened fire we had let her have 100 rounds but the steamer was still afloat. The ship appeared deserted and drifting in the heavy seaway, her entire stern section in flames. It fell quiet as we closed in. At a range of 400 yards Bleichrodt told Maureschat to resume the shelling: Leibling handed me a decoded signal and grinned:

Wireless Monitoring Service reports; grid square DD3145 steamer *Halcyon* sending 'I am being attacked by enemy warship.' American unit has left Bermuda to assist. BdU.

I took the message to the bridge. The grey dawn was breaking and we had again ceased firing while we made a short voyage round the stern of the *Halcyon*, which had a list of 40°.

Bleichrodt read the signal and said, 'Damn, she's still not sinking,' then shouted down to Maureschat, 'How many rounds have you got left?'

'Twenty, Captain.'

'Get ready, Maureschat. I'm going to go in really close and I want you to give her a final battering.' Bleichrodt called out to the stern, 'Berthold, I'm going in close. Keep shooting at her waterline.'

The wreck dwarfed us as we went close by her. Her sides were enormous for such a small ship. Now we knew why the torpedoes had passed beneath her; she was only 3,531 BRT and carried no cargo. Shell after shell was now pumped into the tough old nut. Abeam on either side she had a gaping hole large enough to drive a bus through, but still she wouldn't go down. Then the guns finally fell silent.

Leibling threw me a look. 'Yes,' I said, 'they've finished off all the ammunition and the steamer's still afloat.' Leibling shook his head. 'Where's her crew?'

'I don't know. Perhaps they got away in the darkness. There's a Jacob's ladder and davits dangling over her side.'

I returned to the bridge and watched the gun crew on the foredeck collecting the empty shell cases together. I heard Maureschat shouting, 'Don't let any of them go overboard or I'll have to write out a 10-page memorandum with thirty copies about each one.'

It was now daylight and we all gazed at the burning derelict nearby. Bleichrodt said to me, 'We'll have to leave now. The boys from Bermuda will be here soon.' With that he bent down to the manhole and issued his course and speed instructions to the helmsman. The diesels roared and the bow swung round to an easterly heading towards the waiting *U-130*. I wondered what would happen to the *Halcyon*; she would never survive a tow but we had left her afloat and so couldn't claim her as sunk, only damaged.

U-109 began to pick up speed and Maureschat paused as he came out of the control room, his face blackened with powder and smoke from the gun. As usual he asked if there was anything in the latest news bulletins. I shook my head and then asked him, 'Were there any survivors?'

'Yes. I saw two men get away in a small boat, but I lost sight of them during the shooting.' He took a deep breath and continued, 'Imagine it, Wolfgang, I think I destroyed the big lifeboat with the rest of the crew in it.'

'How did that happen?'

'It was while it was still dark. Just as we fired I saw the boat being lowered. It came right into the cross wires.'

'Perhaps they were lowering it empty.'

He shook his head. 'No, they were just letting it down and I think it was full.' It had affected him deeply. He would carry the memory of it with him always. 'I'm so sorry for those poor sods,' he said.

'Yes, Ede, but that's war! If they had got to their gun first, they'd have shot us to pieces.' He said nothing and, just as he was about to go, a voice on the bridge shouted, 'Steamer's sinking by the stern!'

'Thank God for that,' said Maureschat. 'Now I can get some sleep.' We had expended 200 10.5-cm and 100 3.7-cm shells in the effort to sink the *Halcyon*.[26]

At about 0800 we dived when the battle-mast of a cruiser appeared. In the hydrophones we could hear her approaching at high speed. The Commander sat at the periscope swearing softly. 'Boys, boys, a cruiser, perhaps 9,000 tons. All by herself and we haven't got a torpedo.'

'She's looking for the German cruiser that never was,' smirked Keller.

After she had stormed out of sight we surfaced and headed eastwards towards Kals, homing in on his D/F signals and locating him at dusk.

He congratulated us on our most recent success and suggested that we should begin with the oil transfer immediately, since we had no means of knowing how long the good weather would last. Bleichrodt agreed and we went alongside *U-130* as close as we dared. Lines were thrown to Kals' boat and then the hoses were hauled across by his crewmen. Next, both boats turned into the wind and *U-130* proceeded at slow speed ahead, towing us on her port quarter so as to keep the hoses slack between us. By early morning we had 64 cubic metres of fuel and the replenishment was completed. When the lines and hoses had been stowed we watched *U-130* make off at speed into the darkness and we followed her tracks on one diesel to conserve our bunkers, gradually losing sight of her tiny shadow in the night.

By 9 February, when we were north of the Azores, we began to realize that we had a serious food shortage on our hands. I was unable to understand why the stocks were so low. We were supposed to have been supplied for ten weeks and in the seven weeks of the voyage so far we had by no means fed ourselves sumptuously. I was suspicious that some of the Admin people might have diverted a share of the provisions. It was decided to impose an even stricter rationing of the food per man. Järschel wasn't happy about it: as cook, he was in the front line.

Otto Peters suggested drawing up a short list of crew members we could quietly dump overboard without endangering the boat in the event that rations fell below subsistence level. With a great deal of mirth we eventually settled for the torpedo mechanics, all the midshipmen and Arnetzberger, the Assistant Coxswain. We didn't like to tell them in case we hurt their feelings.

The pubic lice infestation had caught hold and all the men in the stern were reporting to me for treatment, but unfortunately my large bottle of Kuprex was finished. Because several men had to share the same bed on the shift system, the blankets were the medium by which the problem was transmitted from one man to another.

Schewe announced that we could increase speed a little. He had deceived the engineers on *U-130* into parting unwittingly with an extra 5 cubic metres, but, because of the contrary winds and high swell, Bleichrodt kept our progress down to a crawl.

On the evening of 15 February we reached position 44°17′N 23°10′W. It was here that Lieutenant Commander Rollmann in *U-82* had been on the same course as ourselves for Lorient when he reported a weakly defended convoy. The BdU had ordered him to keep contact but since then nothing more had been heard from him for over a week. Bleichrodt spent some time reading through the various signals and poring over the charts.

'What's your opinion, Hirschfeld? Do you think they can get an accurate fix on our transmissions?'

'Certainly, sir. When I was in the Monitoring Service in 1937 we needed an extremely large antenna for short wave direction finding. Personally I'm convinced that they can do it now from a destroyer, but . . .'

'But what?'

'Captain Meckel doesn't think so. Lt Seidel told me. And Meckel's opinion is the one which carries weight in the Signals Branch.'

The Commander nodded and went to his nook, where he stared at the photo of his wife which was pinned on his side of the corridor dividing wall. Whenever he was on the bridge, Ferdinand and I often used to look at this photo. Carla Bleichrodt was more than just a beautiful woman, she was a Goddess before whom one might be seized by the impulse to fall on one's knees in homage. Ferdinand told me she was a family practitioner in Lünen. Otto Peters, who also used to stare at the picture, said, 'I can't understand it. Such a beautiful woman. How could she marry such a corrupt sailorman?'

The next morning the Commander decided to allow Senior Midshipman Bruns another chance as watch officer. I joined Berthold Seidel on the bridge for a quiet smoke. The sea was calm but the horizons were very milky. Berthold would occasionally give a worried glance into the distance. 'I say,' he called out to Leading Seaman Zank, one of the stern lookouts, 'has the Old Man been told about this poor visibility?' Zank shook his head and Berthold told the midshipman to report it at once. At about 0900 a thick mist began to gather and by midday visibility was down to about 400 yards. Bleichrodt was very disquieted. His sixth sense took him to the bridge. In this area fog was very unusual.

At 1500 a lookout shouted, 'Shadow ahead!' The fog was now so dense that it was often difficult to see the bow.

'Hard to port! Starboard diesel full ahead!' the watchkeeping officer roared. Towering above us suddenly rose the huge side of a merchant ship. She was heading north and crossing our bow. As we turned we ran parallel with her for a short distance.

'Hard to starboard!' came the order. Ferdinand was at the hydrophones listening out for the Asdic. Soon he reported that, despite the noise of the mashing propellors all around, he could hear numerous Asdic emissions.

'Corvette to starboard!' We were in the middle of a convoy in the fog. When I went to the bridge to report the Asdic to the Commander he said, 'I thought so. We can't dive or they'll get us straight away. We'll have to steer our way out of it on the surface.'

The starboard corvette seemed to be the forward sweeper and had turned to starboard again. We followed her through the swathes of fog and suddenly glimpsed a steamer materializing to port, a vessel with a high stern, clipper bow, a short funnel and high wheelhouse. As we continued our turn to starboard another dark shape became visible.

'Slow ahead!' barked Bleichrodt. The convoy seemed to be sailing in a very tight formation, probably two corvettes and two merchant ships using ultra short wave transmissions to keep their positions. Bleichrodt was continually adjusting our speed and heading until another corvette was at last spotted. This would be the rear sweeper. The warship crossed our wake to the east and we were free. We made off fast to the south.

Bleichrodt continued to study Rollmann's signals. 'He was exactly here, where we just met that convoy,' he reflected.

'Really we should have made a contact report,' I said.

He looked at me almost contemptuously. 'And for whose benefit would that have been? No, we won't signal in.' I hadn't really expected him to say anything else.

As we neared Biscay we began to spend much more time submerged. In the distance we could hear the unending depth-charging as British aircraft dropped explosive on every tin can. The men were cursing at our slow progress to port; the coxswain shook his head to hear it. I knew what he was thinking.

For four days we fought a storm head-on as we pitched and rolled towards Lorient on our last drops of oil. The bilge pumps were working furiously; for some reason the internal ballast tanks kept filling and the Chief sweated as he tried to keep the trim. Eventually, when he grounded the boat at 120 feet off the Ile de Croix to wait for the minesweeper escort, the keel hit with a spine-jarring crunch.

On 23 February, 1942, an R-boat led us through the Kernevel Narrows. It was quiet on the electric motors; we had no oil left for the diesels. Officers waved their caps to us from the villa of the BdU, the band played on the crowded hulk of the *Isere* and newsreel cameras recorded our arrival for cinema. A tremendously happy feeling swept over us as we realized that we had reached home safely once more. The screws whirred a few times and then we tied up. It was cold in France.

In the U-boat bunker at Keroman we patted *U-109* as if she were a faithful pet. She had brought us across the ocean, withstood whatever the enemy had thrown at us and had remained intact. Some of the planks were missing from the free-flooding deck; the covers were open and cables ran everywhere. The air was filled with the dust and clatter of drills and riveters.

Unexpectedly, the BdU arrived and had us parade as we were, unshaven and in our dungarees. We stood in the courtyard of the Salzwedel Barracks with several other crews in a half-circle around him. Dönitz told us that a fresh wave of boats had already arrived on the American coast while another group was operating in the Caribbean. This had tied up the American Atlantic Fleet and thus left Japan with a free hand in the Pacific.

'If the defences along the American coast become too strong,' the BdU said, 'we will withdraw into the Atlantic and resume the convoy war with renewed vigour. *The outcome of the war depends on your success.*'

A cold shiver ran up my spine. Were we supposed to decide the war with these boats? They were too slow. Surely he knew that. We would have to have new boats – and new torpedoes too.

After we had been dismissed Otto Peters drew me aside with a grim expression. 'If he thinks we're going to win the war with these boats things look pretty black for Germany,' he muttered.

They threw a celebration party for us in the barracks mess – roast turkey, Beck's beer and a lot of liquor. It was quiet while we were eating, but soon the alcohol got to work. An Austrian ordinary seaman and Maureschat began to sing a nursery song about a child who wanted a pony. 'Isn't it sweet?'

Ferdinand said to me, 'We'll all be sniffing in our hankies next.'

Bleichrodt shouted, 'Since when have you been an Austrian, Maureschat?' but the boatswain ignored him. When they started to sing the third verse Bleichrodt jumped up and exclaimed, 'Enough of this wailing! Comrades, let's not make arses of ourselves! We must be hard, the terror of Barbary! Long live the U-boat spirit! Prost!' We sprang to our feet, eyes shining. One single cry echoed around the hall: 'Prost Ajax!'

In Kernevel we found that we had been credited with the *Empire Kingfisher*. There had been no other boat in the vicinity and the BdU thought it likely that our stray torpedo had eventually found a mark. Our total haul for the voyage was therefore five ships of 33,700 BRT.[27]

– 7 –

'TODAY IS THE FÜHRER'S BIRTHDAY'

I arrived back in Lorient from my leave early on 20 March, 1942. It was very mild and pouring with rain, a contrast to the icy cold in Germany. Many acquaintances in Hamburg had scarcely been able to conceal their surprise at seeing me. One of them remarked quite openly, 'I thought you were a prisoner.' When I asked him the reason, he told me in the strictest confidence, 'From the BBC. They reported *U-109* sunk and that the crew had been made POWs.'

'Well, now you know what liars they are,' I told him, 'and I wonder how many people listen to the British radio as you do and believe the shit they serve up.'

As always when I came to Hamburg, at the request of the Commander I would visit the regulars' table at the 'Hanseaten' in St Pauli in order to convey the good wishes and respects of Lt Cdr Bleichrodt to the old sailing masters who used to meet there every Sunday morning. Captain Hermann Piening and his colleagues knew Bleichrodt from his voyages in 1926 aboard the Laeisz four-masted bark *Peking*. They would urge me for stories about our Atlantic patrols and nod understandingly when I described the terrible winter storms. Yes, they said, they had experienced it so often themselves off Cape Horn.

On 10 March Bleichrodt had given a radio interview and on 14 March the arrival of *U-109* at Lorient had been shown on national cinema newsreel. The commentator said, 'Captain Bleichrodt, reported sunk by British radio, returns from a successful voyage to the east coast of the United States.'

Aboard *U-109* there had been many changes. Lt Wissmann had gone on the U-boat commanders' course and the coxswain, Bruno Petersen, had left to become an officer. Dönitz had not forgotten his promise. I was not to see the coxswain again until after the war.

Boatswain Walter Gross had been promoted and was to be the Senior Boatswain on a new Type XIV tanker U-boat. 'If I have to refuel *you*, you won't do the dirty on me like you did with Kals,' he said to us in parting, 'I know how Schewe does it.'

Of the midshipmen Wex had gone for officer training, but we kept Hengen, as the Commander considered him too immature to recommend at this stage. The first watchkeeping officer was Lieutenant Werner Witte whom I knew well from my minesweeping days, and I liked him very much. We had also acquired a 21-year-old engineering Sub-Lieutenant, Albert Heyer, who would do one voyage understudying Martin Weber before being appointed Chief Engineer elsewhere.

Lorient had begun to receive regular visits from British bombers and we did not think it likely that the town would last much longer.

At the U-boat Clinic in Carnac Fleet Surgeon Dr Lepel inspected the red spots on my arms and asked when I had first noticed them. 'On the last voyage,' I told him. 'We'll have another look at it when you come back next time. It looks like a fungus.'

As the boat's medical team, Ferdinand and I visited the Flotilla doctor, Ziemke, and received the latest information about the treatment of venereal diseases.

On the evening of 25 March, 1942, we had the usual big send-off from the *Isere* and put to sea. Bleichrodt stood on the bridge staring stolidly ahead as the grey iron shark followed in the wake of a big mine-destructor ship towards the Fortress of Port Louis. Adalbert Schnee in *U-201* was a short distance behind us. With a final wave towards the villa of the BdU, the crew went down into the belly of the submarine. Early next morning, after we had made the trial dive, the commander told me to play the record 'New York' to the crew after which he would announce the operation. They knew what the music meant – America! This time to the coast of Florida.

On the third day out the depth-charging in the Bay of Biscay was almost incessant. That evening a returning U-boat reported seeing three unidentified destroyers and ten MTBs making for the French coast. Early next morning U-boat Command ordered:

All boats to the east of 29°W head at fastest speed to grid square BF6510. English landed tonight at St Nazaire.

Bleichrodt handed me back the signal log. 'I don't think it's a big action. We'll go on a bit.'

'But the BdU knows we haven't passed 15°W,' I said. Bleichrodt smiled in amusement. 'Hirschfeld, if it's the real invasion, we'll go back.' He patted me on the shoulder like a father. 'You'll see. They'll soon countermand the order.'

On reflection I thought he was right. We had heard only of light forces and not an armada, and what was the sense in recalling outward-bound boats which needed every drop of fuel? But when no countermanding order had arrived by 0645, the Commander turned the boat around with a bad grace and we headed back towards France. At 0743 the BdU signalled:

FT 0655/28. English attack on St Nazaire by destroyers and MTB's beaten off. Air recce at dawn. Await orders.

We drifted and waited. In the NCO's Mess Werner Borchardt said, 'I'm surprised that they let the BdU occupy the villa on that spit of land. Would it surprise you if their commandos came one day and nabbed him?' We all laughed but realized that he was right. An hour afterwards we received orders to resume the voyage.

We crossed the Bay of Biscay and on 31 March signalled to the BdU that we were clear, having passed 16°W. There was a west-north-west breeze under overcast skies with the occasional break in the cloud through which a patch or two of blue could be glimpsed.

The Commander introduced a series of exercises and emergency drills to sharpen up the new men and during the midday pause Seidel went to the foot of the conning tower ladder and requested permission to visit the bridge for a cigarette. Just as he did so he saw a bomber framed in the circular manhole above him and he cried out, 'Aircraft!'

Lt Witte chased the lookouts into the boat and sealed up as the bows cut steeply under, but once the submersion had been accomplished they all relaxed because they thought it had been just another drill. Suddenly there was a dreadful explosion dead astern.

I ran from my bunk to the radio room. Seidel was standing there.

'They were depth charges,' I said.

'From a plane.'

'Well that's nice, if even their fliers can drop them now.'

Lt Witte said, 'My God, Seidel, that was a close thing.'

Berthold nodded. 'My 13th U-boat war voyage. But even this time we'll all be coming home safe and sound.'

On 1 April the wind shifted to the north-west and it began to blow strong on the starboard bow. Endless mountains of green water rolled towards us and for four days we made no headway. We ate our soup from ladles and tin cans to conserve the crockery when we were on the surface, and chafed at the enforced idleness when we sought refuge from the storm in the depths.

From signals traffic we learned that the first U-tanker, *U-459*, had put to sea. This Type XIV boat carried 700 cubic metres of oil. Later that month she would be followed by three sister vessels. This was the response to the destruction of the surface tanker fleet in the wake of the *Bismarck* disaster;[28] it was urgently necessary to find a way to increase the period we could remain on the enemy coast between the 8000-mile round trip out and back to France.

On 6 April the weather was calmer and the sun beamed down from a clear sky. We sailed through fleets of Portuguese men-of-war, exotic, translucent and vividly coloured jellyfish, and in the stillness after the storm we felt at peace with the world.

In the evenings we often used to tune in to the BBC German Language broadcasts. Although it was strictly forbidden, few U-boat commanders enforced the order, and I was certain that Dönitz knew and laughed about it.

The programmes were pure propaganda, a neatly served cocktail of fact and lies, and the most popular item with us was 'Secret Transmitter No. 1'. When this came on even Bleichrodt would draw up a chair in the radio room. The programme would begin with the words, 'Achtung! Achtung! Here is Gustav Siegfried One! The Chief speaking!' The Chief was supposed to be the old SA leader. He mocked the failures of the Party bosses and castigated the SS, but never insulted the Führer. He was extremely well informed on certain matters and would hammer these for all they were worth. Once, using the most disgusting personal details, he recounted the goings-on at a sex orgy involving Bömke, the Bürgermeister of Bremen and a number of Polish fisherwomen. In conclusion he would always say, 'Comrades! Don't let this go on! Report it to Minister Dr Lammers in Berlin. He will be interested to hear from you!'

The Chief insisted that he was operating from a mobile transmitter on the Continent but our Wireless Monitoring Service had plotted the source of the signal to London.

On 8 April the barometer fell and the wind strengthened to hurricane force and howled and wailed for five days, while the sea rose angrily and hurled itself with massive force at the conning tower, forcing us to submerge.

Three days earlier, on the eleventh day of the voyage, Ordinary Machinist Gerstner had reported sick with gonorrhoea. Bleichrodt found it incredible that it had taken him so long to report it. The man was relieved from his duty and we began the Albucid cure. I appointed Karl Will, the oldest hand in the stern section, to make sure Gerstner took the tablets.

When I saw Gerstner again on 12 April, I found that the cure had not taken. This was strange because the medicine had been proved in practice. I started a second course, which was also a failure.

The same day Leading Seaman Goldbeck reported stomach pains and had a high temperature. After consultation with Dr Bleichrodt my diagnosis was appendicitis. We gave the patient an iced water bottle and then prayed for him to get better. Otherwise I would have to operate.

The Commander gave me another regular task, typing-up the War Diary. Apparently the BdU Staff found it too much of a struggle to have to read handwriting. Bleichrodt shook his head in anguish when Hardegen sent a signal stating that he had sunk 74,837 BRT of shipping off the American coast; eight tankers, a passenger freighter and a Q-ship, and had survived two depth charge attacks.

'Right in our operating area,' he groaned. 'When we get there the traffic will have been diverted and they'll be lying in wait for us.'

On the twenty-second day out we entered an area of calms and the flak gun crews were exercised; there had been reports of small airships or 'Blimps' engaged in aerial reconnaissance around Bermuda which might have to be dealt with. Bleichrodt requested the BdU:

Gonorrhoea patient second Albucid cure not effective. Request meet with returning U-boat for transfer.

We were to the north-east of Bermuda on 16 April when we sighted a small merchant vessel on a easterly course which was not zig-zagging. We made an attack approach and then the Commander cursed.

'She's flying the Swiss flag,' Maureschat told me. We surfaced and Maureschat's team manned the deck gun while Lt Witte used a lamp to order the steamer to stop and send across a boat with the ship's papers. This seemed not to be clearly understood, for the steamer turned her bows towards us and her screws kicked up a heavy wash astern. She only stopped when we fired a machine-gun burst across her path.

It took an hour for her lifeboat to row over. The steamer's first mate climbed aboard; he looked a real scruff, nothing like a Swiss. Bleichrodt gave him a long, penetrating stare, then read aloud from the manifest for me to write down; 'Swiss steamer *Calanda* with 6,420 tons of wheat in sacks and loose, New York to Genoa.' Her officers were all Dutch and the crew a mixture of Portuguese and Eastern Europeans.

'Are these the true papers?' Bleichrodt demanded, 'or do we have to search your ship?' The Dutchman protested that the papers were genuine.

'Good,' said Bleichrodt. 'If you are found off your course you will be sunk.'

'He's lying,' Witte said, after the lifeboat had begun pulling back to the neutral steamer.

'Yes, I'm sure you're right,' Bleichrodt agreed, 'but it's too dangerous for me to send people over there to search when we can be caught on the surface at any moment by their air reconnaissance.'

The Captain reported the meeting with the *Calanda* and the next day the BdU answered:

Bleichrodt. First, transfer of your patient not possible. Doctor orders bedrest and repeat Albucid cure after one week. Secondly, no refuelling will be possible.

Bleichrodt was outraged about the oil and wrote in the War Diary:

So, I have at my disposal on the American coast only 20 to 28 cubic metres, which will soon be consumed without my being able to search any great length of area. This may mean that I have to bring the torpedoes home. A somewhat unproductive exercise.

Next day Maureschat appeared at the radio room and said with a grin, 'You know something about fish, don't you Wolfgang?' I nodded. 'Can you eat flying fish?'

'Certainly. They have an excellent flavour.'

'Good. I'll get the fish and you prepare them.' With that he went. I didn't think he was likely to catch any, but a short time later he reappeared with a large cloth filled with the flapping creatures. Leibling and I rolled our eyes.

'How did you do it, Ede?'

'They just keep throwing themselves against the tower. All you have to do is collect them.' I took them off to the kitchen without waking the cook.

As we eagerly started to gorge ourselves the Commander appeared.

'What have you got there? Fish?'

'Flying fish, sir,' said Eduard with a laugh. 'May we serve you some?'

The Captain stroked his beard. 'I don't think I can say no.'

We were at 34°57′N 63°51′W. 'It's Adolf's birthday the day after tomorrow,' said Otto Peters at dinner, 'and we haven't got a ship for him. I think we should have quietly sunk that Swiss steamer. Nobody would have known and they wouldn't have declared war on us just for that.'

19 April, 1942, was a Sunday and, as always on Sundays, we had ham with asparagus. Otto Peters told me that Järschel was complaining about having to give everybody a small tin of the vegetable. When I asked him what was the problem, he explained, 'Petty Officer, if we continue eating like this the provisions won't last twelve weeks.'

'But Järschel, don't worry about it. In a few days we'll have shot off all our torpedoes and, as there's no possibility of our receiving any more fuel, we'll have to go home.' This appeared to mollify him.

The BdU made an urgent request for all U-boats at sea to report their successes. Apparently there was to be a Special Announcement on 20 April, the Führer's birthday. We were asked to report the successes of *U-109* because they assumed in Paris, which was to where the BdU had been removed after the St Nazaire affair, that we would already be in our operational area. Bleichrodt snapped the log shut in disgust.

We were 200 miles north of Bermuda at midnight on 20 April when Bleichrodt rummaged in his trunk and brought out a bottle of rum. With three glasses he came to the radio room.

'Today is the Führer's birthday,' he said with a smile. 'We must drink to that.' He offered a glass to Leibling and myself and filled them both to the brim. 'We have no successes to report, but we won't let that worry us, will we, Hirschfeld?'

'Commander, we have until 0700 to report in. The Special Announcement isn't being made until midday.' Bleichrodt stuck out his lower lip. 'There are no ships round here. They all hug the coast.' He tucked the bottle under his arm and went forward to the NCO's Mess.

Half an hour later the bridge watch reported a smoke trail on the port bow and the Commander came back down the central gangway and stowed the bottle of rum under his bunk.

'If the Devil wills it, Hirschfeld, it will surely happen. Keep watch on the distress frequency.'

'Yes, sir. Let's only hope it's not a Swiss again!'

We made for the steamer at high speed, but after only a short while I heard Lt Witte curse, 'We've lost him, sir!'

There was a moment's silence. 'Keep calm, he can't have gone far.'

On the bridge they studied the darkness with their powerful Zeiss glasses. Leibling said to me, 'If we don't find him again soon we'll miss the Special Announcement.'

'Just wait,' I told him. 'We'll pick him up on the hydrophones if necessary.' The minutes dragged by and then I heard Berthold Seidel say, 'There he is, 30°.'

'Where?' Witte asked. 'Can you see him, sir?'

'No. Damn this darkness. Have you still got him, Seidel?'

'No. I just saw a door open and a man in a white jacket came out. That was at 30°.'

The bows came round to point at the presumed position of the ship and we went to half ahead. Then they found the dark shadow once more.

'Witte, I'm going in as close as possible. He's not going to escape us again.'

We manoeuvred into a surface attack position with the moon behind the steamer, closing in quickly. I heard Witte calling out the range.

'800 yards! 600 yards! Fan of torpedoes ready!'

Otto Peters called to me from the control room. 'We might as well save the torpedoes and finish him off with the ram!'

'Torpedoes running!' The three eels had left their tubes with a loud hiss.

'They got it off all right but even at this range they'll still miss,' Otto called out. The Chief Engineer gave him a blistering look.

The torpedo running time had elapsed. On the bridge there was a tense silence. Through the voice-pipe Maureschat said to me in a low voice, 'They missed, Wolf. For the first time in German U-boat history they missed at 600 yards with a fan of three torpedoes.'

'What's up, Wolfgang?' Otto Peters asked.

'Missed her.'

'Ha, what did I tell you? Another 75,000 Reichsmarks up their arses!'

When Arnetzberger came into the control room, I went over to him and asked, 'How was that possible, Coxswain?'

He gave me a stare and said, 'Incredible, eh? Possibly we got the range wrong. I think the torpedoes were set too deep.'

'And now?'

'Fresh attack from the stern tubes.'

The boat went to full speed, throwing up a thick, curling wake.

The steamer ought to have spotted it if she was keeping a proper lookout, but it remained quiet.

An hour and a half later we tried again. As we moved in at low speed for the kill, the moon slipped behind a bank of cloud. We loosed two torpedoes at 1000 yards.

'Torpedoes phosphorescent!' someone shouted. Just like the dolphins at Biarritz. If the steamer's lookout saw the tracks early enough and reacted, there would still be time to avoid them. After 28 seconds it was too late. There were two explosions in quick succession. I had just put my stop-watch aside when a tremendous blast struck the boat and I was hurled to the floor from my perch on the gramophone record cabinet.

As the bridge watch plummeted into the control room Bleichrodt was shouting 'Down! Down!' Detonation followed detonation in the distance. We looked at each other wide-eyed. Maureschat came to the radio room doorway.

'Terrible, Wolf, terrible. The steamer just disintegrated.'

'Where's Witte?' the Captain shouted. 'Did he get hurt?'

'I'm under the periscope housing. The steamer's gone down.'

I went to the sound room where Ferdinand handed me the hydrophones. I listened to the awful grinding and bursting noise and the occasional explosion. Minutes after the volcanic eruption, splinters were still pattering down on our decks in a minor blizzard from the skies. The bridge watch went back up into the pitch black night. Close by us there drifted two calcium light buoys, all that remained of the mystery ship.

'I wonder what his cargo was,' Bleichrodt said, staring at the scene from where the steamer had vanished. 'Did he wireless?'

'Not a peep, sir.'

The Commander and First Lieutenant swept the wave tops with their binoculars. 'Not much point in looking for survivors, Witte. None of the poor devils could have got away from that.'

Witte lowered his Zeiss and nodded. 'She must have taken them all with her. The steamer went down in ninety seconds.' Bleichrodt ordered the diesels stopped for a few minutes while he listened, but all he heard was the sigh of the wind. Turning to me, he said, 'Make a signal: "Just sank a 10,000-ton steamer in grid square . . ." and so on. Get the position from the coxswain.'

'I think he was bigger than that, sir,' Witte interjected.

'Possibly, but we don't have the name, so we'll leave it at that.'

While I was composing the signal and waiting for a vacant frequency, Leibling was decoding the latest traffic. Among this there were three messages from other boats with an almost identical text:

'Have just sunk a 10,000-tonner in grid square . . .' and so on. It seemed to have been a very productive evening. I looked at Leibling's face and saw an outlandish grin light up his features.

'Read this one, Petty Officer,' he said.

To all boats from the BdU. In estimating the tonnage of a steamer do not permit the wish to be the father of the thought. We are a solid firm.

This was typical Dönitz, I thought. The Commander came to the radio room.

'Have you sent that signal yet, Hirschfeld?'

'No, sir, frequency is still occupied.' I handed him the latest batch of decrypts. He glanced through them and then bit his lip.

'Amend our signal. Put in 7,500 tons.'

'But sir, she was over 10,000 tons,' I protested.

'On a night as dark as this everything looks bigger. It makes no difference, Hirschfeld. When we get home the BdU will already know what ship it was we sank. Then we will be credited with the correct tonnage. Better if we don't have to reduce our claim.'[29]

The British ship had been unlucky. Perhaps we might never have found her again in the darkness if the man coming out on deck had switched off that light before opening the door. A small omission, but it had cost every man aboard his life.

Next morning we checked the torpedoes and guns over and examined the boat. In a few days we would be at the American coast. We found that we had been slightly damaged. A large iron plate from the steamer had crashed down on the foredeck and we had been hit by a multitude of small metal splinters. Possibly as a result of this a fuel tank had been slightly torn and we were trailing a thin oil slick.

Oil was transferred from tank to tank in the effort to find the leak and, after flooding all the empty tanks, the engineers managed to eliminate the problem for a time, but by evening it was again shimmering in the wake. Otto Peters said it was probably no more than a small tear in a seam somewhere.

'Our oil leak off Gibraltar was a lot worse,' I reminded him.

He rolled his eyes in exasperation. 'The sea was rougher there. Man, we've had a lot of luck already. Just suppose those first three torpedoes had hit when we were at 600 yards instead of 1000. That would have split some of the tanks clean open.'

On the night of 23 April we sighted the outer channel buoy at Cape Lookout. It was a bright, moonlit night and the sea shone like silver. In this area Mohr and Hardegen had sunk nearly 100,000 BRT of shipping. We rubbed our hands together in anticipation and waited. When dawn threatened we were still waiting. There was nothing around here and before the first streaks of light burst upon the eastern horizon we slunk off to deep water south of us. Because of the oil slick, it wouldn't be safe to spend the day dozing in the shallows.

What I remember about the Florida patrol is the tremendous heat we had to endure in the boat, often up to 45°C while we tried to sleep by day, and the amount of aviation we saw, mostly land machines of all shapes and sizes. The Commander thought they were probably from training schools, some of them flying unofficial vigilante patrols along the coast.

Usually we would surface at dusk and approach the shore, following the 60-foot contour southwards looking for merchant shipping. On the second night we cruised from Cape Lookout to Cape Fear. It was completely deserted.

'We've certainly got the right operational area again,' Bleichrodt commented.

In the early hours we saw a destroyer and our diesels suddenly stopped. When I asked Arnetzberger the reason he said, 'It's very quiet around here. You can hear the engines for miles. He'll be listening through his hydrophones for us.' This was a new problem about operating in very shallow sub-tropical coastal waters that we hadn't thought of.

26 April, 1942, was a day of incident. We had spent the previous evening close inshore near the 27-foot shallows at Cape Fear marked by two red-flashing light buoys and we suspected that the duty destroyer was probably lurking around the *Frying Pan* outer channel buoy. Witte and Keller were in a very bellicose mood about this destroyer but Bleichrodt was not keen on attacking, principally because we wouldn't be able to approach within 4000 yards without being detected.

At dawn we retired to deeper water and had 180 feet beneath the keel when the alarm bells rang and we submerged to periscope depth. Ordinary Seaman Zank told me, 'It's a destroyer on a collision course. He came from the *Frying Pan* buoy. Witte thinks he's following our oil slick but hasn't seen us.'

The Commander was seated at the periscope and ordered the Chief Engineer to concentrate on keeping the depth accurately. After a while Bleichrodt said, 'Boys, boys, he's running straight in front of our tubes. We can't let this one escape. Chief, the periscope's cutting under. Will you keep the depth! Destroyer bearing 200 to 210°, speed 14 knots.' For a moment there was another pause and then Bleichrodt resumed, 'I can see his bridge, funnel and guns. He's approaching quickly, *Flusser* class. Chief, your damned depthkeeping!'

The crew went to battle stations and Borchardt came past the radio room reminding me to listen to the torpedoes.

I sat beside Leibling at the hydrophones and heard the familiar sound of the twittering screws approaching.

'Damned near, isn't he?' I said.

'And damned fast. Cross your fingers,' Leibling replied.

The Commander ordered a spread of two single torpedoes to be fired at depths of six feet and nine feet respectively at a range of 800 yards. Although I knew the very dangerous situation into which we had put ourselves, I did not believe that anything could go wrong at this range. The destroyer wouldn't be able to hear the torpedoes because of his high speed.

Both torpedoes were shot off and we set our stop-watches running. Suddenly the Commander swore. 'The periscope's cut under, Chief! What's going on?'

'We're at 55 feet, sir,' Weber called up.

'Shit! Who ordered that? You tilted the bow too soon! Get the periscope up, quick!'

'*Jawohl!* Boat is rising,' the Chief reported in a dejected voice.

Leibling gave me a meaningful look. We both had the horrible feeling that Weber had made a decisive error. If he had put the bow down too quickly after the first shot the second torpedo might have leapt above the surface.

Leibling nudged me; the destroyer's bearing had changed. A few seconds later the periscope broke through.

'Damned shit,' the Commander shouted. 'He's turning towards us, bow on! Go to 400 feet!'

'When we dived, the sea bed was only 180 feet,' Leibling reminded me calmly. I sprinted to the control room and turned on the echo-sounder. Bleichrodt was ranting at the Chief Engineer, 'Weber, you idiot! The boat's rising! Periscope is three feet above the surface! I told you to dive!'

The sweat ran ice-cold down my spine. Behind the periscope well Otto Peters rolled his eyes and smacked his forehead with the heel of his hand.

'Get us down, Weber, or he'll ram us!' the Commander screamed. Warrant Officer Alfred Winter stood at the chart table with his arms folded, shaking his head. 'I've never seen anything as stupid as that,' he said to me in a voice loud enough for the Chief to hear. Martin

Weber's eyes were like organ stops, staring in panic at the depth gauge. He had bungled the compensatory flooding: this could now cost us our lives. Suddenly he snatched the microphone and shouted, 'Everyone forward!'

Winter gave a deprecating smile. 'Type II sailor,' he jeered.[30] The off-watch men came stampeding forward. Karl Will gave me a laugh as he stormed past: astern they had no inkling of the deadly danger we were in. The boat toppled forward and began to spear downwards. In the confusion the Chief had flooded too many of the forward tanks. I stared at the echo sounder; the valves had warmed up and it was now giving a reading.

'60 feet to the sea bed!' I called to the Chief.

He stared at me in disbelief. The depth gauge was showing 180 feet.

'45 feet to go,' said Winter.

'Rise! Quick, quick, get the forward depth rudders up!' the Chief screamed. The electric motors were humming at full speed; the broad upper deck had a hydrofoil effect and half the crew was in the bow room. It was far too late to bring the long boat to trim. We plunged deeper.

'Hold tight!' Winter bellowed forward. Any second now we would hit the bottom.

Lt Witte and Pötter, the Quartermaster, came down from the tower and the Commander secured the lower hatch. At that moment the boat trembled and the ratings called out 'We've grounded!' There was a see-saw effect and then the boat settled with a bow-down attitude of about 30°. I went to the hydrophones and heard a distant explosion as one of the two torpedoes hit the sea bed. We could hear the destroyer's propellors with the naked ear. The Commander had perched himself athwart the pressure doorway so that he could maintain contact with the men in the control room and the hydrophones room.

'Give me his exact bearing, Hirschfeld.' Bleichrodt was perfectly calm despite the impending catastrophe. A depth charge attack at 240 feet on the sea bed gave little expectation of survival.

The destroyer sounded very faint in the hydrophones and it was much easier to hear him without them. Leibling shrugged. 'He was tremendously loud just now,' he assured me. In desperation I swung the indicator steering wheel around the full circle. Surely the equipment couldn't have gone out of commission before a single depth charge came down?

'He's approaching from the starboard quarter astern,' I told the Commander. 'We can't make out the exact bearing, the reception is too dispersed and weak.' Bleichrodt nodded and passed a fresh course to the helmsman in the control room.

'Boat doesn't answer the helm,' Pötter called out.

'That's a good start,' said Leibling.

'Boat does not answer the depth rudders,' Berthold Seidel reported. I saw the Commander bite his lower lip. The thrashing propellors were very loud. All eyes stared upwards. The thrashing was directly overhead, then wandered quickly away to port. Just as I took a breath, there was an appalling thunderclap and the boat rolled and reeled. The hydrophones dropped from my head. A second, third, fourth thunderclap. Our heads withdrew into the cradle of our arms. A giant's fist shook the boat. It sounded like the dissolution of the universe. I was choking, thinking it was the end. Here we were going to die. Slowly the main lighting failed. Around us it was now darkest night. The emergency lighting flickered on and shone with a weak glimmer. The thunder was still rolling away through the depths. The control centres reported in. No damage forward, no damage aft. This was incredible. We didn't have a single leak.

'Stop both engines and all machinery except the hydrophones transformer,' Bleichrodt ordered. It became deathly quiet in the boat. In the sound room we could just about hear the destroyer's propellers.

'Can't you get a bearing on him?' demanded the Commander.

'We can't get a maximum accuracy, sir. He's at about 290°. Must be to do with the receivers in the bows.'

Bleichrodt nodded. 'The bows must have bored into the mud. There's no other explanation for it.'

From a seat in the radio room Lt Witte said to the Commander, 'What do we do now, is he gone?' The Commander gave a grim smile. 'He's coming back, Witte. We will keep completely still. If we stir up the mud, he'll know where he has to drop.'

The destroyer was manoeuvring nearer. Lt Keller was perched on a stool near the sound room. 'Nice piece of shit we're in,' he whispered.

'Yes,' I whispered back, 'specially when I think about our oil slick.'

The thrashing noise was becoming louder. Bleichrodt looked at me enquiringly.

'Soon he'll be overhead,' I said. I glanced downhill into the bow room where the men were all curled up in naked fear. Järschel was slowly stroking his beard. The propellers were overhead again. Leibling was rolled up on the floor like a hedgehog. We stopped breathing. I gripped the wheel of the hydrophone equipment. A crash of thunder and a huge fist shook the boat again, trying to crush the pressure hull. I tensed, expecting to hear the dread cry, 'The sea's breaking in!' The terrible thunder sawed at our nerves.

Keller had blocked his ears, but as the awful noise rolled away he grinned at me. 'They were very close that time. But their charges seem weaker than the cans the British threw at us off Greenland.'

Incredibly, we had survived again without serious damage; just a few smashed instruments.

A third attack followed, in which the shock wave and thunder were even more powerful than previously; the lights went out and stayed out and we could hear the vents leaking a little water. Then the destroyer was gone.

Bleichrodt came to the radio room, picked up the microphone and said, 'Comrades, he seems to have given up. We will now free the boat and continue. Out.'

The Chief attempted to free the boat first by running the electric motors furiously in reverse while the men in the bow room stormed down the central corridor to the stern, roaring with laughter. How soon they forgot the mortal danger in which we had just found ourselves! But the boat wouldn't budge.

Witte said to me, 'The whole eastern seaboard of America has many deep holes. Scientists think that the world once had a second moon which fell to earth and exploded here.'

I crept to the control room and looked in. The Commander was leaning on the chart table, looking at the Chief Engineer's back.

'How long are you going to keep the motors running at full speed, Chief?'

Sweat stood out on Weber's forehead. He stopped the motors and swivelled round on his stool. 'We must blow the tanks, sir. Otherwise we'll never get the boat free.'

'But you'll stir the mud up. If they've got a plane up there, they'll drop a bomb on us.'

There was a long silence. We could hear the water dripping through the vents.

'We've already stirred up the mud with the propellers. We're very deep in it, and probably being slowly sucked deeper. If we are ever going to escape, we can only do it by blowing the tanks. I see no alternative.'

'Well blow them then,' said the Commander. 'It's all the same to me if we slowly suffocate down here or get blown to pieces.'

Peters opened the valves and the compressed air rattled through the piping. The motors went to full astern again. Witte gave me a sceptical glance. The boat wasn't moving. Once the air was finished, we were done for. But at last *U-109* shuddered. There was a sucking noise in the bow, then, after some heavy whirrings with the propellors, we slowly reversed out of the burrow in the mud of the sea bed, the keel bumped along the sea floor and we slithered into deeper water.

When we were well offshore the Commander surfaced the boat, and as he opened the bridge hatch he cursed loudly. The whole tower was still clogged with mud. The forward part of the boat from the peak of the bow to the Winter-garden must have worked its way deeply into a soft mud bank and this had saved us during the depth-charging.

Later that evening the BdU reported to all boats:

According to B-Dienst, US Navy Unit sank a U-boat south of Cape Fear.

Bleichrodt read the signal with a frown.

'They probably mean us,' I suggested.

'It can only mean us,' he replied. 'We're the only boat in the area.'

Keller grinned. 'These people aren't like the English, Commander. They would have concentrated on us rather longer.'

Bleichrodt nodded. 'A bit of luck for us then. Otherwise we wouldn't be here now.'

It was a wonderful summer night as we ran in towards the coast at Jacksonville. Using the night optical aiming device we could see right into the front rooms of the houses. We drifted to save fuel. Witte handed me his binoculars and pointed to the houses on the beach. 'The real Jacksonville lies much further back,' he said, 'the really rich types live here.'

As we returned to deeper water at dawn I was typing the Commander's notes for the War Diary and I re-read one particular sentence:

The Chief Engineer is a poor depth-keeper.
He will never learn to control a large U-boat.

Suddenly I became aware of a warm breath on my neck and I turned and saw Lt Weber. 'Unheard of,' he sniffed. I told him at once that he should not have read it and he went off in a rage. Shortly afterwards he tackled the Commander about the entry: the telegraphists could hear the whole conversation in the Captain's private nook.

'What do you want me to do, Weber? What I wrote is correct,' Bleichrodt told him. 'Think of that incident off Newfoundland when we were marooned with the stern out of the water. If that aircraft had had a bomb you would have got us sunk on that occasion as well.'

At dusk on 27 April we transmitted a very long signal to the BdU and about an hour later a destroyer turned up, having presumably homed in on our transmission. The order was given to clear the tower after we had dived to 120 feet and when I went to the control room doorway I saw Paul Pötter taking up the lower helm position. He was dripping wet.

'What's up?' I asked him.

'There's something jamming the bridge hatch cover open and water's getting in'. The boat manoeuvred for a while but the destroyer was too far away for an attack. When we surfaced Witte found that a French beach slipper was lodged in the hatch, one of a pair in which Leading Seaman Zank was accustomed to perform his lookout duties. He was given a stern instruction not to wear them again.

We spent the night of 28 April transferring five torpedoes from the chambers on the upper deck down into the interior of the boat; the sea was like a duckpond, ideal weather for the operation. The following evening we kept the bright lights on the coast to starboard as we followed the 60-foot contour south from the Hetzel Shoal. The Commander was very interested in a fast steamer heading south but it outdistanced us easily.

We sweated in our bunks in a temperature of 45°C during the day. The boat lay quietly on the sandy sea bed at 28°38'N 80°04'W at 200 feet.

Shortly after picking up the Cape Canaveral light on the evening of 30 April I located a ship through the hydrophones. The diesels pounded us towards the enemy steamer which was making wide zig-zags, and at 3000 yards we shot off a torpedo which broke surface and sheered away uselessly to port. In the darkness behind the target a tug with a low silhouette was chugging to the south.

The next torpedo threw up a huge silver track. It was astonishing that on a calm summer night with perfect visibility the steamer had neither heard our diesels nor seen the wake, but the silent distress frequencies were mute proof that she considered nothing to be amiss.

We fired two more torpedoes at her. I was listening at the voice-pipe and heard Witte shout, 'He's seen us, he's turning away!' Leibling grimaced; I called out to Ferdinand in the hydrophones room, 'Are the torpedoes still running?'

'Yes, time's almost up!'

There was an explosion and the shock wave rocked the boat. We had scored a hit astern, and the victim began to signal on the 600-metre frequency:

SSS SSS *La Paz* torpedoed Cape Canaveral sinking fast SSS SSS

I shouted the name of the American vessel into the control room.

'The other torpedo is still running,' Ferdinand told me. There was a muted rumble in the distance, quite a few miles away. The coastal stations had come to life, repeating the *La Paz* distress call. Suddenly I picked out another one, much fainter than the first:

SSS torpedoed off Canaveral SSS *Worden* sinking SSS

In their excitement, the coastal operators had not heard this one; it went unrepeated. We thumbed through Lloyds Register: *La Paz* 6548 BRT; *Worden* 433 BRT, motor lighter.

U-109 turned away to the east: the crew of the *La Paz* were abandoning ship, but they needed no help, for the coast was clearly visible from the lifeboats. When the Commander summoned me to the bridge I told him about the second SSS.

'Did you hear that, Witte?' Bleichrodt said with a laugh. 'We never saw the tiddler. We can claim her with a good conscience since there's no other boat round here. A torpedo hit on a small ship like that. Must have torn her apart. Did he wireless very long, Hirschfeld?'

'No, sir, just the usual message once, broken off in mid-sentence when it was being repeated.'

Bleichrodt nodded and resumed his binocular observation of the *La Paz*.

'That ship hasn't sunk yet,' he said to Witte. The freighter was touching bottom in 50 feet with her stern, but the bows were well clear of the water.

'They'll never tow her in, sir.'[31]

'Let's hope so,' said Bleichrodt, 'but we have to get out of here before it gets light. They're sure to start up a big search for us.'

In the radio room Leibling showed me his note pad. 'They're calling up the *Worden* and asking for her position. But she doesn't answer.'

'Yes,' I said, 'that little ship had bad luck. We would never have wasted a torpedo on a small motor lighter of that size.'

That evening we re-visited Cape Canaveral and during the early hours of 3 May spotted two shadows, one ahead, the other astern. We went a little offshore to get a broadside view of them; the southbound steamer was the larger and making about 13 knots. The diesels thrashed furiously as the pursuit was taken up. When the hunted ship rounded the Hetzel Shoal buoy to get to the landward channel parallel to the coast Bleichrodt began the attack.

It was close to dawn as we fired a fan of two torpedoes. There was a slight shock almost at once and some cursing on the bridge.

The telephone snarled in the bow room and Bleichrodt asked, 'Where's the second torpedo?' Borchardt explained that it was stuck in the tube but running. The torpedo mechanics managed to release it and send it on its way but it was of course of no use in the attack.

The first eel hit the steamer astern and she immediately wirelessed:

SSS *La . . . es* SSS torpedoed SSS

Her radio operator seemed to have gone haywire and was keying extremely fast; the name of the ship was a jumble of dots and dashes which we couldn't untangle, and neither could the shore station which repeated her distress call.

As the crippled steamer wasn't settling, a third torpedo was fired to finish her off and we turned away quickly for the open sea.[32]

That morning the boat's medical team met for a conference. The third Albucid cure for Gerstner's gonorrhoea had not taken and Karl Will informed me that, although Gerstner had been taking the tablets, he had also been drinking beer regularly. When I heard this I decided to change the treatment to the old method using perman-ganate of potash in a urethral syringe. This seemed to have worked because the patient no longer had a discharge, but Dr Bleichrodt was of the opinion that the gonococci had merely encapsulated. The things that a U-boat commander had to know! Later, in Lorient, Gerstner would have to undergo a treatment known as 'the Koll-mann', the details of which I would prefer not to give.

The next evening we were so close to the shore that we had less than 60 feet under the keel and the boat followed a southerly course between the Hetzel Shoal and Bethel Shoal buoys. At about 0400 hrs we saw a small warship approaching us bows-on. We couldn't turn out to sea because by doing so we would present our broadside to her guns. The only solution was to turn 180° to the north and run for it. I sprinted to the control room and turned on the echo-sounder. 45 feet! We could tell that the American vessel had seen us by the huge wash that appeared at her bows. The diesels hammered furiously and we touched 19 knots, a speed it was only possible for us to achieve in a millpond. Eventually we showed her a clean pair of heels. She had to be a pretty tired old tub to be outrun by a German U-boat.

During 5 May we heard a number of passing merchant vessels and our mood that night was optimistic. A large aircraft with navigation lights set made for us from the coast and described a wide circle around the boat at heights between 300 to 900 feet. Several times he droned directly overhead. We manned the flak guns and watched his antics.

'Why don't we dive?' Peters asked the Second Lieutenant.

'Peters, you know perfectly well that there's no depth under the keel. And can you guarantee that the boat won't be phosphorescent like those torpedoes we fired on the Führer's birthday? Then they would see our outline from above.'

Otto nodded. 'So we just sit here and bite our nails.'

'The Commander thinks that the pilot has identified us as a patrol vessel. Possibly it's just a training flight. There's a flying school not far away.'

The water was highly phosphorescent and the boat crept towards the open sea at a few revolutions. The aircraft buzzed us again at a very low altitude, but I saved the Commander any further worries on the matter when I reported an echo-sounder reading of 120 feet. We submerged, landing on the sandy bottom with a gentle thump. The aircraft which spoiled our evening's hunting was a Martin PBM 1-2 flying boat. These pilots under training played a dangerous game with their lives.

At about 0330 hrs on 6 May we sighted a tanker and positioned ourselves at the seaward end of a long sandbank which we knew she would have to negotiate. We drifted in the gentle swell and waited. The tanker came up and one torpedo hissed out of a stern tube. Her lookouts must have spotted us, for she suddenly turned towards land and the torpedo missed. The distress frequencies remained silent. I wondered whether this was a naval oiler. In the control room I found Arnetzberger leaning on the chart table with a worried expression. He tapped the chart and said, 'That tanker's going to run herself aground. And if we're not bloody careful, we'll be alongside her.'

I warmed up the echo-sounder as the boat came round in a semi-circle to bring the forward tubes to bear.

'Echo-sounder! Depth?' came the enquiry from the bridge.

'45 feet,' I replied. Our torpedo exploded in the distance. Suddenly there was a shout. 'Tanker has run aground! Big list! Hard-a-starboard!' As Arnetzberger had predicted. Now we were running through the shallows at full ahead, heeling heavily as we turned.

'36 feet!' I cried.

The Coxswain gave me a meaningful look. 'High time we were out of here,' he growled. 'There's only 24 feet in places.' The beached tanker was firing off red distress rockets which had begun to attract the interest of passing aircraft. At the 250-foot contour we dived. Witte said we were trailing an oil slick again.

We had just settled down in our bunks for the day at 27°36'N 79°59'W at 330 feet when Leibling told me that there was some external activity audible through the hydrophones. A merchant vessel escorted by three destroyers was passing on a northerly heading. Almost at once there was another noise – torpedoes. They ran for several minutes and then two hit home.[33] The destroyers went berserk and depth charges began to thunder down; fortunately there was no Asdic. Bleichrodt gave me a worried frown: he was thinking about our oil slick. If an aircraft flew overhead and saw it . . .

We had to wait until long after nightfall before we surfaced. A nest of destroyers was still hunting the U-boat that had knocked off their valuable steamer. Fairly soon after reaching the coastal shallows a lookout sighted a long tanker of at least 10,000 tons, but before we could close in we noticed a destroyer approaching and were forced to turn away to sea; it was very dark and we were not observed. After a safe period we set off for the tanker's estimated position, pounding down the 60-foot contour but without success.

Peters joined me at the echo-sounder. 'Damned little water under the keel again,' he said with some concern. 'Think what would happen if a destroyer came along on a parallel course but just a bit seaward of us. Then we'd have no choice but to run her up the foreshore.'

'Yes, Otto, and then we can write home from behind barbed wire and tell them we were caught sunbathing on a Florida beach.'

The 60-foot contour drew ever closer to the coast where the city lights were twinkling as if it were peacetime. I was on the bridge taking the salt air when a strong smell of oil became apparent. The Commander sent for the Chief Engineer and said, 'Our fuel's leaking out.'

Weber took a knowing sniff. 'That's not from us, sir.'

'No,' Seidel added. 'Look, the sea's sloshing around really heavily. We're in an oil spill.'

'Do we have a wreck warning for this area, Hirschfeld?'

'No, sir. Nobody's reported sinking a ship here.' Bleichrodt examined the black waters with his binoculars as we ploughed through the oil.

'Masts to starboard in the water!' Berthold cried suddenly. We spun round. Seventy-five feet from the hull a derrick stood crookedly above the surface.

'Another here to port,' said lookout Karl Will quietly.

I froze as I thought of the wrecked ship just beneath us in 60 feet of water. Was there clearance enough or would she rip our underbelly? We passed close to the port side mast without mishap and left the unknown casualty in position 27°22'N 80°02.5'W.

'That's not been there very long,' said Bleichrodt. 'We were lucky. It could have sliced us open.'

'But we could have easily paddled ashore in our rubber dinghies,' Berthold told him with a laugh.

At high speed we maintained the hunt for the elusive tanker. At 0300 hrs on 7 May we passed the Jupiter Inlet light and checked our position by two tall radio masts. And then we saw her ahead of us.

Peters pulled a face as the Commander ordered full speed ahead.

'What's wrong?' I asked, 'Are you worried about the fuel?'

'It's the couplings. I wanted to have them overhauled three days ago.'

I went back to the bridge and Witte whispered, 'Palm Beach over there.'

The coast was very near; we could see the lights in the houses. There seemed to be a coastal road. We could see the headlights of a lot of motor traffic. The boat was edging ever closer to the foreshore. The purpose of this was to prevent the tanker we were following from attempting to beach herself after our torpedoes had hit. We couldn't position ourselves for the textbook attack because she was too fast for us. We would have to fire from an oblique angle almost alongside and it would be dawn before we could manage it.

The headlights were much closer to us now. I watched a car drive off the road and down to the beach. As it manoeuvred, its main beams swept the sea, played over the tanker and then swept along the length of the boat. Then it was dark again. Bleichrodt cursed loudly.

'Perhaps we should try a stern shot right now,' suggested Witte.

The Commander shook his head and watched the tanker through his Zeiss.

'His wake is kicking up.'

'Yes, Commander,' said Witte, 'there's no doubt. He's turning away.'

'Then he's seen us,' Bleichrodt muttered.

I went below and Peters told me, 'It's finished, Wolfgang, the diesels are too hot, the couplings are sliding. We can't keep up the speed.'

The boat was losing way. Bleichrodt had given up with the tanker. He came down from the bridge without speaking and threw himself on his bunk.

'Commander, *U-564* is south of Miami. Shouldn't we send her a signal?'

He glanced at his watch. 'Good, make this short signal: "Tanker, course south, escaped at 18 knots." Give our position and my signature.' Then he drew his green curtain across his private compartment.

We set a submerged course towards the Bahama Islands. At about 0830 there was a sharp report in the distance.

'There's someone who can shoot straight,' said Peters through a mouthful of food.

Maureschat nodded as he chewed. 'Underwater shot. Cheeky type.'

Borchardt nudged me. 'I didn't think there was anybody else around here. Who would that be?'

'It can only be Teddy Suhren,' I told him. 'He's south of us. Perhaps he just bagged our fast tanker.'

'He's obviously sunk the ship we just spent the whole night running after,' Seidel exclaimed loudly.

Seven minutes later there was a second explosion.

'Another hit,' said Otto.

At 0840 a third sharp rap. 'And that's the coup-de-grâce,' Otto murmured in triumph.[34]

We spent the next day cruising around Key West, but the sea was deserted and the prospects appeared far from promising. We were pestered on several occasions by aircraft which were fitted with some sort of radar aerial.

If we had had enough fuel the Commander would have gone to Aruba. Witte suggested a circuit of Cuba and then out through the Windwards, but that was too far with only 75 cubic metres of oil. We had no prospect of being replenished and the provisions were low, so with a heavy heart Bleichrodt decided to head for home.

I discussed with Järschel whether we should start rationing the food. We had plenty of semolina and macaroni but a voyage of 4,000 miles lay ahead of us.

For four days we sailed through glassy seas with empty horizons under clear skies, still trailing our oil slick, and passed through the outer fringes of the Sargasso Sea where not only did we meet great beds of weed but also the wreckage from marine casualties of war recently destroyed here by gun and torpedo.

On 15 May, west of Bermuda, we dived on sighting a small airship. There was a discussion at some length on what to do next, since the situation was a novel one. Maureschat suggested shooting it down with the main deck gun. Keller laughed at this. 'That would be a good one for Goebbels. "German U-boat shoots down American Airship".'

Bleichrodt stroked his beard. 'And what would we do about the crew? Let them drown? No, Maureschat, our food stock is very low and we've got a long way to go.'

'Shame,' Maureschat said afterwards. 'It would have been good practice for the gun crew.'

We surfaced two hours later and cruised onwards through more wreckage. We were harried by a Consolidated flying boat which the Blimp had undoubtedly called up to attend to us.

Bleichrodt was still fuming about the oil, explaining not for the first time that with another 50 cubic metres he could have operated in the Caribbean. It was no help to him when he saw the results signalled to the BdU by Würdemann in *U-506* (52,000 BRT in the Gulf of Mexico) and Schacht in *U-507* (50,000 BRT in the Caribbean).

I was tuning in the transmitter just after midnight on 20 May when I felt a nudge in my back. Unwillingly I turned round. It was the Captain, holding two glasses of rum. 'I congratulate you on your 26th birthday, Senior Petty Officer Hirschfeld.'

'Thank you, Commander, I hadn't realized.'

He raised his glass. 'I give you the wish that you survive the war.'

'Thank you, Commander. I wish you the same.'

Bleichrodt smiled darkly and poured out the glasses afresh from the rum bottle under his arm. 'We can't stand on one leg, Hirschfeld. Prost!'

The alcohol ran down my throat like fire. He poured out a third round. 'We will probably have to sail together for a good while yet. Prost!' Three glasses of rum on an empty stomach. I felt weak at the knees.

A 4,000-mile voyage in a U-boat short of fuel and food called for desperate measures. We needed to supplement our staple diet of peas, macaroni, lentils and semolina. When I came to the bridge on 22 May Maureschat said, 'Look astern. We've had three sharks trailing us since dawn.'

'They probably like the taste of our oil slick,' I said. Then I remembered that other boats had reported catching shark, which were found to be delicious. The Commander gave permission for an attempt to be made with the shark hook and Järschel agreed to sacrifice the last side of bacon as bait. The cook was fitted out with a bridge harness and some rope and cast the baited hook into the sea from a point on the after-deck. The sharks took the bait but the hooks failed to take the sharks and the operation failed.

'Järschel, hang the hook round your neck and jump in. Then we'll catch one!' the Captain shouted.

Next morning we sighted an empty float which the gunners sank with machine-gun fire and then an upturned lifeboat was reported which turned out to be a turtle. We closed in for the kill on the electric motors, and Bleichrodt called up the flak crew.

'Man, turtle flesh!' exclaimed Peters.

A short rattle of fire ensued and the boat drew alongside the turtle. A bestial stink told us that the shooting had been unnecessary. Witte gave me a grim look. 'So it's stew again then,' he said, and I nodded.

The source of the oil leak had been identified as a small tear in a pipe leading from port fuel bunker III and Schewe estimated that it had lost us 3.5 cubic metres of fuel.

'What's the situation?' Bleichrodt asked him on 25 May.

'With this north-westerly wind, we can make El Ferrol or Vigo in an emergency, Commander.'

'OK, Spain if you're sure. Otherwise I ought to head for the Azores.'

'That would please the BdU,' Schewe grinned.

The stiff following winds and swell were pushing us eastwards. The seas were as high as a church and the bridge watch cursed each time they went up for their four-hour dunking. But Bleichrodt only laughed at them and blessed the storm.

Schewe rubbed his hands. 'We can definitely make it to El Ferrol,' he said with a smirk, 'and from Spain we can get home by train.'

'Is the oil as short as all that?' I asked him.

'Yes,' he said. 'We lost more through that rip in the tank than we first thought.'

Järschel called me to the galley and said, 'What shall I prepare, semolina or macaroni, remembering that they're going to lynch me whichever it is.'

I laughed. 'Do macaroni and give them all the remaining tinned grapefruit. We can't take that back again.' The crew loathed grapefruit.

'My God,' said Järschel, 'I'm not going to see France any more.'

On the morning of 29 May the wind dropped and visibility became appreciably poorer. In position 44°N 23°W we crash-dived upon sighting a convoy which consisted of a destroyer and several other shadows in the murk. Leibling reported from the sound room that he could hear numerous Asdic emissions.

'Go deeper,' said Bleichrodt, 'go to 350 feet.'

'But we must report it and keep contact,' Witte protested.

Bleichrodt shook his head. 'That would be our last signal. I'll show you why. We're in grid square BE8371. The BdU Instructions warn of a U-boat trap masquerading as a convoy here. We are not supposed to attack it. In February Rollmann in *U-82* reported a convoy in this square. Since then nothing more has been heard from him. On 15 April Lerchen, in *U-252*, coming round from Kiel, signalled the presence of a lightly defended convoy in this area and disappeared.'

'Could be coincidence,' said Witte.

'Commander,' I said, 'in February we ran into a convoy in the fog around these parts.'

Bleichrodt flicked through his notes. 'Yes, here it is. 16 February, ran into convoy in thick fog at 44°17'N 23°19'W. Look, Witte, the same position as Rollmann. It was lucky for us that we had no torpedoes that day.'

After we had left the convoy far astern, Bleichrodt reported it, but the BdU showed no interest.

The storm and following sea had compensated us for the loss of fuel and it now seemed certain that we could make Lorient.

The BdU signalled:

To all boats. Remain submerged by day in Bay of Biscay.

Already we could hear a great rolling of underwater thunder to the east, interspersed with the occasional crack of a bomb. The British had total air supremacy over the Bay and the approach to Lorient was very dangerous.

In the Officers' Mess Witte remarked, 'Once we had a marvellous Luftwaffe.'

Keller nodded. 'The worst thing about it is that Goering has also grabbed the Naval Air Arm. All they think about is the land war and leave us here to rot.' It was Keller's last voyage with *U-109*; on return to Lorient he would go to the U-boat commanders' training course.

We surfaced once to change the air in the boat; it was overcast. When we dived to 180 feet three aircraft bombs exploded close by.

Bleichrodt was standing at the entrance to the radio room. 'They can't have seen us through the cloud, Hirschfeld.'

'They dropped on a radar fix,' I told him, 'and the sooner the BdU realizes they can do it the better.'

'In that case it's more dangerous on the surface at night than under clear skies by day.'

I went cold as I realized the implication. 'Of course it is, if they're also flying at night . . .'

Forty-eight hours from home the bow hands found some tins of vegetable and a large can of ham in the bilges and Järschel made a wonderful soup, accompanied by tea and ship's biscuit.

Under a cloudless night sky on the last day out we ran at full speed towards our flak-minesweeper at buoy *Lucie* 2; we could smell the land. We passed green trees, the massive Keroman concrete bunker and the rotting cruiser *Regensburg*. We motored slowly alongside the crowded hulk of the *Isere* and moored. Music swelled up and on 2 June, 1942, *U-109* was safely home from her fifth war patrol.

On 6 June, 1942, Dönitz came down from Paris just to greet the crew of *U-109*. After the black Mercedes had rolled to a stop in the yard of the Salzwedel Barracks, the Admiral emerged and Bleichrodt reported the crew ready for inspection. For some time Dönitz stood facing us without speaking, his face grim. Then he thanked us for the patrol and urged us to continue the fight with that same spirit. 'Comrades, the fate of the German Reich hangs on your success. The war will not be decided in Russia. It will not be decided in any other theatre. This war will be decided in the Atlantic,' he told us. Four of the *U-109* Petty Officers were ordered to step forward – Maureschat, Borchardt, Liebscher and Wolfgang Hirschfeld. With a handshake, Dönitz awarded each of us the Iron Cross, First Class. But my heart was heavy, for if these obsolete U-boats were Germany's hope, then I knew that day that the war was lost.

Im Namen des Führers
und Obersten Befehlshabers
der Wehrmacht

verleihe ich

dem

Oberfunkmaaten
Wolfgang Hirschfeld

das
Eiserne Kreuz 1. Klasse.

Befehlsstelle, den 6. Juni 1942

Admiral und
Befehlshaber der Unterseeboote
(Dienstgrad und Dienststellung)

– 8 –

OAKLEAVES FOR THE COMMANDER

I returned to Lorient on 5 July, 1942, after three glorious sunny weeks in Germany. In Hamburg I had two surprising encounters. I was in the Ufa Palace to see Zarah Leander in *Maria Stuart* and in the foyer I met Cdr Eberhard Hoffmann, who had made the Labrador trip with us. He was the new commander of the Type IXC boat *U-165*. He got straight to the point and offered me the radio room of his boat. I declined with a laugh, although I thought a great deal of him. Almost immediately afterwards I bumped into Lt Cdr Schwartzkopff, our former First Lieutenant, who invited me to join him in a drinking bout at the Alster Pavilion, where he made me the same offer. He was now commander of the Type IXC boat *U-520* and had no Front-experienced telegraphists aboard.

'But Lieutenant, you know Bleichrodt won't let us go. He keeps his NCOs and the engineers under lock and key.'

Schwartzkopff laughed. 'My last voyage was with Hessler, Dönitz's son-in-law., Through him I have the best contacts possible to the BdU. Bleichrodt can't hold on to his men for ever.'

'Besides, Lieutenant, I want to qualify as a Warrant Officer when I get off *U-109*,' I countered.

'Of course,' Schwartzkopff said with a smile, 'but even the Telegraphist Warrant Officers will eventually have to go to sea. It's already been arranged for them to run the radio rooms of the new U-tankers. The war will go on a long time yet.'

I had no doubt he was right, but nevertheless all my instincts were against sailing with him, and we parted with mutual best wishes for a long life.

Lt Werner Witte had left for the commanders' course. He had been well liked amongst us and we were sure he would make a fine commander. But I was not to see him again; on 15 July, 1943, west of Madeira, his boat *U-509* was lost with all hands when bombed by an American aircraft.

Our new First Lieutenant was Joachim Schramm, a swarthy former torpedo-boat man, and newly promoted Sub Lt Helmut Bruns was our Second Lieutenant and radio officer; the Coxswain, Wilhelm Braatz, was the Third Watchkeeping Officer. Bleichrodt had recommended Midshipman Hengen for officer training and had also managed to get rid of Martin Weber to *U-526*. Albert Heyer was now Chief Engineer.

I asked Peters what he thought about all these changes.

'We can teach the young ones,' he said. 'As long as we keep the long-serving petty officers, we'll get through.'

Warrant Officer Alfred Winter had been listening to this conversation.

'Ah, Hirschfeld, the main thing is, Heyer can keep the trim. Whatever else he can't do, we can cover for him.'

'Wolfgang, it worries me when I think about this next voyage,' Ferdinand confided to me later, 'It's going to be a kindergarten on the bridge.'

In the Prefecture, Bleichrodt told Ferdinand and myself that the scientists had come up with a device called the 'Biscay Cross' for detecting radar-emissions but that it wouldn't be available for the current voyage. They had also accepted that even an aircraft could get a fix on us.

The boat was freshly painted and overhauled. With the benefit of the usual send-off we put to sea on 18 July, 1942, for our sixth war patrol. As we left, Bleichrodt stared stolidly ahead. It was becoming more difficult for him to put to sea with every new voyage.

The danger from aircraft was now so serious that we had to cross the Bay of Biscay submerged except under cloudless skies, when we couldn't be surprised.

At midday on the third day we had surfaced to recharge the batteries in conditions of broken cloud. Schramm advised the control room that the stern lookout had just spotted a two-engined aircraft which was thought to be friendly.

A few seconds later the alarm bells rang and we submerged at a very severe incline with the diesels still running – Heyer's first serious error. We went under so fast that I wondered whether the dive could be controlled. Ferdinand looked at me thunderstruck. At 180 feet the boat was hammered by a tremendous shock wave and the lighting slowly failed. Heyer got the boat to trim and, as the lights came back on, I recognized Schramm standing in the doorway. I must have given him a sceptical glance because he snapped, 'It was definitely a Junkers 88!'

'There's not many of *them* around here, Lieutenant,' I replied.

We weaved an evasive course between fishing cutters, the odd enemy corvette and search groups which haunted the western part of the Bay of Biscay, and began to hear the first depth-charging of the voyage. The new crew members listened to the terrible thunder with large eyes. Because they were not up to scratch, Bleichrodt kept them occupied with continuous emergency drills so that they should be able to do it in their sleep.

We rolled slowly westwards into the Atlantic in gentle breezes and fine visibility still awaiting our operational orders. On the ninth day Bleichrodt was told to head for the Brazilian coast at the most economical speed.

'That's good. Let's hope it pays us to go there,' he said as he read the log.

'Shall I play the America March, Captain?' He looked at me for a moment as though this was a question of some importance, then answered, 'No, put on the tango Bolero, then I'll tell them where we're going.'

The coxswain showed me our operational area on the chart: it would be around the Brazilian port of Natal, where all traffic to and from Rio passed. We headed south in warm, light airs and the sea had a lazy swell. It was hot inside the boat and all the lookouts had sunburn. The Commander was still giving the new men drills and exercises to sharpen them up and we tutted in annoyance.

On 31 July the BdU signalled von Schmidt in the large Type XB replenishment boat *U-116* attached to Group *Hai* to refuel Hirsacker and Schröter and, if he had more than 15 cubic metres of oil left, to give it to Bleichrodt. I was sceptical about getting it, but Bleichrodt said, 'Herr von Schmidt is a gentleman and won't leave us in the lurch.'

It was uncommonly hot and I was wearing a stomach support bandage which attracted a great deal of mirth, but Bleichrodt, who had experience in the tropics, said I was right. He had also rigged up a shower behind the conning tower. It was forbidden to swim in the sea since the Oak-Leaves holder Mützelburg had drowned while bathing from *U-203* in April.

On 1 August the BdU ordered Harro Schacht in *U-507* to the Brazilian coast and I heard the Commander and Schramm discussing the difficulty in identifying neutral vessels. The Commander was firm on the point that, if there was any doubt, he would always leave well alone.

At dawn on 5 August the bridge watch reported the silhouette of a large passenger ship on a westerly heading and making at least 20 knots, a speed we could never hope to match in order to get in an attack. We gave chase for an hour and then Bleichrodt came down from the bridge in apparent dejection.

'Anything on the international wavelengths?'

'No, sir, all quiet,' I told him. 'Pity we couldn't get that ship,' I added.

Bleichrodt gave me a melancholy smile. 'Ah, Hirschfeld, who knows if it wasn't for the best? A big passenger ship, perhaps with many women and children aboard, hundreds of miles from anywhere in mid-Atlantic.'

Cdr von Schmidt had refuelled Hirsacker and Schröter and now signalled the BdU that his tanks were empty. Bleichrodt was very upset. Contrary to his expectations, Herr von Schmidt had left us in the lurch. Berthold Seidel joked, 'If we haven't got enough oil to get home with, we can intern ourselves in Rio. I could tell you some stories about the girls there.'

That evening, on the latitude of Dakar, Cape Verde, we found ourselves in the path of a ship steaming north at 10 knots. We submerged and the Commander observed the steamer cautiously through the periscope a few seconds at a time only because the sea was almost calm.

'It's an armed tanker, British. One stern gun, 10.5 cm it looks like, and machine guns on the aft superstructure.' We waited until she was within 1000 yards and then fired two torpedoes. After 84 seconds there were two sharp detonations.

'Hit leading edge bridge and astern,' the Commander stated.

'Ship has stopped,' Ferdinand called out from the hydrophones room.

'Tanker listing to starboard,' Bleichrodt said, 'two boats being lowered. Five men manning stern gun. They're ready for a scrap.' We waited for a while and the Commander muttered, 'They've equalized the list by flooding. Tanker's now floating on an even keel again but with a deeper draught.'

A few more moments passed and the Captain resumed, 'The hole in the stern is very large, but he's not sinking any deeper. We'll have to sacrifice another eel.' We made a slow half-circle to bring the stern tubes to bear on the crippled tanker, but as soon as we fired the third torpedo she immediately moved off. This was another refined character, I thought; she had avoided the third torpedo. The Commander swore. 'Both motors full ahead!' he yelled and we gave chase at periscope depth for 40 minutes before positioning ourselves for the fourth torpedo shot, which hit amidships with a loud explosion.

The gun on the tanker's poop had been abandoned, but she still refused to sink and we surfaced and closed to 600 yards so that we could shell her waterline. Maureschat got 55 hits from 67 rounds with the 10.5-cm cannon before our victim took her last plunge. While the shell cases were being collected *U-109* motored over to the place where she had disappeared. There was no trace of the crew, only an empty lifeboat with the name *Arthur W. Sewall*. In Lloyds Register this was listed as a 6035 BRT Norwegian tanker registered in Risör. As the boats had presumably made good their escape, we were unable to comply with a new instruction of the BdU to take the ship's master of every casualty prisoner. The sinking was at 08°28′N 34°21′W.

Later that day Leibling decoded signal 1413/8 from the BdU ordering us to concentrate our search for traffic off Freetown and told us that we could not expect refuelling.

'Isn't that typical?' Bleichrodt commented when he was shown the signal. It was incomprehensible to him that they should keep changing the orders. We could have saved fuel by proceeding to Freetown directly from the Azores.

That evening, when reporting his successful encounter with the tanker, Bleichrodt argued, in a very long signal to Lorient:

> as already in grid square ER [midway between the Amazon Delta and Liberia] and cannot expect replenishment consider coastal area FC [Brazil] more favourable for fuel and weather. August in ES and ET [West Africa] very unfavourable month. Frequent heavy rainfall and widely scattered lone vessels. Request free manoeuvre in FC.

That night we languished in a tropical rainstorm. The sea was highly phosphorescent and there was a strong, warm breeze from the south-west. The boat rolled heavily in the swell. The humidity was so high that much of the bread and potatoes had gone mouldy and had had to be dumped overboard.

The BdU replied to Bleichrodt:

> *U-109*. Go to your ordered area via ER 30. Traffic confirmed there most recently. However no report of movement in FC.

The landsmen always knew best, so we began our slow trudge towards Freetown through the rain. The officers were very down in the mouth because they had been looking forward to Brazil very much. Bleichrodt had an inflammation in his right eye. He had refused my offer of an eye-patch because it might give him a piratical appearance, which I thought was a ridiculous objection, and now it was worse, red, swollen and weeping. I gave him some drops, but whether he was taking them I had no means of knowing since he insisted on treating himself.

On 11 August we were to the south of Cape Verde in very poor visibility and had submerged for a hydrophones watch. Ferdinand reported a propeller noise almost dead ahead but faint. When I came down the corridor from my bunk I found the Commander listening through the parallel headset.

'Well, it could be,' he murmured, 'but let's hope it's not the dolphins making fools of us again. You listen, Hirschfeld.' He gave me the headphones and I thought it was definitely a ship. 'About 120 revolutions,' said Ferdinand, 'that is a ship.'

The sound was dwindling quickly. We surfaced and headed through the rain at 17 knots for an hour, then submerged to confirm the bearing.

'What can you hear?' Bleichrodt said.

'Nothing, the sound's disappeared.'

He gave a meaningful look to Ferdinand and myself.

'Yes, yes, telegraphy is shit,' Ferdinand said.

'You said it this time, Hagen,' the Captain laughed.

Nevertheless Bleichrodt believed in the ship and we surfaced to resume the chase on the previous bearing.

'We'll never find him in the rain,' Otto Peters groaned. 'Pity about our fuel.'

Late that afternoon the lookouts sighted the mastheads. Bleichrodt's determination had paid off and the relentless pursuit now began in deadly earnest through slashing rain. Suddenly the cloud cover dispersed and the visibility improved like magic. We crash-dived, knowing that if the tanker was keeping a proper lookout she couldn't have failed to see us. She changed course and we manoeuvred to get ahead of her at top speed underwater, almost draining the electric batteries. We succeeded and fired two torpedoes from the stern tubes. After two minutes I heard a metallic click followed by a huge explosion.

'A hit!' yelled the men in delight.

'The stern has parted completely from the rest of the ship,' the Captain told the Coxswain, scribbling feverishly for the war diary, 'Gun on poop unmanned. Tanker is sinking quickly by the stern.' There was a silence before he resumed, 'Sea sweeping over stern section. Crew in the boats. Tanker is lying broadside to the swell.'

We remained beneath the waves until the lifeboats were clear of the wreck. When the bridge watch went up at last to examine the scene they reported that the tanker was fiercely aflame with a burning oil spill on the surrounding sea. A huge black column of smoke was rising vertically into the evening sky, flattening out like a mushroom cap at the top.

We picked up Captain Norman Ross Caird from a ship's boat and made off to the east. His ship had been the 5,728 BRT *Vimeira* of Glasgow registry, bound for Freetown from Aruba with a cargo of heating oil. Ten of her crew of forty-three had been killed when the torpedo astern hit the magazine for the stern gun. The position of the sinking was 10°03′N 28°55′W.[35]

For the next six days we rolled on a series of different headings on a mean course towards the port of Freetown. The skies were leaden and the rain heavy and virtually incessant. On 14 August, when I went to the bridge in my oilskins for a smoke, I was astonished to see the sun.

'It's summer, Hirschfeld!' Lt Schramm laughed, but soon we had a fresh breeze from the south-west and with that the rain returned.

The news bulletins from the Russian Front were always very encouraging. Our panzers were rolling across the steppe towards the Caucasus and brushing aside all resistance. Yet Bleichrodt always looked very worried when he heard these reports no matter how optimistically they were presented. Once I head him say to Schramm, 'Remember how long the supply line will be when the winter comes. Last year the whole Front nearly collapsed.'

Captain Caird had adapted readily to U-boat life, although he admitted to an uncomfortable feeling whenever we dived very deep. He appeared to relish Järschel's cooking, and when he politely declined any more of our German cigarettes, I let him have some of my cigars instead.

On 18 August Schacht in *U-507* reported sinking five ships totalling 17,000 BRT off the Brazilian coast.

'Look, Schramm,' I heard Bleichrodt say in the Officers' Mess, 'Schacht sank them one after the other, right where we were supposed to be.'

'I don't know,' the First Lieutenant replied thoughtfully, 'It doesn't feel right to me somehow. They're probably all Brazilian neutrals.' Bleichrodt laughed. 'We'll be hearing more about it if that's the case,' he said.

By 19 August we were closer to Freetown in a better area of weather. The wind was southerly and the horizons were misty, but of the Sierra Leone traffic there was no sign and our fuel was visibly diminishing despite our most stringent economy measures. It was making the Captain nervous. He reckoned we would have to start back in six days.

We spent much of the summer cruise under electric propulsion on the surface, when it would be as quiet as a sailing ship on board, with only the creak of the yards missing. The telegraphists relayed march music and news bulletins to all rooms to ward off the creeping lethargy of the tropics. On the Elbrus, the highest Caucasus peak, mountain troops had raised the swastika flag. If they could seize Maikop and Grozny in the lowland to the east the oilfields would be ours and the war against the Soviets would be won. Manstein and his panzers had reached the banks of the Terek and General Paulus' 6th Army had dug in at Stalingrad. In North Africa Rommel was advancing on Alexandria. It was victory on all Fronts. They all seemed to have enough oil; only the U-boats were short of it. How were we supposed to win the Battle of the Atlantic on our meagre allotment was beyond me.

On 22 August Würdemann in *U-506* signalled that he had sunk a fast independent far to the south of us and Bleichrodt was interested enough to order a southerly heading.

That day Brazil declared war on Germany and Italy. Reuters reported that it had been caused by the sinking of five Brazilian merchant vessels just outside their territorial waters by a German U-boat. Captain Harro Schacht was responsible but the full circumstances had naturally not been explained by Reuters.

As from the German declaration of war on the United States on 11 December, 1941, Brazil had ceased to be a neutral in the conflict within the meaning of the term in international law because she was not impartial. From that day she permitted the US Naval Air Squadron to use the airport at Natal.

At the end of May, 1942, Brazil adopted the attitude of undeclared war against Germany that had characterized America's demeanour in the latter half of 1941 and announced that her aircraft had attacked, and would continue to attack, German and Italian U-boats encountered in international waters off her coast.

On 4 July, 1942, a Supreme Command directive authorized U-boat commanders to attack all Brazilian merchant ships without warning as retaliation for the activities of the Brazilian Air Force and the arming of Brazilian merchant vessels. Although the sinking of five Brazilian merchant ships by Schacht in August had caused Brazil to declare war on Germany on 22 August, 1942, this had merely regularized the undeclared state of war that had existed since May at least.

Whether the German action was in any way connected to the successful effort to dissuade the neutral Portuguese Government from leasing air bases to the Allies in the Azores is very much open to conjecture.[36]

On 24 August the BdU drew Bleichrodt's attention to Würdemann's signal of the 22nd, which meant that Bleichrodt was at liberty to operate much further south, but our oil situation was causing him increasing concern. We were south-west of Liberia under clear skies but the horizons were deserted: the mood of the officers was grim. I asked Schewe whether we had enough fuel to get back to Lorient and he said, 'We've got enough to get to Tenerife. What do you want to go to Lorient for?'

'It always used to be the Azores, now it's the Canaries.' I told him.

On 26 August the Commander gave the following short signal to transmit:

Have begun return to base on account of fuel situation. *U-109*.

As we were still on a course to the south-south-east, however, I was a little surprised. A few hours later Dönitz requested our position and bunkers, and by return we informed the BdU that we were in grid square ET89 with 68 cubic metres. That afternoon, Dönitz replied:

Bleichrodt. Your return to base is premature. Remain in ET 38. You can rely on another 30 cubic metres.

The Commander returned the log to me without speaking. I could see that he was annoyed by the implied censure, but then he laughed and called out to Schramm that the report about returning to base had done the trick.

During the night we brought down into the torpedo rooms the six remaining eels stowed under the upper deck planking and then Bleichrodt began charting a new course after I handed him a signal decrypt containing secret British course instructions for their Cape Town-Freetown shipping which Kals in *U-130* had found in the papers of a ship's master he had taken prisoner a few days earlier.

We were forced to dive that afternoon when a large biplane overflew us; it appeared to have no warlike intent and was soon gone, but during his descent through the manhole Bleichrodt had taken a nasty knock on the shin.

The wound was very painful and I treated it with cod-liver ointment and then bandaged it. For reasons best known to himself he was sceptical about the Peru Balsam and wouldn't let me use it. A number of crewmen had developed boils which I treated daily with Ichythol. Berthold Seidel told me that my diagnosis was wrong and that it was the Black Death from which none of them would recover. The Quartermaster, Paul Pötter, had a large one on his face which could be potentially lethal and the Captain was so concerned for him that he insisted on visiting the morning clinic to watch Dr Hirschfeld administer the treatment.

On 29 August, south of the Pepper Coast, we met up with *U-506* and Bleichrodt and Würdemann gossiped for an hour through their megaphones while the free watch of each boat sunned themselves on deck. It was rare now that two U-boats could socialize like this and we soon went our separate ways. The aircraft two days previously had been a warning.

We were deep in the Gulf of Guinea and slowly approaching the Equator. On 31 August the commander showed me his painful injury which had not been improving and consented to a trial with the Peru Balsam.

'Where did you get that poisonous stuff?' he asked.

'The naval surgeon Dr Ziemke gave it to me in Lorient after the first voyage. It's very difficult to get hold of.'

'God help you if it doesn't work,' the Captain said.

When I completed my surgery that day I gave myself an examination and found that my fungal infestation had now spread over my whole body.

At dusk on 1 September we sighted the widely-spread masts of a large steamer making 14 knots, but soon lost her to sight against a dark cloud bank, which caused much swearing on the bridge. They had estimated her course and a probable interception point and at daybreak we submerged when we found all our assumptions correct and the mastheads ahead on our starboard bow. All day the steamer made wild and irregular zig-zags about her mean course and it was not until the late afternoon that we fired off a fan of three torpedoes with a 100-yard spread at a range of 1800 yards. This coincided with one of her irregular changes of course and all three missed. A single shot shortly afterwards suffered the same fate. At dusk on 2 September the steamer was still in a good position for us and we knew her course. At midnight our fifth torpedo was a rogue which sheered astray but the Commander reacted instinctively to shoot off the sixth and this hit the target astern after an 85-second run. She morsed:

SSS SSS *Ocean Night* SSS 00° 57'N 04° torpedoed by submarine, sinking over stern, SSS.

We were unable to find the ship's name in Gröner's *Merchant Fleets of the World* or Lloyds Register, possibly because we had incorrectly taken down the transmission but more likely that the British radio operator had got the name of his own ship wrong. She was, as we later discovered, the 7173 BRT *Ocean Might*. I went up to the bridge to give the information to the Commander and saw the stricken freighter: clipper bow, long superstructure amidships, a short oval funnel and numerous loading masts.

'Her lifeboats are away,' said Schramm.

'We'll wait a bit,' said Bleichrodt, 'then we'll finish her off.'

When I went below Ferdinand told me that the ship had ceased transmitting as the coastal stations had acknowledged her SSS. Some time later we fired the seventh torpedo which struck in the engine room and she began to go down on her portside and by the stern, finally making a vertical descent. The lifeboats meanwhile had disappeared into the darkness.

'Pity,' said the Commander to Lt Schramm. 'I'd like to have got to know her skipper. Must be a really experienced type.'

We left the scene and headed south and *U-109* was probably spotted by a large land aircraft of unknown make which bumbled over at midday searching for survivors. We crossed the Equator at 1800 and permission was given for Neptune to visit the control room for a short baptismal ceremony a few hours later.

For several days after that we cruised the glassy sea along the supposed Freetown-Cape Town track. It was very hot, but the provisions were now so low that Järschel was reduced to preparing a daily stew. On 6 September the Commander, whose leg wound now looked much better and had ceased to trouble him, decided to head north-east back into the Gulf of Guinea. At dusk the bridge watch sighted the masts of a large, fast steamer crossing our bow to the east, and at a range of 800 yards we loosed off two torpedoes which both struck astern with a sharp explosion.

The steamer stopped, hove-to and got her boats away as she settled by the stern. Ten minutes after the torpedoes had hit she used her emergency transmitter to send her last message:

SSS SSS 01°34N'11°40'W *Tuscan Star* torpedoed – sinking quickly SSS SSS.

She was an 11,449 BRT refrigerator ship registered in London. The Commander allowed me to observe the wreck through his binoculars. She had a heavy list and was already being lapped by the waves abaft the funnel.

'She's going down by the stern,' Schramm reported. I went below and heard the Commander give orders to make for the lifeboats in order to take the ship's master prisoner. There were women and children in one of the boats and Bleichrodt summoned Ferdinand to the bridge and gave him some instructions.

'I've got to get some provisions together for them, milk and bread for the children,' the Captain said. 'I don't know where they're supposed to come from.'

'Give them the cans of condensed milk. There isn't any other kind aboard,' I told him, 'and the kilo tins of boneless chicken meat.'

While we were waiting for Ferdinand and Järschel to get these supplies together a cry for help was heard in the darkness and in the beam of the searchlight a man was seen struggling in the water amongst the wreckage. He was obviously in serious difficulties. At once Maureschat roped himself up, gave the free end to Berthold Seidel to hold and jumped into the sea. With a few strokes he got to the drowning man and signalled to Seidel to haul them both in. When they bumped against the hull the bridge watch dragged them aboard. It was the ship's second radio operator; he was taken down to our engine room for a rub-down and a change of clothing.

Järschel lugged two sacks of provisions into the control room.

'We've hardly got any fuel left,' Otto Peters observed, 'so it obviously makes sense to get rid of the food as well.'

'But Otto,' Schewe admonished him, 'we can still go to the coast and pick ourselves a few bananas. They can't.'

The lifeboats were alongside the bow and the provisions were handed down. Seidel had discovered a very pretty young woman dressed in a fur coat and little else. The coat was open to reveal her bosom.

'Captain,' he shouted up to the bridge, 'shine the searchlight over here! I'd just like one more look at the beautiful girl!' The bridge obliged him, but someone in the lifeboat must also have understood, for the woman coyly drew her fur across her breasts.

The boats were large and stable but overloaded. The ship's master was said to have gone down with the ship. This was not true, but we informed the first officer that we had radio operator Gordon Gill on board, whom we would retain as a prisoner. Then we gave the officer a course to steer for the nearest coast and cast off the lines. The boats drifted slowly astern.

'Thanks and good luck!' they called after us. Forty-one crew, eight gunners and three passengers out of a total of 113 persons aboard the *Tuscan Star* were lost, but happily all the survivors in the lifeboats were eventually picked up alive and well. The *Tuscan Star* had a cargo of 11,000 tons of frozen meat from Buenos Aires for London.[38]

We had only 33 cubic metres of fuel and six torpedoes left and the next day we received the BdU's order to return to port via grid square DS30, which was south-west of the Canaries opposite the Rio de Oro. This would be where we would have our refuelling meet. Bleichrodt sent for the First Lieutenant and showed him the signal.

'It's incomprehensible,' said Schramm. 'Go back now, when in all probability we've stumbled across their arterial route?'

Bleichrodt nodded. 'And we're going to bring six torpedoes home. This nonsense with the fuel is enough to make you puke.'

We cruised at a few knots through mist and glassy sea and in a signal the following morning the Commander protested:

FT 0952/8 To BdU: Request remain here and later refuel like Schacht. Bleichrodt.

to which the BdU replied

FT 1236/8 U-109. Ensure you return to DG50. No prior refuelling possible.

DG 50 was even further north than DS 30. Bleichrodt sighed in resignation.

Next morning I was awoken by the trembling of the boat and the thumping of the diesels. We were racing towards an interception point with a *Duchess of Bedford* class ship making over 18 knots, but the opportunity passed us by. We had the chance to fire, but only at a range of six miles or not at all. Our slow U-boats were not up to a challenge like this.

We cruised slowly onwards towards the Cape Verde Islands, desperately devising new ways of conserving the fuel. Already we were only performing the daily trial dive twice a week and Schewe was juggling the fuel round the various tanks to rid ourselves of all unnecessary water.[39]

Early on 13 September Ferdinand brought to my attention a signal he had just copied down on the America Frequency:

To BdU. Sunk by Hartenstein British *Laconia* grid square FF7721 unfortunately with 1500 Italian POWs. So far rescued 90. Request instruction. Hartenstein U-156.

'Where's that position?' I asked. Ferdinand waved a hand vaguely. 'A long way astern. About 500 miles north of Ascension Island. We don't need to wake the Captain.' We tuned in to the international frequencies, but it was all very quiet. A few hours later the BdU signalled:

FT 0340/13 Schacht, Group Polar Bear, Würdemann, Willamowitz, go at once to Hartenstein FF7721 high speed ... BdU.

At 0600 a transmitter started up on the 600 metres distress frequency:

CQ CQ CQ ...

I nudged Leibling. 'That's a U-boat transmitter.'

To everyone! If any ship will assist the ship-wrecked *Laconia* crew I will not attack her providing I am not being attacked by ship or aircraft. I picked up 193 men. 4°53′S 11°26′W. German submarine.

'Crazy,' Leibling said. 'There's never been anything like that before. That must be Hartenstein.'

When I showed Bleichrodt the signal log when he awoke, he said, 'My God, that Hartenstein. I wouldn't want to be in his boots.' He passed it to Schramm who said, 'That's suicide for Hartenstein. They won't give two hoots for the survivors and their planes will go and shit all over him.'

Schacht in *U-507* had reported that he was 700 miles away from Hartenstein and heading towards him at 15 knots; the Italian boat *Cappellini* was also joining in the rescue operation. There would be a large assembly of Axis U-boats. I wondered if there would be a bloodbath.

On 15 September we encountered a head wind which kept our speed low. In the afternoon we drew some comfort from a signal reading:

To Schnoor. Go to DS 30. There meet Bleichrodt. BdU

Whether we could actually reach DS 30 was a little doubtful. Schewe had calculated that we had only three days' fuel left and after that we would have no option but to rig a jury mast and sail. We had never been so low on bunkers as this before.

Hartenstein reported the number of *Laconia* survivors as 1500 which he had in tow in twenty-two large and overcrowded lifeboats and on numerous floats. No vessel or aircraft had been sighted. The BdU told him to expect a Free French cruiser, and at least one merchant vessel from Dakar soon.

On the 16th we made little progress in the strong north-east trades; if the wind increased, we wouldn't even make the Cape Verdes. Schewe suggested to the Commander that at night we should only use the electric motors as this would help save fuel. We were riding very high in the water because we had only six torpedoes and the remaining fuel was concentrated in a few full tanks while the rest had been emptied to help reduce the surface displacement of the boat as much as possible, but in a head wind and sea it was a serious disadvantage. Bleichrodt was keeping the BdU informed:

FT 0101/17. 8 cubic metres fuel left; using diesels only to recharge batteries, otherwise travelling on electric motors. Request instruction for Schnoor in event gale force 8, when arrival DS 30 not guaranteed.

to which the BdU responded:

Steer 340° most economical possible.

That night Hartenstein sent a signal which confirmed Schramm's opinion of his rescue attempt:

Despite 4 metre square Red Cross Flag on bridge, good visibility and towing four full lifeboats, Hartenstein attacked five times by American Liberator aircraft. Both periscopes damaged. Abandoning assistance. All survivors off boat. Removing to west to repair.

'It's a miracle he's still afloat,' said Schramm. Würdemann in *U-506* had also reported that he had been bombed twice even though he clearly had several hundred survivors in boats and on deck.

At midday on 17 September our lookouts sighted mastheads astern and, despite the fuel situation, the Commander had no hesitation in ordering full speed to the south. The steamer was steering south-south-west at 10 knots. Within an hour we were submerged and awaiting her approach.

'He coming up just right,' I heard Bleichrodt say. 'He has two guns astern by the look of it and several Oerlikons.' Two hours after we had first sighted the ship we fired three torpedoes at a range of 800 yards and hit her with all three. She immediately assumed a heavy list to port, got her boats away, capsized and went down by the bows.

We surfaced and approached the lifeboats which were stable, well-equipped and capable of reaching the Cape Verde Islands. The ship's master was asked to identify himself, invited aboard and made prisoner. The steamer was the 5221 BRT British vessel *Peterton* from Hull to Buenos Aires with coal, armed with a 10.5 cm cannon and two 4.7 cm Oerlikons. She was also fitted with four depth-charge throwers. Eight of her crew had been killed in the attack and one survivor in the boats died later in hospital. The *Peterton*'s captain had with him a pouch containing the ship's papers which included secret course instructions for Freetown. He was pleased that we had wasted a number of torpedoes on his ship; one would have been sufficient to sink her, he told us. Below decks he joined Captain Caird and Gordon Gill where he told them that if we had made a surface attack he would have destroyed the U-boat with his Oerlikons. Captain Caird observed that he was sure his fellow captain would understand if he was not too disappointed that the plan hadn't worked out as hoped.

We turned about and crept northwards for several days at a few knots, engaging the diesels only to recharge the batteries. The Commander wanted to retain a small reserve of oil for the ultimate emergency, but on 20 September, when that was nearly all we had left, he told us that, should we not be replenished by that evening, we would have to rig a sail. Where we would actually sail to was not discussed. The problem was that Schnoor in the supply boat was not answering signals. If he had been sunk we were in the most dire straits, for everything depended on him. When he eventually conde-scended to contact us that afternoon, arranging a refuelling meet for the evening, a trendous sigh of relief swept through the boat.

At 2000 we met up with the fat Type XIV U-tanker *U-460* and, after a swift exchange of pleasantries, the oil transfer went ahead. The weather was favourable and the men of *U-460* worked quickly. On her foredeck I recognized our former boatswain Walter Gross, now Senior Boatswain of the other boat, and we waved to each other. We received 38 cubic metres of fuel and provisions for five days. Shortly after midnight we parted without ceremony. A U-boat rendezvous was a very dangerous place to be.[40]

On 23 September Ferdinand gave me the signal log with a grin and pointed to FT 1508/23:

To Bleichrodt. In grateful appreciation of your heroic participation in the struggle for the future of the German people I award you as the 125th Soldier of the German Wehrmacht the Oak Leaves to the

Knights Cross of the Iron Cross. Adolf Hitler. My heartiest congratulations. Dönitz.

'Give the signal to the First Lieutenant,' I said, 'it's for him to announce it.' The Commander was deeply moved as Schramm read it aloud in the Officers' Mess. That evening all hands and the prisoners celebrated with a minor banquet from the provisions that U-460 had given us.

During the early hours of the next morning we sat up decoding a hail of signals congratulating the commander: from Naval Command in Berlin, the Commander North Sea and the Flotilla.

'My God,' Leibling groaned, 'now this really is what I call signals traffic. The British will definitely think we're up to some dirty business.'

On 25 September, when we were south of the Azores island of Sao Miguel on course 42° for Biscay, we sighted mastheads and turned due east to follow. There was a very steep sea running from the east and the boat began to buck and toss viciously as we crashed through the mountainous rollers.

'Onwards to the last battle,' Borchardt laughed, 'and to rid ourselves of our last three torpedoes. But we won't be able to make a submerged attack in these seas.'

I agreed. We would just have to keep chasing and hope for a change. We were lucky that the pursued vessel was going east, but we were unable to maintain the high speed in the conditions without drowning the bridge watch and when towards evening we lost the Gibraltar-bound tanker in a squall the pursuit was abandoned on the grounds of the drain on the fuel.

Cdr Eberhard Hoffmann in U-165 had reported that he was only 48 hours from Lorient after a strikingly successful trip to the St Lawrence. He had earned his Iron Cross, First Class, and we looked forward to celebrating with him when we arrived home too.

Sub-Lt Bruns asked me for my assistance in encoding an Officers-Only signal which read:

To 2nd Flotilla. Recommend Boatswain Seidel, Berthold, for the German Cross in Gold. 14 war patrols totalling 80 weeks at sea. Participated in the sinking of 61 ships totalling 405,000 BRT. Bleichrodt.

Berthold was to know nothing of this.

The weather conditions worsened appreciably as we neared the north-west cape of Spain. The fuel situation was giving rise to concern once more and the engineers were permutating the various combinations of diesel/electric propulsion to conserve what we had left in the bunkers.

On 28 September Schewe reported to the Commander in a highly emotional state and alleged that *U-460* had given us short-measure of fuel, requesting that the matter be entered in the War Diary for investigation ashore.

Bleichrodt said, 'How could you let them do it to you, of all people, Schewe? But no, I won't put it in the report; remember how you embezzled that five cubic metres from Kals at Nantucket?'

As I overhead this, I remembered what Walter Gross had said to us as he left *U-109* for the last time: 'If I have to refuel you, you won't do the dirty on me like you did with Kals. I know how Schewe does it.'

'If these storms keep on like this,' Schewe told Alfred Winter afterwards, 'we'll have to ask for a minesweeper to tow us in.'

'That's providing we get across the Biscay first,' Winter replied, 'Personally I don't trust your calculations any more.'

For five days we slunk across Biscay submerged at a few knots, every so often visiting the surface for a tense period of recharging the batteries and then returning with relief to the depths. As we approached the French coast the depth charging and bombing grew more oppressive. At first the three British prisoners listened to it in appalled disbelief, but when a few random sticks of bombs exploded close to the boat the same afternoon the two ship's captains affected not to have heard it.

While recharging the batteries on 3 October we were surprised on the surface by a British bomber which for some reason did not attack, after which Schramm gave the prisoners a life-jacket each 'in case we have to go outside', he said with a kindly smile.

We were quite close in under the coast: we had to remain submerged because above us there was a sea mist and the British could locate and bomb through the fog. Bleichrodt enquired by signal:

FT 1821/4 To BdU. On 6 October for approach run 1000 hours Point Kern to 1600 hrs Point Lucie. Question: Can we expect Luftwaffe air cover? Bleichrodt

Leibling laughed as he encoded this message. 'He'll really annoy the BdU Staff asking them something like that,' he said.

Braatz was uncomfortable about the navigation. He hadn't managed to get an accurate fix for days and had estimated our position by dead reckoning. Our radio bearings on coastal beacons soon showed that we were not off the correct place by much but ultimately the crew preferred to rely on Bleichrodt to bring us home with his sixth sense.

I heard Schramm tell him, 'We'll never win the war with these boats if we've lost air supremacy.'

'Don't say that on land, Lieutenant,' Bleichrodt said quickly. 'However, you would think that the Luftwaffe could at least keep some control over the Biscay coast, but they can't even protect us in the approach channel. They haven't responded to my signal of yesterday.'

Soon after we went to periscope depth to take in the signal repeats, with only the retractable radio aerial above the surface, we were detected and twice received near-misses from a bomber. We wondered how they could distinguish between a U-boat and a French fishing vessel on their radar.

On the morning of 6 October, 1942, we reached Point Kern and surfaced. The cloud was high and scattered, which was favourable for us. At 18 knots we made the eight-hour dash along the swept channel to Point Lucie where we would meet our minesweeper escort. The bridge watch and the Captain all wore life-vests and ceaselessly observed both the sky and the wave-tops, under which lurked the British submarine nuisance.

On time we met up with the minesweeper and followed her past the Fortress of Port Louis, suddenly realizing the joy of having beaten the accursed Bay of Biscay once more. From our extended periscope tube fluttered five pennants showing the 35,600 tons of shipping we had sunk on this voyage. There was a huge crowd on the *Isere*, laughing, shouting and clicking cameras. For the first time I could remember, the Commander came to the bridge wearing a white-crowned naval cap. Normally he wore a side-cap bearing the eagle and swastika, the national cockade and the unofficial *U-109* cap badge of a lighthouse. He had shaved his cheeks and trimmed his moustache and black goatee beard so that he had the appearance of a Czarist officer.

'Ajax!' the officers shouted down from the *Isere*, 'surely you can't have brought that old derelict safely back yet again?'

After we had secured alongside the hulk a plank was placed between the *Isere* and our Winter-garden and the Flotilla Chief, Viktor Schütze, came aboard to greet the Commander. The band played and Schütze made a short address of welcome, but we weren't listening. We stood in our three ranks on the after-casing and looked up at the faces of our flotilla comrades and the legs of the girls. Then we were dismissed.

A guard party was waiting to take away the three British prisoners and Bleichrodt took his leave of them personally. Captain Caird pressed something into his hand. It was a lighter and a note on which was written, 'As a token of respect and admiration for Cdr Bleichrodt, his officers and the crew of *U-109*. N R Caird – SS *Vimeira*'

- 9 -

WARRANT OFFICER:
I JOIN U-234

O n 7 October, 1942, Ferdinand and I attended the Telegraphists' Debriefing Conference at Kernevel and afterwards we
visited the cipher rooms. To my question where Cdr Eberhard Hoffmann's boat was, the Telegraphist Warrant Officer gave
me a grave look. 'That was a terrible thing,' he said, '*U-165* reported
on 26 September that she was 48 hours from the rendezvous with
her escort, but she never turned up. Since then, she's missing.' He
showed me a list of eighteen U-boats which had been lost to the 2nd
Flotilla since July. We returned to Lorient in a state of shock.

At the Salzwedel Barracks Lt Schramm was waiting for me.
'You're supposed to report to the hospital today,' he reminded me.

'But I want to go on leave first, Lieutenant.' He shook his head.
'Then you won't be well again until after we've sailed, will you?'
The dark-haired officer clapped me on the shoulder. 'Now go, before
the Captain comes back and cancels it.' I gave Ferdinand my
documents and went off straightaway to see the Flotilla Surgeon.
That same afternoon I was certified unfit for U-boat duty by Dr
Lepel and admitted to hospital for treatment of my skin disease.
They burned my skin down layer by layer with Cignolin Vaseline
because the fungus had eaten down very deep. Bleichrodt's hopes
that I would recover in time for the next voyage were dashed and he
left my bedside in a very bad temper. When I was transferred to the
out-patient list at the beginning of December, 1942, *U-109* had
already sailed on her seventh mission. I felt a keen sense of desolation
that for the first time *U-109* was at sea without me. As the disease
had not yet been fully cured, I remained unfit for U-boat duty and
could not be assigned to another boat. For the time being I was
drafted to the Cipher Room at Kernevel as a supervisor.

On 2 December, 1942, Lt Cdr Herbert Schneider brought his boat

U-522 home from her first patrol with an unusual success of 57,000 tons of shipping sunk, despite a tight convoy defence. When I greeted the crew of the boat on the *Isere* I was reunited with Kuddel Wenzel, who had been one of the *U-109* boatswains on the first Newfoundland voyage. Now he was Coxswain of *U-522*.

At Kuddel's suggestion, I was invited to join the crew in their Christmas celebrations in the U-boat barracks. Lt Cdr Schneider seized the opportunity to entice me to become his senior telegraphist. When I objected that I was still unfit for operations, he dismissed this with an airy wave of the hand. 'It's no problem if you volunteer. Just the one voyage, Hirschfeld, until my radio crew have got it off pat.'

Although I was very hazy because of all the alcohol I had drunk, I asked for 24 hours to think it over. Afterwards Kuddel sidled over and warned me, 'This boat hasn't got very much more time. The skipper does things that make your hair stand on end, like taking bow shots at approaching destroyers.'

I was convinced. When the First Lieutenant of *U-522* arrived for my answer, I politely declined.

At the beginning of 1943 the new Signals Officer of the 2nd U-Flotilla, Lt Gugelmeier, summoned me to Lorient and informed me that I had been selected as a Warrant Officer candidate, but that I would have to remain in the Cipher Room at Kernevel until sent for.

On the evening of 14 January the U-boat base at Lorient was subjected to its first heavy air attack. The two-storied bunker in the Salzwedel Barracks shuddered like a ship in a seaway under the hail of landmines dropped by the British, but the bunker held. All U-boats were hauled into the shelter of the concrete pens at Keroman. The following evening the British returned with a fresh delivery of explosives and incendiaries but we felt safe in our bunker.

As the Senior NCO on the waterfront, I was summoned to the telephone that evening by Cdr Friedrich, a staff officer of the Flotilla, who ordered me to remove all the hand grenades from the arsenal. I objected that I could still hear some explosions outside, but he assured me that it was perfectly safe since the bombers had left. I took two men and went to carry out the order. The alleyways were on fire and it was as light as day, with the flames leaping out of the barrack windows. I realized at once that I would need a much larger gang for the job, and so the three of us trooped back to the bunker. No sooner had I shut the armoured door than the building trembled under a very violent blast outside. The staff officer phoned again. I took the instrument, controlling my anger with difficulty. 'You told me that the attack was over, sir. But now we have just heard an explosion so loud that we thought the walls would cave in.'

Cdr Friedrich sighed as though he were addressing a complete dullard. 'Those were the limpet mines on the waterfront,' he explained quietly. 'The aircraft have gone.'

I could hardly believe what he was telling me. 'Limpet mines? This is the first I've heard about them. Do you realize that if I'd been out in the open when they went off I wouldn't be alive now?'

I set out from the bunker again with the two ratings and found it necessary to tie a damp handkerchief over my nose and mouth because the quality of the air had deteriorated so much. All Lorient was burning.

'My God, the poor Frenchies,' said the Leading Seaman to me. 'Yes,' I replied, 'they're all suffocating in their basements.' Friedrich came running up and demanded, 'Where are your men?'

'In the bunker still. They didn't come with me.'

'Then round up all the men you can find and get them to clear the French Mills bombs out of the arsenal. There's a lorry coming for them shortly.'

'But who'll take any notice of me on a night like this?'

Friedrich glanced at my dyed RAF battle-dress and nodded. 'I've got to get back to the Prefecture,' he said, placing his own cap on my head. It fitted perfectly. 'Now they'll obey you,' he called out as he went off.

I managed to gather together fifteen men. The lorry arrived and parked near the arsenal while at the other end of the alley the flames were leisurely making their way towards where my gang was working. In feverish haste, shortly before it got too hot for us, we completed the task.

I kept the officer's cap; as a Warrant Officer I exchanged the peak with its gold trimming for a shiny leather one and wore it until the end of the war.

These two air raids were sufficient to transform Lorient into a smouldering ruin, and only the actual target, the U-boat pens at Keroman and the U-boats sheltering within them, survived unscathed, protected by a ceiling of concrete some 22 feet thick. Our accommodation had been completely gutted and we were transferred to a new camp at Pons Skorf, from where we commuted to Lorient by staff bus each morning.

Lt Gugelmeier selected me to act as a courier. All the transmission turning curves had been destroyed in the shipyard and I was sent off to the Lorenz and Telefunken works in Berlin to fetch a replacement stock. The engineers with whom I spoke there were visibly depressed at the grim news from Stalingrad, but then they cheered up and, clapping me on the shoulder, exclaimed, 'Well, never mind! You'll still win it for us with the U-boats!' I was appalled by their misplaced confidence. They simply had no idea of how dominant the enemy anti-submarine defences had become, nor of the horrendous scale of our losses. I could, of course, hardly tell them that we ourselves no longer believed it possible to win the war at sea with the present fleet of old boats. Perhaps only a few officers thought it could still be done.

When I returned to Lorient on the morning of 27 January, 1943, after one of these messenger outings, I found the city still alight after an air raid the previous evening. This time the British had pinpointed our well-camouflaged camp at Pons Skorf and it had been bombed by low-flying Mosquito aircraft. But, nevertheless, the U-boat spirit remained unbroken and the community functioned as before.

U-109 had put into St Nazaire along the coast. Off Trinidad Bleichrodt had finally cracked. He had signalled U-boat Command that he was a little unwell and Dönitz had told him to hand over his command to Lt Schramm if he felt unable to continue. The Captain had ignored this instruction and had instead decided to transfer his stock of torpedoes to other boats in the area and then sailed home. He was very upset about the fuel situation, he said. Once *U-109* had tied up, they fetched Bleichrodt off his boat and a surgeon certified him as a psychological case. Another commander might not have been so lucky.[41] A large proportion of the crew, including Otto Peters, Schewe, Alfred Winter, Maureschat, Berthold Seidel and Järschel were remustered either to other boats or to shore positions, and all of these NCO's eventually survived the war.

Ernst Kals had been appointed Chief of the 2nd U-Flotilla, and Siegfried Keller, the former Second Lieutenant of *U-109*, was given *U-130* as his first command.

U-109 set off on her eighth operational mission under Lt Schramm, but before very long she was back in Lorient with depth rudder problems. 'They should scrap this boat,' Walter Vetter, one of the engine room hands told me, 'It's had enough once parts start dropping off just because the sea's a bit rough.' But *U-109* was repaired and had to sail again on the Atlantic.

In front of my desk in the Prefecture bunker there hung a framework of pigeon holes containing a card system for the radio crews attached to all boats of both the 2nd and 10th U-Flotillas. Whenever a boat was posted missing, I would find the cards lying face downwards on my desk the following morning.

Early in March, 1943, Warrant Officer Geissmann laid the cards of *U-522* face down on the table. It affected me deeply. Under the influence of too much bonhomie and champagne, I had been close to joining her crew for that one voyage. A few days earlier Lt Cdr Schneider had been awarded the Knights Cross. Then he was depth-charged and sunk with all hands off Madeira.

At the beginning of April the cards of *U-130* were absent from their pigeon hole. On 12 March, 1943, Lt Keller, who a week earlier had sunk four ships of 16,359 tons of convoy XK2, a special Gibraltar convoy for Operation Torch, was the contact boat on convoy UGS 6 west of the Azores.

Towards midnight he was detected by radar at two miles and visually at just over one mile by the US destroyer *Champlin*. When the American warship opened fire, Keller appears to have been caught in the dilemma of whether to run or dive. When he eventually did decide to submerge, the destroyer was closing fast. *U-130* was sunk with all hands in the ensuing depth-charge attack.

Lt Volkmar Schwartzkopff, the former First Lieutenant of *U-109* who had been so eager for command, was surprised on the surface by an aircraft in the vicinity of Newfoundland. His boat, *U-520* was lost with all hands. It was Schwartzkopff's first voyage as a commander and he had no successes to report.

On 14 April, 1943, I stood with a crowd of U-boat men from the 10th U-Flotilla on the *Isere* to welcome home *U-526*. Her Chief Engineer was Martin Weber, formerly of *U-109*. Suddenly a pinnace came in from the outer harbour with a foaming bow wave and a voice shouted through a megaphone, 'No music! All dismiss! *U-526* has blown up in the approaches!' The boat had been mined and sank at once in shallow water. Some of the crew in the forward compartment had survived and divers established contact with them, but it had not been possible to do anything to free them since all the hatches had buckled in the explosion and could not be opened. So they died there, even though the boat was only a few metres down.[42]

It was a glorious June morning when, entering the bunker, I glanced automatically at the pigeon-hole for *U-109* and saw to my grief that it was empty. The cards lay face down on the table. *U-109* was gone. I turned on my heel and walked out into the sunshine.

I remembered Ferdinand Hagen. When we had shared a last drink together before *U-109* left on her last voyage he had said to me with a resigned smile, 'Wolfgang, believe me when I tell you that we won't be coming back from this trip.'

'Don't talk nonsense, Ferdinand. *U-109* always comes back. You must believe in that.' He shook his head. 'No, don't ask me how, but I know it for certain. Do me a last favour and tell my fiancée when you hear for sure.'

On 7 May, 1943, Lt Schramm was heading for a convoy north west of Cape Ortegal. At about 12.28 in the afternoon, at position 47°06′N 10°58′W, *U-109* was detected fully surfaced by Sunderland aircraft W3993 of 10 Squadron RAAF piloted by Flight Lieutenant Geoffrey Rossiter. The flying boat tracked *U-109* through cloud at a height of about 2,000 feet, broke cover at four miles and approached the U-boat from astern at about 50 feet. Two lookouts, wearing sou'westers and oilskins, were seen staring at the aircraft, apparently transfixed with horror. The situation reminds me of Ferdinand Hagen's remark on seeing the replacements sent to us at the beginning of the sixth voyage: 'Wolfgang, it's going to be a kinder-garten on the bridge'.

The aircraft dropped four shallow-set Torpex depth charges to straddle the boat amidships and then circled before dropping four more from broadside. *U-109* began to manoeuvre in tight circles at about five knots as if her rudder were jammed, trailing oil and gradually slowing to a stop with her stern awash over a period of about twenty minutes. At 1300 hours she sank stern first in a widening pool of oil. The whole incident covered a period of about half an hour, throughout which the boat had been fully surfaced, so it can only be assumed that the depth charging had buckled the hatches, leaving the crew entombed on the surface – a most tragic end for Schramm and his men.

On 29 July, 1943, I boarded the train at Lorient. My orders read: four weeks' platoon commander training in Emden, then a four-month Warrant Officer Telegraphist course in Flensburg-Mürwik. Lt Gugelmeier promised me that he would secure my return to Lorient if I passed the course.

I obtained permission from the Flotilla Chief to travel to Hamburg first to collect my uniform from home, although word had got round that four days previously the city had suffered a saturation air raid. Towards midnight that day the U-boat train stopped at Buchholz just outside Hamburg and all passengers for the city had to detrain there and wait for a connection while the express continued to Kiel via Lüneburg. From the station platform at Buchholz in the early hours of 30 July I watched a fresh aerial bombardment of Hamburg. The skies above the city were illuminated by tracer and the beams from a hundred searchlight batteries. I could clearly hear the thunder of the heavy flak and the crump of the ordnance falling from many hundreds of bombers – an inferno of fire. We stared silently towards the red glow in the distance and thought of the families there.

At 0400 the Front leave train arrived and took us the final stretch of the journey into Hamburg. I walked across the Berliner Tor to the Hammersteindamm and found the ruins of the house in which my family had lived. In the porch someone had pinned a postcard which read, 'All the occupants of this house escaped alive.' While I stood there gazing at the remains of the street, an infantry captain wearing a uniform coated with dust ordered me to join a small group of servicemen searching the basements for survivors and subsequently we succeeded in rescuing a number of women and old people who had been entombed. Whenever anybody speaks to me of atrocities against civilians in war, I remember what I saw that day. The British had been using phosphorus in their bombs and I saw the bodies of countless women and small children burnt beyond recognition by this chemical.

In the afternoon the infantry captain allowed me to go so that I could get out of the city before the expected air attack that night. In the Hammerpark I came across a lorry which someone had been preparing for the removal of domestic furniture to the Baltic coast. The furniture had been incinerated and the vehicle was now commandeered by a large number of refugees. At the park gates I found a young woman in evident distress sitting on a bundle of clothes.

'Are you waiting for somebody?' I asked. She looked up at me with empty eyes and shook her head. 'Well, you'd better come with me before the next air raid starts,' I told her, and lifted her up to the tailboard of the lorry and pushed her aboard. When I had climbed up, I sat beside her and let her rest her head on my shoulder. She was the wife of an Army officer missing at Stalingrad and she had now just lost both her parents in the bombing of Hamburg. The lorry headed north, stopping at Ahrensberg, where Red Cross sisters handed out hot coffee and buttered rolls, and at Timmendorf I got the Red Cross to take her off my hands. In a small village near Plön, in Holstein, I found my family sheltering with relatives. Happy in this knowledge, I now made my way to Emden for the platoon commander's training course.

*   *   *

It was at about this time that the German submarine *U-180* arrived at the French Biscay base of Bordeaux. On 18 February, 1943, Cdr Musenberg had taken his brand new Type IXD boat to sea from Kiel and, after breaking into the North Atlantic through the Iceland-Faroes Narrows, headed for the Indian Ocean. Aboard his boat were the Indian Nazi sympathizers Bose and Hassan.

On 27 April Musenberg met up with the Japanese submarine *I-29* under Captain Yoichi at a point south east of Madagascar. Bose and Hassan were transferred to the Japanese boat and were replaced aboard *U-180* by two Japanese naval officers, one of whom was Captain Hideo Tomonaga. The luggage of these two men consisted of three one-man torpedoes, a 3-cm gas-pressure self-loading cannon and, in a large number of smaller cases, a substantial quantity of gold ingots destined for the Japanese Embassy in Berlin and said to be payment for German technology.

There was, in fact, so much gold that the U-boat's Chief Engineer found it very useful for trimming the submarine. Probably there was several tons of it. Subsequent research has shown that the Japanese submarine *I-52*, which left Kobe in March, 1944, for Lorient and was sunk with all aboard on 23 June, 1944, near Cape Verde, carried a shipment of 4409 lbs of gold in bars. She had a crew of ninety-four, plus thirteen Japanese scientists.[43]

Captain Hideo Tomonaga came to Germany ostensibly to inform himself about U-boat development. He was a Samurai and in Japan was credited with the invention of an automatic depth-keeping device, a sort of iron Chief Engineer. But time, as we shall see, was to prove that his interests were somewhat wider.

* * *

On 1 September, 1943, I began my Warrant Officer's course at Mürwik. One of the few instructors who had Front experience was Robert Rüter, who had been Würdemann's senior telegraphist aboard *U-506*. 'You will have to be very circumspect,' he told me, 'most of the instructors here haven't got a medal and they've got it in for petty officers with the Iron Cross, First Class, Otherwise it's the same here as it was before the war.' The school taught and examined High Frequency technology which was never used at the Front. All candidates who failed the intermediate examinations were rejected. There were only two U-boat men; the remaining candidates came from the Fleet and land stations. The course ended just before Christmas, 1943, and I was successful, receiving immediate promotion to Warrant Officer Telegraphy (*Oberfunkmeister*). The class went to Le Touquet for further instruction, but the U-boat Arm kept its own and we two U-boat men were attached to the 3rd U-Training Section at Schleswig to await our new orders.

My drafting to the 2nd U-Flotilla at Lorient had been confirmed as early as October, 1943, by the U-boat Personnel Officer at Kiel and Lt Gugelmeier told me in a telephone conversation that I was expected at the Signals Headquarters soon.

There was talk too of new, streamlined U-boats already nearing completion, with a phenomenal underwater speed of 18 knots. This was almost incredible. I wondered if this could be the turn in the fortunes of the U-boat fleet. With such boats as these, a convoy could be penetrated to its heart with impunity, leaving the escort vessels floundering. The only question was, how long would it be before these wonder-boats arrived at the Front in large numbers, and why should the current stock of old, slow boats have to bear the merciless killing techniques of the Allied navies until they did arrive?

On 19 January, 1944, my Senior Officer handed me a telex.

'Your posting. You leave tomorrow.'

I thanked him and tucked the paper into a pocket.

'Wouldn't you like to read it?'

'Thank you, Lieutenant, but I already know where.'

'I should have a look at it if I were you,' the officer said with a grin. I unfolded the paper and read:

Warrant Officer Hirschfeld to report on 20 January, 1944, to the 1st *Baulehrcompanie*, Kiel, Germania Werft, for *U-234*.

This was a hammer blow. Quickly I rang a contact in the Personnel Office in Kiel.

'I can't talk on the phone,' he said. 'You'll have to come to Kiel first.'

'Just answer me this. This *U-234*, is it a streamlined boat?'

'No, it's a large Type XB, a 2,000 ton minelayer. She got a bomb hit on the slip in 1942 and has only just been finished. She's entitled to have a Warrant Officer for her telecommunications and that is you.'

I replaced the handset with a feeling of deep gloom. I arrived in Kiel the next evening in the middle of a heavy air raid. Flak thundered from a thousand barrels. I sprinted to the great Hummel-wiese bunker, but they wouldn't let me in. Only for women, children and civilian males, said the watchman, and slammed the door in my face. So I took to my heels again through a rain of flak splinters in a desperate run to the Germania Werft.

'We don't have a bunker,' said the man at the door, 'only some slit trenches. They're in the shelter of the overhang of the aircraft carrier hulk B. They seem to be pretty safe.'

In the darkness I stumbled into one of the trenches and found a place to sit next to an engineer officer. The ground was quaking and the great hull of the carrier trembled in the blast of the enormous explosions. In the pale light of a candle I saw all the care-worn faces. They were nearly all of them U-boat men. It was just like a depth charge attack under water, only here you couldn't be drowned.

Once the bombers had gone the engineer glanced at my shoulder-straps and asked my name. When I told him he said, 'Well, you're one of us then,' and introduced himself as the Chief Engineer of U-234, Lt Cdr Horst Ernst.

We went off together to the accommodation ship *Holstenau* where the officer arranged a cabin for me. Then he explained how my drafting had been changed. Although the boat's telegraphy section was complete, the Commander had noticed upon reading the operating specifications that he was entitled to have a Warrant Officer in charge of the radio office and he had gone to the Personnel Bureau in Kiel to find out if there was one available with U-boat experience. Only I was on the list and so I was 'volunteered'.

The following day I met the Captain of U-234, Lt Cdr Johann Heinrich Fehler.

Fehler was 34, a Berliner like myself, the first of three children and the son of a judge. His ambition from childhood onwards had been to become a Merchant Navy officer, but a boy had to be under the age of sixteen years to qualify for nautical school and his father had compelled him to complete his education.

By his nineteenth birthday he was too old for sail training and discovered that in order to sit his mate's certificate it would be necessary to serve fifty months at sea, of which at least twenty months had to be in sailing vessels. He signed on as deck boy with the small 140-ton oak-built galeasses which plied the ports of the Baltic until after twenty-seven months of this cold, harsh life he could finally become apprenticed aboard the motor ships and steamers of the great German shipping lines. Soon he was in the Far East aboard the 7,600-ton North German Lloyd motor ship *Havel*.

On one of his infrequent returns to Germany in November, 1933, he was recruited into the Nazi Party during a membership drive, although no deep political conviction lay behind his decision.

On 2 April, 1936, Fehler entered the German Navy as an officer cadet and by the outbreak of war had command of the minesweeper *M-145* operating out of Welhelmshaven. By the turn of the year he had been drafted as Mines and Explosives Officer to the raider *Atlantis*. Between March, 1940, and November, 1941, Fehler spent 622 days at sea aboard the *Atlantis* in a voyage which twice circumnavigated the globe, sinking twenty-two Allied merchant vessels. For a short while he commanded the tanker *Ketty Brövig* which the *Atlantis* took prize, but this was sunk under him in the Indian Ocean.

Returned to Mürwik in 1942 as an instructor, he impatiently importuned the authorities for a U-boat to command and qualified as a U-boat commander in September, 1943. In conversation with me, Fehler said that he was disappointed to have been assigned *U-234*, a minelaying submarine, when what he really wanted was a fighting U-boat. I was also disappointed to learn that Fehler had no previous operational U-boat experience. I liked his buoyant optimism and warm personality but I was doubtful whether he would keep us alive very long once we hit the Atlantic.

Of the officers, only Ernst, the Chief Engineer, had ever even been on a training boat in the Baltic, although all the Senior NCO's were old U-boat hands and there was a highly experienced nucleus amongst the junior NCOs as well.

The seven boats of the Type XB were the largest in the German Navy, displacing 2,700 tons laden submerged, and had been designed as minelayers, equipped with 30 mineshafts capable of carrying 66 mines. In general, however, they saw service as ocean replenishment boats, the 'milch cows'. 294 feet long and 30 feet in the beam, the class had diesel-electric propulsion providing a maximum surface speed of 17 knots and 7 knots submerged. The most economic cruising speed was 10 knots, which gave them a range of 21,000 miles and made them ideal for long-distance cargo missions to Japan, which could be reached from Germany without refuelling.

Armament consisted of two stern torpedo tubes and a complement of seven torpedoes. There were two twin 20-mm cannons and one twin 37-mm flak gun on the two platforms abaft the bridge.

U-234 had been seriously damaged by a bomb hit in May, 1943, while under construction and was not launched until 23 December. By the time of her commissioning on 3 March, 1944, four of the fleet of seven had already been sunk. After the commissioning we spent two months in and out of the builders before we fetched up at Rønne on the Baltic island of Bornholm on 27 April, confined in the harbour because of an uncleared minefield outside. We were joined by three E-boats. It was a great pleasure to discover that the commander of one of these vessels, *S-208*, was our old boatswain, Eduard Maureschat, now a Warrant Officer. He had been discharged from the U-boat Arm as medically unfit.

We arrived at Hela for working-up exercises on 25 May, 1944, and here I met Otto Peters who was attached to the U-boat Training Staff. He explained what the exercises would entail; mostly they created emergencies to accustom the crews to working under pressure. In beaming sunshine on the morning of 20 June, 1944, U-234 set off for a position just seawards of the Hela mole for a practice dive. The depth was 180 feet. The alarm bells rang to start the exercise and we submerged with an extremely steep inclination of the bow, boring deeply into the mud on the sea bed within a few seconds. When we were stationary the Captain raised the periscope and calmly informed the Chief Engineer that the stern was still above water. The Quartermaster, Paul Rische, was raging in the control room. 'We've been training for four weeks and all the Chief has learned to do so far is this. I tell you, Wolfgang, he's a typical learner. Useless! Well, I've had enough of it. I'm getting off this boat.' If only it was so easy. Our plight had been noticed from the shore and a launch had been despatched, her commander enquiring on arrival if there were any survivors. It seemed an age before the Chief got the boat to settle horizontally and the only comfort we drew was from the continued presence of the launch slowly circling above us.

I seized the opportunity to slip ashore at Memel for three hours with the Captain on a private errand on 19 July and found the place almost deserted. The remaining townspeople had aged noticeably since my last visit here, with lines of worry and anxiety etched in their faces. They were weary and nervous, for, although they could not yet hear the artillery, they knew that the Soviets had reached nearby Mitau, and when the Red Army did eventually sweep into Memel they feared for the women and girls. Returning before time to U-234 aboard the Commander's launch, Fehler said to me, 'Take a good long look at it, Hirschfeld. You may not get another chance.'

I looked at him in astonishment. 'Don't you believe that the Army can hold the Russians?' I asked him.

He gazed across the harbour. 'It was a long way from Stalingrad to Mitau. And now we have a European war on two fronts. Do you want me to spell it out?'

It was on the following day, 20 July, 1944, while pounding through the Baltic chop en route to Palmnicken for the tactical exercises with the U-boat depot ship *Waldemar Kophamel* that we heard of the attempt on Hitler's life. We were all relieved to hear him speak to the nation in a radio bulletin that same day, and we took an extremely dim view of the actions of the officers involved in the plot. Whereas they were undoubtedly acting from the best motives in seeking a just armistice, 'unconditional surrender' remained Roosevelt's terms, and the Russians would almost certainly have grabbed the chance to roll on over our surrendering armies and not stop until they reached the Rhine. Our watchword was Lenin's adage, 'Who has Germany, has Europe,' and so we preferred to fight on in the hope that Hitler's promised 'miracle weapons' might yet materialize and so bring about the turn in our receding fortunes.

As soon as we clambered aboard the *Waldemar Kophamel* I was summoned to the bridge of the depot ship with instructions to report to her Commander. I had no idea who he was, but when the helmsman pointed to the bridge wing where an officer was standing with his back to me, silently observing the U-boat flotilla manoeuvring alongside the hull of his ship, I reported myself. He turned slowly, and I gasped as I recognised Lt Cdr Wilhelm Wissmann, who had been the First Lieutenant aboard *U-109* for her third and fourth voyages and had then commanded *U-518*. We shook hands and Wissmann told me he thought I had been drowned on *U-109*. I asked him how he came to have command of the depot ship. 'Dönitz relieved me of command of *U-518* because I refused to sail with the ridiculous Biscay Cross device aboard. I told him I wanted a proper radar.'

'Is there such a thing for U-boats?'

He nodded bitterly. 'Yes, the Hohentwiel, which we could have had from the Luftwaffe in 1943. That would have reduced many of our losses. But how did you manage to get off *U-109*?'

'I had a skin fungus which I caught from those damn French Navy hooped jerseys we used to wear. Lucky really. The Fleet Surgeon, Dr Lepel, considered it was likely to be fatal if it penetrated any further beneath my skin.'

Our conversation lasted many hours, and thus we spent a convivial evening before the start of the sea exercises. Speaking to Fehler later of the advantages of ship-borne radar, he promised me that he would ensure that we obtained a set, and later did so. It was to save our lives.

The next day the Senior Telegraphy Instructor began by bluntly describing to the radio crews the deteriorating position in the eastern Baltic and then stated that 118 U-boats had been lost on all fronts in the first six months of the year. He continued, 'If you are aboard one of the new Type XXI or XXIII boats your high underwater speed is your salvation. If you are on any other type of U-boat and you fall into the hands of a hunter-killer group, you are dead.'

We looked at each other in alarm. 'How long would it be until the new Walther boats were actually available in reasonable numbers?' we asked, but the question drew no response.

Once the training period had been successfully completed, we arrived in Kiel on 30 August, 1944, for a refit, and on arrival I went aboard the former cruise liner *St Louis* to see her radio room. That same afternoon there was a heavy air raid on Kiel and the *St Louis*

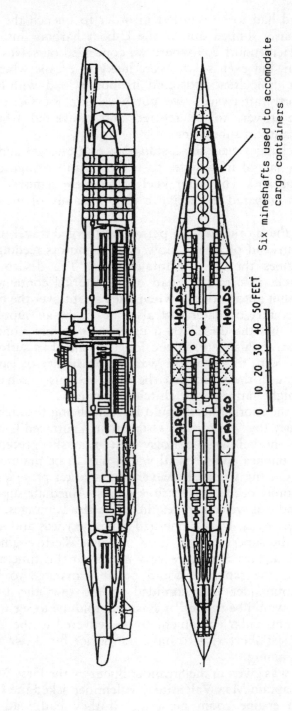

TYPE XB U-BOAT U-234

Six mineshafts used to accomodate cargo containers

0 10 20 30 40 50 FEET

Displacement: 1763/2177 tons
Armament: 2 x twin 20mm cannon,1 x twin 37mm flak
Complement: 45 crew plus 12 passengers (normal for class:52)
Dimensions: 294 x 30 x 13 feet
Machinery: 2-shaft diesel electric BHP/SHP 4100/1100
Speed: 17 knots surfaced/7 knots submerged
Bunkers: 369 tons fuel

was set ablaze and had to be scuttled in order to quench the fire. *U-234* had previously slipped out of the U-boat harbour into the relative safety of Heikendorf Bay where we concealed ourselves in a thick smoke-screen, but even so we were lucky to escape when an enemy aircraft in difficulties jettisoned its bomb load within 30 metres of us. Shortly afterwards, we put back into the Germania Werft where *U-234* was to be refitted and converted from a minelayer into a transport submarine.

The important changes were the installation of a Snorkel and the removal of the 24 lateral mineshafts to make cargo stowage compartments (see diagram). The outer keel plates were removed and the keel duct was prepared to receive a cargo, mainly of mercury and optical glass.

The purpose of the snorkel was to permit submerged travel under diesel propulsion instead of by the slow electric motors feeding air to the diesel engines through an intake mast. The device had numerous drawbacks in use. The head of the snorkel contained a float valve which shut automatically when a sea swept over the mast. This prevented the entry of water, but also cut off the air supply at the same time, so that the diesels then drew their supply from the interior of the boat. If this went on too long, it tended to suffocate the crew. Coupled with this problem was the possibility of carbon monoxide poisoning in the event that the diesel exhaust discharged into the boat, as might happen if the clutches jammed.

During the day the snorkel head could be seen slicing through the waves, but obviously this was far less visible than a surfaced U-boat. When in use the snorkel was so noisy that it masked reception through the hydrophones and a visual watch had to be maintained at the periscope. On the whole, however, the snorkel provided U-boat crews with sorely needed protection against Allied air supremacy over the sea and was welcomed despite all its disadvantages.

On 22 December, 1944, *U-234* emerged from the yards and made a trial run under the supervision of the Germania Werft engineers. The great air-raids against Kiel were very intense at this time and I was surprised that the repairers could possibly manage to keep working. The commander had confided to me that the boat's impending voyage would be to the Far East and told me to see to the arrangements for anti-radar equipment to be delivered to the Yard. Finally, after one last short visit to have the device fitted, we were listed for snorkel training.

Our instruction was given in the Strander Bucht by the First World War U-boat ace Captain Max Valentiner. Valentiner asked the Chief Engineer and the engine room personnel if they had read and understood the Snorkel Instruction Manual and they all confirmed that to be the case. The boat dived and was trimmed at periscope depth. The snorkel exhaust and air intake masts were raised and the boat ran submerged on the diesels. We progressed smoothly beneath a slight swell and Valentiner told Lt Cdr Ernst to have the snorkel cut under the waves.

Initially there was no noticeable effect even though the diesels were consuming the air from the interior of the boat. After five minutes the diesels were still running and this created a partial vacuum which was particularly unpleasant on the ear drums and rapidly became intolerable. Peter Schölch, the Boatswain, found that two fillings in his teeth dropped out.

Suddenly all the men in the diesel room collapsed over the machinery, but fortunately the last man on his feet, Warrant Officer Winkelmann, still had the strength to disconnect the diesel – and without receiving the order to do so. The tanks were blown and the boat rose, but the vacuum remained. The control room petty officer went up to the tower and, when it was reported to him that the conning tower was clear of the sea, he carefully turned on the test-cock and jumped smartly clear. The air came whistling in, but it was some time before the air intake masts could be reopened. When they were, a storm-wind swept through the boat, followed by a strange mist. Our ears 'popped' as their drums adjusted to the change in pressure.

It had all been the fault of the Chief Engineer. Instead of giving the order to cut out the diesels, he had got confused and given the order to put the diesels into neutral, in which state they continued to consume the air in the boat. Lt Cdr Ernst was brought before the assembled crew and given the severest possible reprimand. It was his first snorkel attempt and a complete disaster. It was Valentiner's advice that he thoroughly revise the instructions before we embarked on our voyage and that we keep on practising with the snorkel.

The Commander and the First Lieutenant, Lt Klingenberg, had such a poor working relationship that at Fehler's suggestion their ways parted and Richard Bulla, who had been appointed to the staff of the Luftwaffe attaché to Tokyo, General Ulrich Kessler, who was also to be one of the passengers on the forthcoming voyage, was made Klingenberg's replacement. Bulla had served as flying officer aboard the raider *Atlantis* and Fehler knew him well.

Fehler had been summoned to Naval Headquarters in Berlin to be informed that U-234 was to take twenty-seven passengers to Tokyo. The commander told them that he considered the number to be entirely unreasonable. They would take the place of eighteen crew members, they would be a nuisance and could endanger the mission. After substantial discussions, a compromise was struck in which twelve passengers would travel and eight crew members would make way for them.

In January, 1945, we began the final preparations for the voyage to Tokyo. A Hohentwiel radar set, the Luftwaffe invention that Lt Wissmann had told me about, was installed; its aerial nestled in a slot within the tower coaming from where it was raised by air pressure. This radar gave a U-boat the priceless advantage of detecting an approaching aircraft before its own radar could get a fix on the boat, but it became very hot if left working too long. Later one of the passengers, the telecommunications scientist Dr Schlicke, obtained a reserve set and this helped to eliminate the overheating problem.

It would appear from the American declassified documents that the actual loading of *U-234* and the type of cargo she was to carry was determined by a special commission formed in December, 1944, and entitled *Marinesonderdienst Ausland*. The head of this organization was a naval captain, Becker, who was in charge of all details including liaison with the Japanese and determined what cargo was to be carried, and Lt Cdr Longbein from this commission was the actual loading officer.

In addition to the cargo compartments already mentioned, steel loading containers resembling a large cigar tube were designed to fit into each of the six vertical mineshafts grouped down the centre-line of the foredeck. These were held in place by the original mine-release mechanism.

The cargo was loaded under conditions of the strictest secrecy. Into the keel ducts went the 50lb iron bottles of mercury. Elsewhere optical glass, engineering blueprints, cameras, secret documents in sealed containers, even an Me 262 jet fighter in its component parts were stowed in the holds amidships. Some of the forward upright tubes were packed with *Panzerfäuste*, other anti-tank weapons and small rockets.

The most important and secret item of cargo, the uranium oxide, which I believe was highly radioactive, was loaded into one of the vertical steel tubes one morning in February, 1945. Two Japanese officers were to travel aboard *U-234* on the voyage to Tokyo: Air Force Colonel Genzo Shosi, an aeronautical engineer, and Navy Captain Hideo Tomonaga, a submarine architect who, it will be recalled, had arrived in France aboard *U-180* about eighteen months previously with a fortune in gold for the Japanese Embassy in Berlin. I saw these two officers seated on a crate on the forecasing engaged in painting a description in black characters on the brown paper wrapping gummed around each of a number of containers of uniform size. At the time I didn't see how many containers there were, but the Loading Manifest showed ten. Each case was a cube, possibly steel and lead, nine inches along each side and enormously heavy.

Once the inscription *U235* had been painted on the wrapping of a package, it would then be carried over to the knot of crewmen under the supervision of Sub-Lt Pfaff and the Boatswain, Peter Schölch, and stowed in one of the six vertical mineshafts.

I asked Tomonaga what the lead cubes contained, and he said, 'It is the cargo from *U-235*. That boat is no longer going to Japan.' When I enquired at the 5th Flotilla Office, they told me that *U-235* was a small Type VII training U-boat which had never been earmarked for operations outside the Baltic. So I knew that Tomonaga had lied to me. I mentioned all this to Lt Cdr Fehler that evening, but he told me not to bring up the subject again with the Japanese. Recently I was informed by the naval historian Professor Jürgen Rohwer that the nuclear material had been requested, probably in the military attaché code, at the end of December, 1944, or very early in 1945. The Japanese Military Attaché in Berlin, Kigoishi, organized the transport of the material with the German authorities and from the quayside at Kiel had watched the loading of the ten cases of uranium oxide into *U-234*. This seems to me to confirm that the uranium oxide was of a nature which rendered it of especial value to the Japanese.

When the loading of *U-234* was finished it was estimated that the total weight of the cargo was 260 tons.

The Commander of the 5th Flotilla arranged a reception for Tomonaga and Shosi. In a ceremony aboard the scuttled liner *St Louis* the Japanese ambassador, Oshima, placed Tomonaga's 300-year-old Samurai sword into the custody of Fehler for the duration of the voyage of *U-234*. The eleven passengers boarding in Germany were the two Japanese, Lt Cdr Richard Bulla, a specialist in air-sea cooperation, who was also the First Lieutenant, and the following eight;

Colonel Fritz Sandrath (Luftwaffe); former head of Bremen AA
  defences.
Colonel Erich Menzel (Luftwaffe): technical aide to the Air
  Attaché, communications
Lt Cdr Heinrich Hellendorn (Navy); specialist in naval AA
  gunnery.

Captain (Eng.) (S) Heinz Schlicke (Navy, honorary rank); radar, infra-red and direction finding scientist.

Lt Colonel Kai Nieschling (Luftwaffe): Nazi military judge.

Captain Gerhard Falk (Navy): specialist in shipbuilding and design.

August Bringewald: Senior Messerschmitt engineer, Me262, Me163 and rocketry.

Franz Ruf: procurement specialist for Messerschmitt.

The final passenger was to board in Norway. Nieschling, the judge, was going to investigate allegations against Embassy staff implicated in the Sorge spy scandal and to keep an eye on other passengers during the voyage. The two Japanese, Nieschling and Falk slept in the deck below the NCO's quarters while all remaining passengers slept where they could.

The US National Archive has now declassified a document under reference *373/3679/Box 22/FOLDER "OP-16-Z Day File 1/1/45*. This is a Memorandum concerning the interrogation of Judge Nieschling. No Memorandum regarding the interrogation of Captain Gerhard Falk has ever been released.

Personally I saw very little of Falk who never socialized except with the Judge.

In the Memorandum Judge Nieschling stated that he knew nothing in particular about the uranium oxide, but the fact that he knew so much about contacts and factories in Germany in connection with the material indicates that a number of conversations must have taken place which highlighted its significance. Nieschling said that 'the meaning behind the ore' was known to Gerhard Falk, who had taken some secret courses before he boarded *U-234* and was to be chief technician on all naval matters in Tokyo under Admiral Wenneker.

On the afternoon of 25 March, 1945, squatting low in the water with all the fuel, ammunition, provisions and cargo she had aboard, *U-234* dieseled out of the U-boat basin into the Förde. Flotilla comrades lined the Hindenburgufer in hundreds to see us off. Our destination was supposed to be secret, but everybody seemed to know.

By nightfall we were at anchor on the far side of the Strander Bucht waiting for the escort to take us north. Without any doubt this was going to be the most difficult part of the voyage to Tokyo and we would soon be required to fight our way northwards to Norway on the surface and through waters thickly sown with mines by both belligerents and over which the enemy exercised almost complete air supremacy. It was also the purpose of every Allied aircraft and, once at the portals to the Atlantic north of the British Isles, if we got that far, of hundreds of Allied anti-submarine vessels to hunt and harry every U-boat, including ourselves, to destruction.

In the early hours of 26 March the escort vessels appeared in company with three new Type XXIII U-boats. This group, including *U-234*, was to attempt to run the gauntlet from Kiel to Christiansand in Norway. As Senior Officer of the convoy, Fehler's responsibilities were onerous. Above all he was most concerned at the probability that enemy agents would have reported his departure from Kiel and that he could expect to be attacked in the Kattegat. If located there, the chances of surviving the onslaught would be poor, for the waters were very shallow and the depths offered little shelter. Accordingly, once clear of the land he reduced speed and headed for Copenhagen. The sea was thickly mined, but as soon as he was out of the Great Belt he detached the minesweeper escort on the grounds that she was too conspicuous and, having passed the Danish capital by night, he set his course to run inside Swedish neutral waters wherever he could.

Although *U-234* could make 17 knots in calm conditions, Fehler was obliged to proceed at 10 knots, the speed of the slowest U-boat of the convoy. We passed through the Kattegat in good weather conditions without incident. At about 1500 hrs on 27 March I reported to the bridge that I wanted to exchange the Hohentwiel radar set for the reserve because it was overheating and that there would be a blind period of ten minutes while the valves of the replacement receiver warmed up. The officer of the watch shouted down his permission and I wasted no time in getting the reserve set plugged in, but before the ten minutes had elapsed the aircraft warning siren wailed through the boat and the AA weapons were manned to the thunder of sea boots on the plating. Three machines had been sighted off the bow.

Dr Schlicke, the radar specialist, was standing near me, and I asked him if we could turn the set on immediately. He agreed, and told me that we could get a new tube in Oslo. When at last the radar screen displayed the field I saw that the enemy aircraft were within 5,000 yards and I began to relay the decreasing range to the bridge. At 3,000 yards I heard the Commander calmly give the order to fire. The flak gunners failed to respond and it remained quiet. I sprinted to the bridge and heard Fehler loudly berating the gun crews. Everyone on the upper deck of the boat had heard the order to open fire except the gunners. To our astonishment the enemy aircraft flew on in apparent ignorance of a string of four U-boats below them.

At midnight, proceeding north in the main swept channel off Frederikshavn, we passed a southbound German convoy consisting of four steamers and a number of modern-looking torpedo boats. Half an hour later we watched from the bridge as a cluster of flares dropped from the clouds and lit up the sea astern with a pale, yellow light. Then the bombers came in quickly for one of the steamers, defying the streams of molten flak that spewed at them from the escort, and suddenly, with a tremendous flash, an ammunition ship exploded in a ball of fire and vanished in splinters.

Our radar showed a multitude of contacts at all points of the screen; the Kattegat was swarming with enemy aircraft. Fehler's flak crews waited quietly at their weapons and searched the heavens while the commander raged inwardly on his bridge, unable to run for it because of his responsibility to the other three U-boats and aware that he could not submerge in these shallows.

Next the radar detected an aircraft approaching at low altitude from the west. The trace appeared when the contact was about 6,000 yards distant and barely skimming the surface of the sea. The flak crews were notified verbally, the other U-boats by signal lamp. All we could do now was fire off a lethal curtain of 2-cm tracer and lead for the enemy aircraft to fly into as he attacked. The radar targets intensified the closer the aircraft approached and, in despair, I directed the beam directly on the attacker. At 3,300 yards the aircraft inexplicably pulled off its headlong course and turned away; at 6,000 yards he vanished from the screen.

I looked at my assistant, Senior Petty Officer Werner Bachmann, in surprise.

'I don't think he liked the look of us on his radar,' he said. 'We gave him such a big contact that he thought we were a cruiser.'

Aircraft were continuing to mill around the sky and after thirty minutes there was another approach from the west, but when the radar beam was concentrated fully on the inbound bomber it disengaged at 3,300 yards. The game went on all night; three times it was repeated. It couldn't have been coincidence but I have never discovered exactly what effect this trick caused on the enemy radar screen.

By daybreak it was all over. The four U-boats cruised unscathed into Oslofjord and dropped anchor at Horten.

On 29 March the resident U-boat Training Officer announced an exercise for all boats fitted with a snorkel. In fine conditions with good visibility and a calm sea the submarines glided out to the training lanes at Christiansand where they submerged and the exercise began. After a short while, about a mile offshore, *U-1301*

(Lt Cdr Lenkheit) crossed into the adjacent training lane occupied by ourselves and rammed us abaft the conning tower at the level of Number VII tank on the port side, tearing open the bunker and releasing about 16 tonnes of diesel oil into the fjord. The ramming boat sustained damage to her bow and torpedo tube doors.

Upon entering harbour at Christiansand, Fehler was informed by the port authority that there was no dry dock available and that the boat would have to go to Bergen. Our officers had a long discussion about this on account of two things: it was dangerous to go into dry-dock with a fully laden boat and the voyage to Bergen would involve a three-day limp along the Norwegian coast at the mercy of whatever enemy forces happened to be in the area. Fehler's compromise was to obtain a suitable sheet of steel plate, anchor in a quiet spot near Christiansand, submerge the bow by 20° by flooding the forward tanks so as to lift the stern above the surface – a difficult task with a 300-feet-long U-boat – and have the crew go to work on it.

Over a period of a week in early April, 1945, and then only when a surface calm permitted it, the men succeeded in removing the bent and torn frames, replacing them with substitutes cut from the steel plate and welding the parts together using power from the diesel engines.

The final passenger now came aboard: Luftwaffe General Ulrich Kessler, the new Air Attaché to Tokyo, an extrovert who fulminated against the régime and Goering in particular. I was amused to watch Fehler's horror as he listened to Kessler's frank opinions about both.

During the lay-up at Christiansand I attended at the signals station every morning to collect the messages for the boat. I think it was about 14 April when I gave the captain a signal which read:

U-234. Only sail on the orders of the highest level. Führer HQ.

A short while afterwards, I was summoned to fetch another urgent signal which stated:

U234. Sail only on my order. Sail at once on your own initiative. Dönitz.

At this the Commander went ashore at once to organize the escort and arranged for a fast anti-submarine trawler to take us round the Skaw. On the afternoon of 16 April, 1945, U-234 quietly parted from the pier and left the harbour. Once clear of Christiansand we stopped and allowed a communications launch to come alongside, and the Regional Commander of U-boats (FdU) North, Captain Rösing, came on deck for a swift farewell ceremony. The crew fell in on the after-casing; the passengers remained below.

Rösing wished us luck for the long voyage and then said, 'Comrades, when you return from this mission, we will have our final victory.' Were these just empty words, or was there a definite meaning in this sentence, I wondered. Then he left. The Commander addressed the crew. 'Comrades, you have all heard the latest news bulletins and know how it stands at home. Germany is approaching hard times. No matter how this war may turn out, I promise to do everything I can to bring you safely back.'

The escort arrived and at 16 knots U-234 followed her into the dusk. At Lindesnes Fehler signalled that she was no longer required.

'Then good luck and a safe homecoming,' her Aldis lamp flashed back.

With a final glance to the low mountains to starboard, the bridge watch went below and Fehler secured the hatch lid. The boat was trimmed at periscope depth and then started the long underwater voyage to the Equator by snorkel. I wondered if I would ever see the light of day again.

ON COURSE FOR JAPAN: SURRENDER

From the telegraphists of an inbound boat at Christiansand I had obtained extra useful information regarding the location of radio beacons down the South Atlantic coasts and right across into the western Pacific, but, in a discussion with Fehler, he told me that he had liberty to choose his own route to Tokyo and as the enemy sea and air presence in the Indian Ocean and western Pacific was now so overwhelming that he proposed to sail to Tokyo around Cape Horn.

On the first day out the motor of the main bilge pump caught fire. Although the flames were soon extinguished, there was an appalling electrical stink in the boat and the crew found difficulty in breathing. As we could not surface in these waters, Warrant Officer Winkelmann came up with the saving idea of disconnecting the snorkel from the diesel so that the engine drew on the foul air in the boat, while the snorkel discharged fresh air from the surface into the bow and stern rooms.

Off Bergen at midday the Commander brought the boat to 50 feet to take in the signal repeats and during the precautionary periscope sweep saw a very large aircraft curving towards us at a low altitude. We dived at once to 300 feet and prepared for depth-charging, but despite the excellent audibility we heard nothing but three gentle splashes one after the other, then silence. By intensive hydrophone observation I located the emission of an occulting beam consisting of a five-second hum and a longer period of silence. This came from three different bearings.

I had a quick search through the 'Novelty Catalogue' which I had been given by the Radio Supplies Office in Kiel and concluded that the aircraft had dropped three sonar buoys equipped with a microphone and a transmitter for sending back its findings. From these the navigator of the aircraft could then obtain the position of the submarine by triangulation and drop his depth charges on it.

Only in the possibility that there might be a warm water layer beneath us which would refract the sonar beams was there any hope of escape. Fehler took the boat to her maximum operating depth of 550 feet and we found that we were not attacked.

Later that night we narrowly escaped being run down by a steamer. The Coxswain, Jasper, had the periscope watch and was late to see the tumbling bow-wave and give the order to dive deep. We passed directly beneath the belly of the freighter, cringing as we imagined the suction forces tending to drag our conning tower into her mashing propellers. This would never have happened if we had been using the electric motors instead of the diesels because we would have been deeper and the hydrophones would have been manned.

At the head of the snorkel mast was a dipole aerial for the detection of radar emissions. The device could also be used as an aerial to receive the *Funksonne* radio navigation aid transmitted from Norway, which enabled the boat to be navigated accurately while submerged.

On the first occasion when we used this aerial, an argument arose between myself and the assistant Coxswain. A course had been laid to snorkel through to the Atlantic Ocean by way of the Iceland-Faroes Narrows and Paul Rische had used an estimated starting position obtained by dead reckoning. This point was materially different from the one I had calculated using *Funksonne* bearings obtained by means of the dipole. It was my opinion that, if we followed Rische's course, we would pass through the shallowest part of an area known as the 'Rosegarden', which U-boats were advised to avoid at all costs, since it was notorious as a spot where Allied aircraft dumped unwanted bomb loads when returning from missions. It had long been favoured by them for that purpose because U-boats returning to Germany from the Atlantic were known to pause there for rest and recuperation after breaking back into the North Sea.

Fehler, in common with almost all Seaman branch officers, held radio navigation in low regard and dismissed what I said until, with the aid of another telecommunications device, the echo sounder, it was proved that the boat was clearly approaching the 'Rosegarden'.

This convinced the commander, and he now decided to abandon caution. In defiance of his operational orders, which required him to reach the Equator submerged at all times, he declared that he proposed to proceed on the surface and break out into the Atlantic as soon as possible.

He had found that the snorkel was proving a mixed blessing in the high swell and, as the boat was difficult to spot in these high latitudes because of her low form and camouflage, particularly if the hull could be kept awash, he intended to remain on the surface even if attacked by an enemy warship. He would trust that the natural inclination of a heavily-laden U-boat to carve through the Atlantic rollers would enable him to foil even a destroyer which would tend to climb over and around the seas, losing both the ability to bring her guns to bear effectively and the advantage of speed.

We blew the tanks and surfaced. The snorkel was withdrawn into its socket on the foredeck, the radar mattress was extended and set revolving and the diesels growled loudly with a puff of blue exhaust smoke to mark the effort. At full speed we hammered through the Iceland-Faroes Narrows, an area where many U-boats had come to grief. During the first night we were obliged to dive twice because of aircraft, but our radar detected them long before they could get a fix on us.

We broke through into the Atlantic on the same day that we learned of the death of the Führer and the accession of Admiral Dönitz to succeed him, and realized that this presaged the imminent end of the Third Reich.

On the evening of 4 May, 1945, I copied down the order of U-boat Command that all German submarines were to observe a cease-fire with effect from 0800 hrs German Time the following morning. All attacks were forbidden and any current pursuit was to be abandoned forthwith. All attack U-boats were to return to Norwegian harbours.

In accordance with his secret orders, Fehler merely noted these instructions. *U-234* was not an attack U-boat, so he could proceed on his mission, submerged by day and surfaced at night under the protection of our radar.

The last Long Wave transmitter, 'Goliath', at Magdeburg, had been destroyed upon the approach of enemy land forces and naval telegraphists were now obliged to rely on Short Wave senders. When instructed to tune to the 'Special Frequency' for a message of the utmost importance, we were suddenly cut adrift from U-boat Command because I discovered that we had been provided with an incorrect table of frequencies. Whether this was an error or intentional I had no way of knowing. For a while Fehler was reduced to informing himself as to the war situation by listening to English language radio broadcasts from the United States and Canada until

Bachmann finally succeeded, by a patient process of elimination, in identifying the new wave-lengths.

On 8 May, 1945, U-boats at sea received notification of Germany's capitulation. Rulings newly in force prohibited the sending of enciphered messages; a signal addressed to all U-boats and to the beleaguered naval garrisons at Lorient and St Nazaire required the destruction of all old cyphers and the surrender of all current and forward-dated code-books.

Late that same evening the FdU North, Bergen, Captain Rösing sent Fehler a signal in the Japan Cipher:

U-234. Continue your voyage or return to Bergen. FdU.

When I showed him the log, Fehler shook his head and said, 'I'm definitely not going back.'

We continued to head south at full speed.

On 6 May, two days earlier, an American news broadcast had reported the Japanese Foreign Minister, Tojo, as having made an official declaration that Japan considered herself free from all contracts and treaties concluded with the German Reich and would fight on alone. On the evening of 8 May Reuters issued a communiqué to the effect that Japan had severed relations with Germany and that, as a consequence, German citizens in Japan were being arrested.

Taking the two reports together, Fehler was now of the view that the purpose of the voyage had been frustrated and he told his officers that he was accepting the capitulation. His immediate problem was the two Japanese officers. They were likely to consider it to be their duty to take action to prevent the cargo from falling into the hands of Japan's enemies and Fehler informed them both of the political developments and placed them under arrest.

In return, Tomonaga and Shosi expressed understanding for Fehler's dilemma and generously wished him an honourable solution. In asking him to reconsider his decision, Shosi gave his personal undertaking that the crew of *U-234* would not be imprisoned on the completion of the voyage, but would receive especially favourable treatment. Fehler had no confidence in the Japanese Government, however; he felt sure that, following the capitulation of Germany, the eastern Axis partner, considering German citizens on her territory to have outlived their usefulness, would correspondingly treat them no better and perhaps much worse than other Europeans who had also been unfortunate enough to fall into the hands of the Emperor.

The Captain heard out the plea of the Japanese officers, but shook his head with a smile.

Subsequently it transpired that Fehler's assumption was uncharitable; on 15 May, 1945, when the diplomatic missions and Party organs of the defunct Third Reich were finally closed in East Asia, German citizens were interned for the remainder of the conflict under the most hospitable and generous conditions.

When I went to the radio room later, Bachmann told me that the two Japanese had made their way through the boat taking their leave of the crew, Tomonaga distributing among them the watches he had bought in Switzerland. At that time it was not suspected what all this might portend. The Japanese officers could not practise the suicide rite because the Captain had possession of Tomonaga's Samurai sword and they had no other weapons. Before the voyage Fehler had taken the precaution of depriving even the German passengers of their sidearms so that only officers and warrant officers of the crew had service pistols.

The Allies had signalled to U-boats at sea that they were to comply with the following requirements when surrendering:

1. All torpedo pistols were to be removed and jettisoned, but the disarmed torpedoes were to be retained.
2. All flak ammunition was to be jettisoned and the guns lashed facing astern.
3. A black flag was to be set at the extended periscope tube.
4. Navigation lamps were to be set.
5. The exact navigational position was to be reported and all further movements were to be made whilst surfaced.

Following these, there was a string of instructions for interpreting the harbour of surrender for each particular sea area. The surrender port for *U-234* was Halifax, Nova Scotia. Upon reading this signal, Fehler called a conference of his officers to discuss the implication of the black flag, since this was the designation of the sea pirate. We had heard a great deal of depth-charging and bombing through the hydrophones and the possibility had to be considered whether the boat would be attacked and sunk when offering to surrender with a black flag at the periscope. The Commander postponed any decision on the matter and we continued to sail southwards. For the next five days Fehler and the first lieutenant, Bulla, who both spoke good English, sat in the radio room every evening listening to American and Canadian news bulletins in order to obtain a broad view of the international situation.

A week after the general capitulation the following message was transmitted over all U-boat frequencies:

Whoever does not capitulate now will be treated as a pirate and put on trial.

There was no signature, but the manner of keying indicated a British operator. Once again there was a long conference involving the officers and some of the passengers. Fehler expressed no opinion as to which course of action he preferred. General Kessler and Colonel von Sandrath wanted to proceed with the mission to Tokyo, but in any case not to surrender; if necessary they could suggest places in Argentina where we would be sheltered once we got ashore. Bulla and Pfaff wanted to sail to an island in the South Pacific. Dr Walter, the boat's medical officer, and Judge Nieschling, who were the most fervent Nazis aboard, were both adamant for surrender. My personal feeling was that we should obey the last order, which had been Captain Rösing's signal of 8 May ordering us to continue with the voyage or put back to Bergen.[44]

There was no consensus aboard the boat and on 13 May Fehler gave me the following signal to transmit:

Halifax. Here is *U-234*.

The Canadian station responded immediately by requesting our position and, once this had been supplied, we were given a course to steer for Nova Scotia. But Fehler had not the least intention of going there and we now headed at full speed to the south-west in order to cross into the American sector.

The diesel hands had dyed a bedsheet black and fastened it to the periscope, and the German battle flag had been hoisted at the jack on the upper gun platform. The running lights were also set, but none of the other requirements of the surrender were complied with.

The stern torpedo tubes were loaded and the flak weapons positioned ready to fire. We maintained a permanent radar watch to preclude the possibility of a surprise approach from the air.

At about 2300 hrs I was summoned to the radio room to see an aerial contact on the radar screen. Fehler gave the alarm, the gun crews closed up and I beamed the radar directly at the approaching aircraft. Just before entering the critical defensive zone of the boat the machine altered course and patrolled a circle round us at the maximum range of our flak weapons. A white flare soared into the night sky and burst, after which the aircraft departed. Shortly, Halifax called:

U-234. Your reported position and course are not correct. Steer 340° to Halifax. Report position, course and speed every four hours.

Fehler read the signal and merely grinned. He would continue towards the US sector.

Judge Nieschling, who lodged in the lower deck, reported to Fehler that Tomonaga and Shosi were lying in adjacent cots, their arms linked, breathing stertorously, and couldn't be awakened. An empty bottle which had contained Luminal sleeping tablets had been found on the deck plating nearby. Now the reason for their leave-taking became clear. The Boatswain, Peter Schölch, was sent to search the Japanese officers' sea-bags and in one of them found a note addressed to the Commander asking him, 'Should he find us alive here, to leave us alone, please, and let us die.'

They had taken their action so as to avoid captivity. In closing, they requested that their bodies should not be allowed to fall into the hands of the Americans and that their diplomatic bag should be weighted and sunk, as it held secret papers useful to the enemy. There was a will confirming the assignment of certain property to members of the crew and for the Captain a sum of money in Swiss francs to be used to inform their relatives that they were dead, but not dishonoured.

Fehler merely said, 'We will do as they have asked.'

Dr Walter later confirmed that both men were still alive. The overdose would have killed a European, but the constitution of the Japanese was stronger.

As Fehler had disobeyed the Canadian instructions to report in every four hours, I now began to find myself inundated with signals from the station at Halifax. The Commander waved me away when I arrived with the log, saying, 'Let them call.' Later that evening he decided to mollify them with a position report. Giving me a slip of paper with coordinates on it, he said, 'It's false, and send it at low volume.'

I tapped out our call sign and Halifax responded at once, confirming good reception, but, as soon as I set to the task of keying out the message, it was jammed by a very powerful transmitter which stopped and started whenever I did. Halifax wirelessed:

U-234. I am being jammed. Change to frequency . . .

Bachmann tuned the set to the ordered wavelength, but when I resumed sending the jamming continued. It was no coincidence; it was definitely deliberate. I reported the fact to the Commander who said, 'Turn the set off then. That's our excuse for not reporting in.'

Not long after, the stern lookouts reported the approach of a destroyer on the port quarter. This was the USS *Sutton*, which gave us orders by lamp to head for the Gulf of Maine and ignore all further communications from Halifax. Obviously the *Sutton* had been responsible for the jamming.

Fehler sent for the doctor and said, 'Tonight we must get the Japanese overboard. If the Americans get to them, they'll do everything they can to bring them round. See to it that they die peacefully.'

Dr Walter descended to the lower deck without comment and a few hours later reported the death of the two Japanese officers.

The Commander acted swiftly. Each corpse was sewn into a weighted hammock, while the diplomatic pouch and the Samurai sword were bound to the body of Tomonaga and then laid on the deck under the red sunburst flag of Japan. The order was given to stop engines and we observed a ten-minute silence for the fallen, after which the bodies were committed to the deep.

When *Sutton* enquired why we had stopped, a signaller flashed back that it had been 'engine trouble'.

The destroyer gave us a course to steer and sailed close alongside us throughout the night. At daybreak on Thursday 17 May, 1945, they closed to 800 yards with all guns bearing on the boat and lowered a launch containing three officers and thirteen ratings. Lt Cdr Bulla announced this through the loudspeakers and I went to the bridge to watch. We lay stopped in the long swell, which from time to time rolled across the fore-deck. As I watched the heavily armed, scowling party in the launch, I felt the sudden shock of our surrender, akin almost to emasculation, a submission to men who, despite the cessation of hostilities between our nations, remained very much our enemies. The launch bobbed across the gap between the two naval craft and was then swept by the swell hard against the saddle tank on the port side, nearly overturning. The helmsman managed to retrieve the situation, manoeuvred the launch round the stern of *U-234* and threw a small anchor upwards. It lodged and the occupants heaved themselves aboard.

'God, look at the weapons they're carrying,' said Bulla. 'In one hand a machine pistol, in the other a Colt revolver and round the shoulders three crossed belts of bullets.'

Dr Schlicke had quietly joined me on the bridge and tossed a few rolls of microfilm into the sea. We watched them slowly sink. 'And there goes the rocket that could fly the Atlantic,' he told me.

'Look at them as they come aboard,' Bulla said. 'My God, they looked worried. If they didn't have their chewing gum you could see their teeth chattering.' The Americans prowled cautiously from the stern to the conning tower, keeping their machine guns aimed at the bridge party as they advanced. 'Of course they've known for some time about this boat,' Bulla continued, 'but they don't know the Japs are dead.' And this point accounted for much of the Americans' behaviour.

When I looked at the destroyer I noticed for the first time that all her guns and flak weapons were trained on the boat. The Americans feared that our surrender might be a trap because they knew from the passenger list which had been sent to them from Kiel that there were two senior Japanese military officers aboard.

The American prize officer bravely clambered up to the bridge of *U-234* and demanded to see the Commander. He was followed by one of the boarding party dragging a long iron chain which was made fast around the periscope stand and dropped into the interior through the bridge manhole to prevent it being closed. In the control room the Americans wound the chain round and through the large hand wheels which operated the depth rudders. I watched them in amusement. They thought they had done what was necessary to prevent us scuttling the boat, but they were unaware that, in addition to the manual wheels, the Type XB U-boat had push-button controls for setting the depth rudders.

The prize officer asked where the Japanese officers were and Fehler told him that they were in Davy Jones's locker. Then the American officer gave his orders. From now on the loudspeakers and internal telephone system were not to be used; Lt Cdr Bulla, Lt Pagenstecher, the Chief Engineer and one engine-room watch would remain aboard *U-234* and all other crew and the passengers would transfer to the destroyer. The prize crew, who were now swarming through the boat, would perform the seaman branch duties. In each compartment a heavily armed sentry was posted, equipped with a chest microphone connected to the control room by cable. The prize officer reported to the destroyer that *U-234* was secure, but I noticed that we remained covered by all her guns.

A very dangerous situation now developed. *U-234* was drifting without way on her in the swell and she slowly came round broadside to the sea. This brought her bows into a position where they were pointing directly at the midships of the destroyer. The *Sutton* went ahead to full speed in order to get clear of this apparently threatening situation. Meanwhile we had begun to roll very unpleasantly and the prize officer ordered the American helmsman to proceed on course 270°. The latter was not yet fully acquainted with the rudder control panel and did not realize that the push button system required another button to be pushed to centre the rudder once the desired heading had been achieved. Accordingly after a further 90° swing, the locking device interceded automatically.

The effect of this error was to bring the bow round until it was pointing directly at the destroyer again, when the rudder locked and the boat picked up speed and headed straight for the *Sutton*.

Panic suddenly broke out among the prize crew as they realized the deadly peril they were now in.

Bulla screamed down, 'We're on a ramming course!' and I saw the destroyer's wake foam up. I went hot and cold; it would seem from the bridge of the *Sutton* that we were preparing to torpedo her. The radio messenger was kneeling over the bridge manhole, shouting down into the control room, and was not visible from the destroyer. 'They will open fire on us in about two seconds,' Bulla said quietly, and then, dragging the American to his feet, gave him an order in English. Standing on the rail of the Winter-garden, the rating waved to his ship and shouted into his walkie-talkie, 'It's just rudder failure, sir!'

We were within seconds of tragedy. The Captain of the *Sutton*, Lt T. W. Nazro had been about to give the order to destroy the U-boat by gunfire, sacrificing his boarding party in order to achieve this object. The Americans were very much the victims of their own U-boat atrocity propaganda. We discovered later that the prize crew members had all made out a last will and testament before getting into the launch because they did not think they could take the boat alive.

The prize officer now ordered Fehler to disengage the rudder locking mechanism. Since he was not allowed to use the loudspeakers or the internal telephone, he had to send a messenger to the stern from the control room. The messenger made his way through the circular communication doorways by seizing the upper coaming in both hands and swinging his legs through and forwards. When the American sentry in the stern torpedo room saw the German coming towards him at speed and in full flight he dropped his machine gun and raised his hands. This type of panic was incomprehensible to us until we saw American propaganda films later during our captivity. U-boat men were rated on a par with Mafia gangsters by Hollywood.

The prize crew now had matters fully in hand and the officer in charge informed Fehler that he would now raise the US flag, after

214

which all Germans having been so detailed would be transferred to the *Sutton*. We were delayed by General Kessler, who insisted on washing and shaving first. When he joined us on deck he was wearing his full Luftwaffe uniform, the Knight's Cross at his throat and wearing a monocle. 'This will annoy them,' he told me. We were allowed to lower the war flag with ceremony and, to our surprise, all the Americans saluted it, while the raising of the Stars and Stripes was performed as if it came as something of a chore to them. The black sheet on the periscope was pulled off by Lt Cdr Bulla and tossed overboard, which caused a furore amongst the prize crew and a determined attempt was made to retrieve it. While this was going on the German war flag was held under water until it saturated and sank. Long enquiries would follow later in Portsmouth, New Hampshire, into its whereabouts; it was wanted as a trophy. A net hung down the side of the destroyer and we scrambled up it. On deck we were searched for weapons and then led into the NCO's Mess where we were guarded by two ratings with carbines who even accompanied us to the heads.

During the first afternoon somebody was shot aboard our boat. The prize crew had been fooling around with our service pistols and one of their telegraphists had been shot in the kidneys. A second doctor was called up for the operation which our surgeon, Dr Walter, performed. Although it was initially successful, unfortunately the man died a few days later.

The next day there was an aircraft alarm. It wasn't a drill. We were amazed. Who would want to attack them here? 'The British,' they said darkly. It was probably a Canadian machine hunting for *U-234*.

Our treatment aboard the *Sutton* was very fair. At first the Americans were very reserved and mistrustful and always carried a shotgun when they had to come close to us, but by the second day the relationship had become almost friendly and the shotguns languished in a corner.

I remember the First Lieutenant of the destroyer in particular. He offered to take custody of all important personal documents, valuable items, jewellery, rings and watches, and each man was given a bag for the purpose. He promised that they would be returned on our release from captivity. He warned us very specifically against the US Army, which was a gang of thieves and would rob us of all we stood up in. I was astonished to hear a US officer talk in such a manner, but only later did we appreciate the difference between the US Navy and Army and realize how well-intentioned the *Sutton*'s officers had been. Few of us had been prepared to hand over our personal treasures and came to bitterly regret it later. I gave in my pay book and telegraphist service book. Later I received these direct from Washington in a CIA sealed envelope. They were the only personal items taken from me in the United States which I ever saw again.

The *Sutton* dropped anchor outside the harbour of Portsmouth, New Hampshire, on the glorious morning of 19 May, 1945. We stared mutely at the foreign shore as the Coast Guard cutters put out to ferry us in. A petty officer of the *Sutton* watched them arrive. 'Look,' he said, 'here comes the gang that never fought a battle but likes to play the big hero.'

Almost as once the hysterical shouting started up as they drove and herded us down into the cutters, threatening us with 'necktie parties' as though a posse had just brought us in. The Executive Officer of the *Sutton* called out something through a megaphone and the shouting subsided. During the short voyage to the quay I sat next to Fehler on a chest in a small cabin. A number of Press photographers were milling around trying to photograph us from all angles. Then a person in Coast Guard uniform thrust a microphone into Fehler's face and pestered him for an interview. The Commander declined in annoyance, protesting in fluent English that we were being treated like gangsters. 'That's just what you are,' shouted Lt Charles Winslow (USCG Reserve), 'and get off my boat!'

Fehler looked at me and shook his head. 'I think I made a mistake surrendering here,' he admitted.

When we came ashore we found a large, hate-filled mob waiting for us, held back by two lines of MPs who made a narrow avenue for us to the waiting buses. Once I had been roundly spat upon and abused, I began to entertain the most serious doubts about Fehler's decision to surrender us to the Americans. In the bus Lt Cdr Bulla sat beside me and said, 'I think it would have been better to have given ourselves up to the Canadians.' When I asked him where we were going now, he replied, 'Straight to jail. There we'll be robbed down to the shirts on our backs.' The *Sutton's* prize officer had warned him what to expect.

The ten specialist passengers were driven off to a secret destination. We located them all after the war with the exception of Captain Gerhard Falk. Possibly, like Peter Schölch, our Boatswain, and Lt Pfaff, who loaded and unloaded the uranium cases, he accepted US citizenship in exchange for his silence. But as Judge Nieschling said, Falk knew everything about the uranium oxide, and he probably knew too much for his own good. His eventual fate after he disappeared into the abyss on 19 May, 1945, remains a mystery.

We got out at the porch to a fortress-like building with barred windows. An American officer stood by the steps and in German bade us enter. 'Come on in, gentlemen,' he said beguilingly. 'Nothing will happen to you.' But as soon as we were in the vestibule the prison staff, naturalized Poles armed with wooden cudgels, beat us towards the trestle tables at the end of the hall where we were to be robbed. Medals, badges, watches, pens, wedding rings, everything was taken from us under the supervision of a senior jail officer and put into bags bearing a label for our names.

But behind a screen the bags were re-opened by carrion who took whatever appealed to them; watches and rings were the favourite.

We were accommodated in single cells which we left only for meals and ablutions. Whenever we returned to the cell after one of these short absences we would find that it had been ransacked. It seemed to me a pretty desperate country if the prison staff had to steal the prisoners' nailfiles and combs. After two days the crews, with the exception of Peter Schölch and myself, were removed to a prison camp.

Next morning I was handcuffed and driven to the quay where the surrendered U-boats were moored. My escort prodded me in the back with a Colt revolver and said, 'Let's go,' indicating *U-234*. At that moment Lt Cdr Ernst appeared at the galley hatch and I raised my manacled hands so that he could see them. He waved and shouted something into the boat and a stocky American naval captain appeared on deck. 'Git on board,' the prison guard said, driving the barrel of the revolver into the small of my back. Speaking good German, the American officer told me to wait: 'Don't go on board in handcuffs,' he said. 'I'll phone the jail.' When he returned a short while later the guard unlocked them. The officer gave me a cigarette and introduced himself as Captain Hatten, US Navy, and offered me a flame from a lighter which had a tiny U-boat soldered on one face. 'Yes,' he said, seeing my glance, 'I've had a lot to do with U-boat men.' I assumed he was an Intelligence Officer. When he led me aboard, the jail guard tried to follow, but the two MPs at the gangplank barred his way.

'That's my prisoner!' he shouted.

'Get lost, you damned Pole,' they replied with a laugh.

The Chief Engineer and the engineering NCOs had not been in the jail and they were astounded when I told them what went on there. Captain Hatten assured me that I wouldn't have to go back.

U-234 looked as though a hurricane had roared through. Locker doors hung broken open and the contents looted, laundry strewn about the plating. My diaries, U-boat leathers and fur outfit were gone. Apparently the US Army had paid the boat a visit the day after the prize crew went ashore.

Captain Hatten told me that two naval officers had arrived from Washington and were very interested in the device we had for sending a signal so fast that it was impossible to get a fix on it. 'In some things you are more technically advanced than ourselves,' he admitted modestly. I was surprised that they simply hadn't taken it. 'It's very simple to remove,' I assured him. 'All you have to do is unscrew it here at the back and clamp the cable to the transmitter.' He smiled nervously. 'We were worried – not me personally, of course – that there might be a booby-trap in it.'

I didn't understand this word and he explained its meaning. I laughed. 'So you are also a victim of your own propaganda,' I said.

'Yes,' he agreed. 'If they keep hammering something into you, some of it is bound to stick. That is the method of propaganda.'

I told him I would take out the device for him if he would get our Boatswain, Peter Schölch, out of Boston jail to join me, and he arranged this.

We were accommodated in an old naval vessel and assigned to a submarine school in the Yards, where we were occasionally asked to demonstrate techniques which they couldn't do on their own pig-boats, but our principal task was the overhaul of the U-boats.

Much of the weapons material, documents and the Me262 jet fighter had been removed from *U-234* during May. One day in July, however, I was standing with Captain Hatten on the bridge watching as the six steel loading containers were lifted from the forward mineshafts by crane and deposited on the quayside.

Peter Schölch was put in charge of the unloading because the Americans feared the containers might be booby-trapped. I saw four men approach the steel tubes carrying small hand appliances and, when I asked Captain Hatten for an explanation, he said, 'They are scientists. They are testing for the uranium with Geiger counters.'

Apparently the scientists discovered that all the steel tubes were contaminated to such an extent with radiation that they could not determine in which of the six tubes the uranium had been stowed. Peter Schölch knew, but did not inform the Americans of this. Eventually Lt Pfaff was brought from Fort Mead Camp and he unloaded the cases of uranium oxide in exchange for an inducement. Shortly afterwards he was repatriated and then returned to the United States as an immigrant, as did Schölch. Neither can ever be induced to speak about the matter of the uranium oxide to this day.

(For a discussion of the implications of this consignment of uranium oxide ore, see Appendix 2)

After the defeat of Japan in August, 1945, the US Navy had no further need of us and the next eight months I spent at a prison camp at Fort Edwards, Massachusetts.

In April, 1946, most of us were transferred from there to New York for our return to Europe aboard the *Rushville Victory*.

In Antwerp we were handed over to the British authorities, who made it clear that we were still military personnel and that we were likely to remain in detention camps for some considerable time. I landed in Camp 2228 near Waterloo in Belgium.

After a month the prisoners in this camp were required to undergo a medical examination for forced labour in England. Every conceivable subterfuge was employed to be certified 'Unfit', which was the only way to get out of it. A U-boat doctor whom I had known in Lorient gave me a supply of tablets which produced a temporary tachycardia and this enabled me to obtain the coveted certificate.

I was discharged from the German Navy on 20 June, 1946, after serving just a few months less than the twelve years for which I had enlisted in 1935.

I looked for the Fishery, but it no longer existed.

– Appendix 1 –

HEINRICH BLEICHRODT –
A BIOGRAPHICAL NOTE

Heinrich Bleichrodt, known as 'Ajax' in German naval circles, was born at Berga am Kyffhäuser near Halle on 21 October, 1909. His father died young and the son of the family was brought up by his mother and elder sister Elisabeth, proving himself a rebel in his early teens.

In 1926, at the age of 15, he realized the dream of many young German boys when he was accepted for sea training at the Finkenwerder Sailors' School. Starting in September of that year, he made several voyages from Germany to the Chilean nitrate port of Iquique via Cape Horn as ship's boy and then ordinary seaman aboard the Laeisz 'Flying P' line four-masters *Peking* and *Pamir*.

From July, 1928, Bleichrodt sailed as an Able Seaman on the Hapag steamers *Heidelberg*, *Oakland* and *Bitterfeld*, visiting Australia, the East Indies and west coast ports of North America. He obtained his mate's certificate at the Hamburg Sea Training College in December, 1931, and was appointed third mate of the *Jonia* which tramped the ports of Africa.

When the sail training ship *Niobe* capsized and sank in a squall off the Fehmarn Bank on 26 July, 1932, she took down with her the majority of the naval cadets of the 1932 entry. The intake of the previous year had been a small one, and Admiral Raeder now called upon the German shipping lines to offer their best junior officers to the *Reichsmarine*. Fifteen of these applicants were accepted into the German Navy in January, 1933, including Bleichrodt and Prien.

By September, 1935, Bleichrodt was adjutant of the Naval Artillery Section at Pillau in the rank of Sub-lieutenant. In April, 1937, he was made a full Lieutenant and served as watchkeeper aboard the three-masted sail training ship *Gorch Fock*.

In the summer naval exercises of 1939 Bleichrodt spent two

months aboard the cruiser *Admiral Hipper* to gain supplementary experience before joining the U-boat Arm in the rank of Lt-Commander at about the time of the outbreak of war.

From July until December, 1940, Bleichrodt commanded *U-48* (Teddy Suhren and Otto Ites were his watchkeeping officers), and in two voyages sank the sloop HMS *Dundee*, and fifteen mercantile vessels of 81,038 tons net register plus two others damaged. For this achievement he was awarded the Knight's Cross.

On the night of 18 September, 1940, *U-48* sank two steamers within a six-minute period, one of which was the 11,081-ton liner *City of Benares*. Aboard this ship were a number of evacuee children, many of them from prominent Jewish families. Seventy-seven lost their lives. For reasons best known to the British Admiralty, the *City of Benares* had not been declared as a hospital ship and was sailing by night in convoy without lights. She was therefore a legitimate target and the entire responsibility for the sinking lay with the British Admiralty.

However, a slander was created that the Germans knew in advance about the Jewish children aboard the *City of Benares* and Bleichrodt had been detailed to lie in wait for the ship. A likely candidate, Frank Laskier, a Liverpudlian steward, who had lost a leg during the sinking of the *Eurylochus* by the raider *Kormoran* in January, 1941, and therefore had a score to settle, was recruited by Terence de Marnay and Eldon Moore of the BBC to record a number of live talks which were broadcast mainly at peak listening time on Sunday evenings during the war. This propaganda was later published in book form and on 78rpm records (BD958 and BD959) by HMV.

In *My Name is Frank – A Merchant Seaman Talks* (published by Allen & Unwin in 1941), Laskier said, 'We know – we sailors *know* – they had waited for the *City of Benares*. I am sorry if anybody listening to me had children on the *City of Benares*. It's opening up old wounds I know, but it's infinitely better that these old wounds should be opened and remain open until the end of the war than we who are left, strong and healthy, should forget about it.' More was to be made of this incident once the war was over.

After a short spell as captain of *U-67*, Bleichrodt was given command of *U-109* in June, 1941, and made six Atlantic voyages with this boat, sinking thirteen ships of 81,133 tons net register plus one freighter damaged but salved.

In September, 1942, he was awarded the Oak Leaves to his Knight's Cross. Otto Köhler, former commander of *U-377*, stated in an obituary that it was about this time that Bleichrodt began to confide his fears for Germany's future and Wolfgang Hirschfeld told the author that it was on the Gulf of Guinea voyage in September, 1942, that he realized that Bleichrodt 'could no longer take the heat'.

Considering the stresses which submarine warfare imposed on a U-boat commander, it is only remarkable that more cases of combat neurosis (formerly known as 'shell shock') have not come to light. Bleichrodt's blind hatred of telecommunication devices, his constant griping about the fuel oil situation and his obsession that any merchant ship which reacted abnormally in response to being attacked with torpedoes must be a Q-ship (a condition I would describe as 'the *City of Auckland* Syndrome') were all symptomatic of the appalling strain to which a U-boat commander was subject.

Eventually, on his ninth Atlantic mission, he suffered a break-down. *U-109* had sailed from Lorient on her seventh war patrol at 1700 hrs on 28 November, 1942. Late on the night of the second day out Bleichrodt attacked a destroyer in the Bay of Biscay. One torpedo jammed in the tube, while those that emerged were all faulty and sheered astray. A severe depth charge attack followed and the boat was damaged but a sudden deterioration in the weather allowed Bleichrodt to make a run for it on the surface. The following day a hunter-killer group joined in the search and passed above *U-109* three times without detecting the boat. Because of the weather conditions much of the outward voyage to the Caribbean had to be made submerged.

Bleichrodt arrived off French Guiana on Boxing Day, 1942, and made an unsuccessful attack on a merchant vessel. This incident appears to have triggered off the medical condition reported to U-boat HQ that night:

Officer-Only Signal. 0012/27. For ten days the commander has been suffering from nervous debility with loss of energy, together with a serious depression. Request return.

The BdU replied that afternoon:

Officers-Only Signal 1157/27. The mission must be carried out under all circumstances.

On the morning of 31 December, 1942 Bleichrodt responded:

Officers-Only Signal 0443/31. At the moment I am not fully fit. Request medical advice.

That evening, the BdU advised Bleichrodt that *U-109* could not expect to be refuelled and at 0400 the next morning told him:

Officers-Only Signal 1131/31. Continue with the mission. No refuelling envisaged. If necessary, transfer command to First Lt with full authority. Medical advice three Luminal tablets daily. Light diet.

Bleichrodt thought about this for a day and then replied:

BdU. Am returning to port for lack of fuel.

When Bleichrodt reported on 5 January, 1943, that he had reached grid square DG 5770, a position south of the Azores on the latitude of Agadir, but had only 50 cubic metres of fuel left, the BdU told him to make for a rendezvous point nearby where he would receive another 15 cubic metres of fuel and be able to hand over his torpedoes to boats of the *Delphin* group.

U-109, *U-463* (Wolfbauer), *U-575* (Heydemann), *U-442* (Heße) and *U-436* (Seibicke) met up as arranged and spent nearly three days attempting to ship Bleichrodt's torpedoes aboard. Wolfbauer refuelled *U-109* while Dr Hoch of the U-tanker attended to Bleichrodt.

The electric torpedoes (Etos) could not be transferred in the sea conditions without a special type of boat which was not available, and in order to transfer the compressed air torpedoes (Atos), each missile had to be wrapped in eighteen life-jackets and left to drift for collection. During the initial lifting operation Seibicke's heaving gear collapsed. Since Seibicke and Heße each had a broken lifting gear, and Heydemann had no lifting gear at all, the parts were cannibalized and a makeshift gear put together on *U-575*, which enabled Heydemann to ship four Atos. The operation was then abandoned and Bleichrodt made for St Nazaire, where he arrived on 23 January, 1943. It shows a certain side of Dönitz' character that, instead of arranging for a most unpleasant command situation to develop aboard *U-109* at sea, he preferred instead to expose five U-boats to extreme danger over a period of three days and to allow Bleichrodt to be hospitalized upon his return. Another commander might easily have faced a firing party.

In his written opinion entered in the War Diary of *U-109* on 6 October, 1943, the BdU stated:

The mission was unsuccessful as a result of the medical condition of the Commander, who gave up his command on his return. As respects the matter on 26 December, the conclusion drawn about the enemy ship was unjustified. The presumed depth charges were undoubtedly the torpedoes detonating at the end of their run after missing.

The author does not have the War Diary extract for the period preceding the 27 December, 1942, the day when Bleichrodt first reported himself to be suffering from lassitude and deep depression, but it is not difficult to guess what must have transpired on 26 December. Following the failed attack on the merchant vessel, Bleichrodt had fallen victim to a delusional state common in those suffering from the *City of Auckland* Syndrome.

Bleichrodt was next given a shore job as a U-boat crew training officer. On 1 July, 1944, he was promoted to full Commander and made Chief of the 22nd U-Flotilla at Gdynia. On 28 January, 1945, aboard the tender *Weichsel*, he supervised the civilian evacuation from Gdynia by sea as Russian forces encircled the town. In May, 1945, Bleichrodt surrendered the Flotilla to British naval forces at Wilhelmshaven.

Later that year Bleichrodt was detained on a trumped-up war crimes charge in connection with the *City of Benares* sinking. The British admiralty alleged that the Germans had known in advance about the Jewish children of the *City of Benares* and had given Bleichrodt mysterious 'secret orders' to wait for the ship to put out. They had no documentary evidence and the only witness was Laskier, who just *knew*.

In the trial of Lt Eck earlier that year a British military court had introduced the precedent that an enemy naval officer accused of a war crime could be convicted and executed on Affidavit evidence without the right to cross-examine the witness.

Bleichrodt was warned privately that the British wanted a show trial and a hanging and his interrogators would need to resort to a perjured Affidavit to secure a conviction as they hadn't been able to find any evidence. Bleichrodt therefore refused to speak during the entire period of his incarceration and eventually the prosecution had to be abandoned.

In marked contrast to the allegations made against Bleichrodt over the sinking of the *City of Benares*, a very different view of him has been given by Gordon Gill, Second Radio Operator of the *Tuscan Star*, who was saved from drowning by the crew of *U-109* and spent thirty days aboard the U-boat as a prisoner.

Following the arrival of *U-109* at Lorient, Gordon Gill was taken by train to North Germany and interned at the Milag-Nord camp, Tarmstedt, near Bremen. He was eventually freed on 28 April, 1945.

At the time of writing (1996) he lives in retirement in Vermont. During his captivity he kept a diary of his experiences and noted the circumstances which preceded his capture.

The *Tuscan Star* loaded for six days at the Abattoir Pier, Santos, Brazil, and sailed for Freetown, Africa, on 30 August, 1942. She had aboard twenty-nine passengers including the British Consul and eight of his staff.

On the evening of 6 September, 1942, the ship was in the Gulf of Guinea, having just crossed the Equator, and was making over 16 knots in a calm sea. The temperature was 35°C, the night as black as pitch. Suddenly Gill, who was writing up the radio log, heard two tremendous explosions about 20 seconds apart, and the ship took a acute angle of heel to starboard.

Gill morsed out three times: 'SSSS SSSS *Tuscan Star* torpedoed position 00°56'N 11°08'W' and then went to his raft stowed amidships on the port side, but was unable to release it. He returned to his cabin for his life-jacket before making his way to the lifeboat stations. There he found the wreckage of one of the boats but the others were already heading away from the crippled ship and out of earshot. As the *Tuscan Star* began to settle, Gill jumped into the sea and watched the vessel sink quickly by the stern. He found himself alone in the ocean surrounded by floating debris and cried out for help in the darkness. He had swallowed seawater and fuel oil. He could hear somebody screaming for help in the distance. The voice was highly distraught. After 20 seconds, there was a terrible scream followed by silence. Probably the first sharks had arrived, he thought.

He swam for perhaps half an hour, orienting on a light in the distance and occasionally crying out for help. At first he thought it was a lamp on one of the lifeboats, then saw that it was a small searchlight sweeping the water. Soon it seemed to hold him in its beam, although he was unable to see clearly because of the film of oil over his eyes. Suddenly he heard the splash of a lifebelt nearby and grasped it, but as he felt himself being hauled upwards the line broke. It was at this moment that he first dimly made out the long grey body of the U-boat. Two stocky U-boat crewmen dragged him out of the sea and laid him on deck to recover before carrying him to the conning tower and down into the bell of the submarine.

'My captivity had begun,' he wrote. 'I asked what time it was. 2245 hrs, I was told. An hour and five minutes had passed since the torpedoes had hit.

'They saw to my eyes and I got my vision back after about half an hour. I had a warm salt-water bath and an issue of U-boat clothing consisting of a shirt, underwear, trousers and a jacket. My own tropical ducks had been ruined by the oil. Next I was given two glasses of cognac and ordered to rest. I had the second radio operator's bunk. I was so exhausted that I fell asleep at once. When I awoke at 1100 hrs I was served a breakfast of liver sausage, bread, marmalade and coffee, and given 50 cigarettes. It was stressed that if I needed any more I only had to ask. I also received soap, a towel and other utensils. When I first met Lt Cdr Bleichrodt I thought, 'This one's a real Nazi', but after thirty days close contact with him, I realized that this opinion was incorrect.'

* * *

In civilian life Bleichrodt found employment as the Director of an ironware factory. He died in Munich on 9 January, 1977. His son, Wolf Heinrich, served as a naval officer and then qualified as a gynaecologist, following in the footsteps of his mother, Carla Bleichrodt.

– Appendix 2 –

U-234 AND HER CARGO OF URANIUM OXIDE

Japanese physicists had worked unsuccessfully on an uranium bomb project since 1941 and had not progressed beyond the early laboratory stage. From 1944 they had the benefit of an efficient atomic espionage network in the United States and possibly from that source had been informed about the plutonium bomb, which could be built at a tenth of the cost and with far fewer complications.

The German naval historian Professor Jürgen Rohwer has confirmed from the first 'Magic' signal decrypts for 1943 and 1944/45 that Japan requested from Germany a quantity of uranium oxide in connection with their atomic research into the fissile isotopes including *plutonium*.[1]

We know from the declassified archive material that what the Germans sent was a small quantity of uranium oxide ore (U_3O_8) in ten metal cases of 560 kilos total weight for containers and contents.[2] Wolfgang Hirschfeld described these as resembling modern radioisotope shipment containers. From his additional hearsay evidence it would appear that they were emitting gamma radiation when examined at unloading and radioactive contamination was detected on all six steel cargo tubes which had been located in the forward mineshafts of *U-234* during the voyage. Uranium oxide ore is inert unless it has been subjected to neutron bombardment in a nuclear reactor. If it *has* been in a reactor core, the isotopes of *plutonium* are bred in the ore.

It would seem that at first the American authorities attached no importance to the uranium oxide, probably assuming it was unprocessed. It is listed on their Unloading Manifest dated 23 May, 1945, but not mentioned in the long memorandum respecting the particulars of the *U-234* voyage and cargo stowage submitted to the C-in-C, Atlantic Fleet on 6 June, 1945.

Both Wolfgang Hirschfeld and the local newspaper *Portsmouth Herald* report that the vertical steel tubes in the foredeck, in which the ten cases of the ore were stowed, were extracted by crane at the wharfside on or about 24 July, 1945, and examined by personnel equipped with Geiger counters, and it was after this that the *U-234* passengers and some crew members were interrogated about the uranium oxide ore. The only interrogation report released by the US National Archive to date, the 'Nieschling Memorandum', is dated 27 July, 1945.

In 1996 articles in British and German publications[3], former Lt-Col John Lansdale, the Manhattan Project's chief of atomic security and intelligence, who handled the disposal of the ten cases aboard *U-234*, said that the American military authorities *reacted with panic* when they discovered the cargo aboard the U-boat. They feared that Japan was further advanced in its A-bomb programme than had been previously assumed. One can imagine that there might easily be some panic when what was thought to be inert uranium oxide ore was found to be emitting gamma radiation.

Lansdale went on to say that the German material was sent immediately to Oak Ridge where the isotopes were separated and put into the pot of material used to make America's first atom bombs. The only fissile isotopes which can be separated from uranium oxide ore are the range of *plutonium* isotopes, from fissioned material.

If the German uranium oxide ore was gamma radioactive, then by implication Germany must have had a working atomic pile. In fact, it would have been surprising if Hitler's scientists had not built a small pilot reactor. By the end of 1940 the authorities had been informed by Professor Paul Harteck[4] that such a reactor could be constructed using about 20 tonnes of uranium oxide ore (U_3O_8) distributed in layers throughout a 30-tonne block of dry ice at a temperature of about minus 75°C, and that Germany had all the material necessary to build such a reactor; and in the same year other physicists[5] submitted scientific papers explaining how the fissile isotope of *plutonium* would be bred in the spent fuel of any atomic pile.

In August, 1941, Professor Houtermans wrote a thesis on the same subject,[6] pointing out that, at such a low temperature, the reactor would produce no heat or energy, only radioactive substances such as *plutonium* in the uranium fuel.

Because the chain reaction in a very low temperature pile depends on the nuclear Doppler Effect, the reaction collapses once the freezing temperature begins to rise and this ensures that the pile is safe enough to be run even in the cellar of a suburban villa, given the appropriate biological shielding.

Professor Houtermans was employed in the private villa of the radio-biologist Baron Manfred von Ardenne at Berlin Lichterfelde. This facility was funded by the German Post Office. The Postmaster-General, Ohnesorge, had a doctorate in mathematics and physics and encouraged von Ardenne's interest in atomic science. Von Ardenne was interested in building a small reactor as a macroscopic source of radiosotopes for pioneering work in medicine and biology, and this was why he had commissioned Professor Houtermans' thesis. In his second paper Houtermans noted the cooperation afforded by Professor J. Jensen, who was a member of Professor Harteck's Hamburg group. In October, 1942, von Ardenne received a contract from Peenemünde to investigate the possibilities of creating an atomic rocket fuel.

In the summer of 1942 he began the construction of several large underground concrete bunkers in the grounds of his villa. They were ready by the autumn of 1942, but what he did in them between then and 1 August, 1943, when he moved his office below ground, he does not say in his autobiography.[7] The fission cycle of Harteck's reactor design would have been about six months.

There are several references to these Post Office activities in the authoritative *Hitlers Tischgespräche*[8] which suggest that, in parallel with an unsuccessful professorial project von Ardenne worked on some sort of atomic project approved at the highest level: his villa was visited on several occasions by Hitler during the latter's periods of residence in Berlin. However, if this was indeed the successful German reactor, it seems unlikely that the advice of Professor Heisenberg would not have been sought at some stage if he did not actually supervise the operation.

From the summer of 1942 onwards the United States had expressed concern that, when the first enemy atomic pile was up and running, reactor fission products would be immediately available and that Germany 'might turn to them in an attempt to avoid defeat.' In December, 1943, Washington's experts were worried that Germany might be planning to use radioactive dust in flying bombs and rockets.[9]

On or about 24 July, 1945, the Americans were suddenly confronted on their own doorstep with their worst nightmare. Whatever the purpose of the German uranium oxide ore aboard *U-234*, there was no knowledge of what stocks of fission products Japan might already have amassed and no guarantee that Japan would not turn to the use of nuclear waste products in an attempt to avoid defeat.

On that day the American Government would have had no option but to order the deployment of their atomic arsenal if they had not done so already. It is one of the great ironies of war that Lt Cdr Fehler had disobeyed his last order and surrendered his U-boat to the United States, presenting them with a possible justification for their terrible action against Japan.

NOTES:

1. Letter from Professor Rohwer dated 28 March, 1996.
2. US National Archive, Box RG38, Box 13, Documents OP-20-3-G1-A dated May, 1945 (Unloading Manifest) and 373/3679/Box 22/ Folder OP-16-Z, Day file 1.1.1945 which includes the Nieschling Memorandum dated 27 July, 1945. The latter document shows that the uranium oxide is the ore.
3. English newspaper *Mail on Sunday* dated 7 January, 1996, and February, 1996, edition of *Der Spiegel*, article entitled *Heiße Ladung* at pages 148–9.
4. Harteck, Jensen J, Knauer and Süß, 19.8.1940, document G-36, Atomic Research Centre Karlsruhe. The best broad review of the German nuclear programme is David Irving's *The Virus House*, (William Kimber, 1972). Most other histories discount the German Post Office project. For Professor Harteck's postwar comments about his wartime work, see Professor J Ermenc's *Atomic bomb Scientists, 1939–45*, published by Greenwood, CT, and for a very informative account of the German experimental work including Harteck's projects see Wirtz, *Im Umkreis der Physik*, published privately by the Karlsruhe Atomic Centre.
5. CF von Weizsäcker, 17.7.1940, document G59, Karlsruhe: Schintlmeister and Hernegger, 10.12.1940, document G-55, Karlsruhe.
6. Houtermans, August, 1941, documents G-94 and G-267, Karlsruhe.
7. Manfred von Ardenne, *Ein Glückliches Leben für Forschung und Technik*, Verlag der Nation, East Berlin, 1972 at pages 156–7.
8. Dr Henry Picker, *Hitlers Tischgespräche*, (Seewald Verlag, Stuttgart 1976).
9. E H Hinsley, *British Intelligence in the Second World War – Its Influence on Strategy and Operations*, Vol 3, Part 2, (HMSO, 1988) at pages 583–592.

NOTES

1   The subject matter of Hirschfeld's diaries included verbatim conversation which was highly incriminating. If the diaries had been betrayed to the authorities the fate of Hirschfeld, Lt Cdr Heinrich Bleichrodt, Lt Werner Witte and Lt Wilhelm Wissmann in particular does not bear contemplation. In January, 1944, the commander of *U-154*, Lt Oskar Kusch, was court-martialled and shot by firing squad for making defeatist remarks to the watchkeeping officer who denounced him. In the German Navy it was the duty of an officer to denounce another officer, including his commander, for breaches of the Naval Code, and the officer who failed to denounce his brother officer could himself be denounced, and so on.

2   Captain Roskill (*The War at Sea, Vol. 1*, HMSO) attributes the sinking of the *Tirranna* to HM S/M *Tuna*, but otherwise makes no comment about the circumstances. For an amusing view of the difference between the conduct of British and German submarine commanders in this regard see *The British Submarine* by Cdr F Lipscomb (Conway Maritime Press, London, 1975):

> in contrast with the observance of our own submarines, the enemy's unrestricted warfare reached a new low level ... our submarine policy was so strongly in contrast to that of the enemy that the effect on neutrals could be said to have sealed their attitude in our favour.

As regards the *Tirranna*, with 274 neutral and British civilians aboard, Cdr Lipscomb, who obviously must have known the details, is understandably coy, modestly refraining from naming her, and congratulating Lt Cdr Cavanagh-Mainwaring, the Commander of HM S/M *Tuna* with the sinking of 'an 8,000-ton supply ship off the Gironde.'

3   GHG (*Gruppenhorchgerät*) was a listening device for underwater

direction finding. In a Type IXB U-boat it consisted of forty-eight crystal receivers arrayed port to starboard around the bow of the boat in the form of an arc. The operator, listening through headphones connected to the equipment, used a small steering wheel to activate a particular group of receivers in a desired direction. The operator adjusted the wheel to obtain the maximum audible volume and an electrical pulse-timing compensator indicated the rough bearing of the sound to within a few degrees by identifying which microphone received it first. (Later U-boat Types were fitted with an array of 96 receivers, and were accurate to within 1°).

In favourable circumstances a single ship might be detected at 15 miles and a convoy at 70 miles, but the critical factor was the acoustic conductivity of the water. The actual strength of an audible bearing gave no certain indication of the nearness or distance of a particular target.

4 This feeling among Hirschfeld and his shipmates reflects a widely held view in the U-boat service at that time. In his *U-boat Commander* (page 83) Cremer uses almost the same words.

5 The capture of Lemp's boat was probably the decisive moment in the U-boat war. All German naval communications were based upon the Enigma system of encryption. The Enigma machine used by the Navy differed from those used in the Army and Air Force. The British cryptanalysts at Bletchley Park had been able to crack the Enigma transmissions of the other two services but the naval machine defeated them for a long time, although, as a result of the capture of some material, a little progress had been made. It was not until HMS *Aubretia* sank Lt Cdr Lemp's *U-110* off south-west Ireland in May, 1941, that the breakthrough was made. The *Aubretia*'s Captain managed to secure a complete Enigma machine, together with all its additional rotors, daily keys and codebooks. This was carried out in such secrecy that the survivors were unaware that the priceless capture had been made. As *U-110* had only recently left port, having sailed from Brunsbüttel just before *U-109*, with whom she had been training in the same group, Bletchley now had the daily keys up to the end of June. The Royal Navy at once took full advantage of this to round up all the tankers and supply ships already at sea to support *Bismarck's* excursion in late May. A further capture of Enigma material in June increased the British advantage and their losses in the Battle of the Atlantic began to fall dramatically, for now they could intercept all the signal traffic, orders and instructions emanating from U-Boat Command Headquarters. Despite a short hiccough in March, 1942, when the Germans introduced a new rotor and keys for Enigma, thereby swinging the balance back in their favour for a few weeks

until Bletchley broke the new code, the British cryptanalysts did not lose their mastery of Enigma again.

6   BdU=*Befehlshaber der U-boote*: Commander-in-Chief of the German U-boat Arm, Admiral Karl Dönitz. From November, 1940, until the time of the St Nazaire raid in March, 1942 his headquarters was at Kernevel, Lorient, in a requisitioned mansion, still standing today, on the western side of Le Ter river facing the Keroman foreshore. Kernevel was rapidly transformed into a fortress, with numerous bunkers and gun emplacements for defence against attack from air and sea. As a result of the raid on St Nazaire and increasing air activity against Lorient, Döntiz was ordered by Hitler to withdraw his HQ to Paris.

7   These capital ships were the 1911-built, 30,000-ton battleships *New York* and *Texas* which formed part of the so-called 'Neutrality Patrol' in the North Atlantic prior to December, 1941, although the author has not yet seen an admission from Allied sources that either ship was on station there before June, 1941. Why would the United States wish to conceal such an apparently innocuous fact?

The *New York* and *Texas* were the only US battleships at that time to be fitted with radar and were in fact used as 'radar training ships' between May, 1941, and the summer of 1942. The *New York* carried the large XAF aerial developed experimentally by the Naval Research Laboratory, and the *Texas* had a parallel development which was the much smaller CXZ aerial, both of which had been fitted in 1938.

The very term 'Neutrality Patrol' was a cynical misnomer, since the real purpose of the American presence in mid-Atlantic was to pass naval information to the Royal Navy, particularly with regard to German movements in convoy areas. During May Churchill was in constant contact with the Americans and there can be little doubt that these two neutral battleships assisted Britain during the search for the *Bismarck*. Even negative reports would have been invaluable. This would have been an act of war without a declaration of war and the analogy to Pearl Harbor is obvious.

The extent to which neutral United States vessels collaborated with Britain in the subsequent destruction of the German tanker chain can only be guessed at. Captain Otto Kölschbach, Commander of the armed Fleet oiler *Spichern*, stated that during the hunt for the *Bismarck* his vessel sighted an American submarine which reported his presence and position. An American coastal station and an American ship repeated the signal. The Wireless Monitoring Service in Berlin subsequently confirmed that the Americans were passing information to the British in this manner.

Roosevelt's other purpose in operating US warships in close proximity to German forces was in the hope that an American vessel would be sunk, thereby enabling him to approach Congress for permission to enter the war. When Topp, in *U-552*, torpedoed the destroyer *Reuben James* during a convoy battle in 1941 Roosevelt attempted to enlist the support of Congress for his crusade but failed.

Eventually, he achieved his objective, although only with the avoidable sacrifice of 4575 American lives at Pearl Harbor.

8 This casualty was the *Marconi*, 7402-tons, owned by Kaye & Co, Cardiff. She carried eighty persons, presumably not all crew members, and thirty-nine of these managed to get away in the ship's boats. Six days later the survivors of these were picked up by the US Coast Guard ship *General Greene* on ice patrol off Newfoundland.

9 Asdic was a device which searched the depths over a range of about 3000 metres using high frequency sound waves to establish the position of a submerged U-boat. *Bold* was a cloud of aluminium strips ejected from the submarine for the purpose of interfering with Asdic reception.

10 The firm of Draeger manufactured the U-boat oxygen rebreathing equipment. It was efficient for escape purposes from a depth of 240 feet.

11 *Rotdrucke*: the German Navy printed its cryptographic documents with a water soluble red ink on a pink paper similar to blotting paper. This would soak up water even if pressed tightly between book covers on a shelf.

12 The Battle of the Denmark Strait (*Grönlandgefecht*) was fought in the early hours of Saturday 24 May, 1941. HMS *Hood* was sunk, with almost total loss of life, by the combined attacks of the battleship *Bismarck* and the heavy cruiser *Prinz Eugen*.

13 Although *U-556* (Lt Cdr Wohlfahrt) had been in the vicinity of the *Bismarck* for several hours, U-boats pitching in the heavy seas could not take accurate bearings on the homing signals sent during the night by *U-556* and *Bismarck*, and the *Bismarck*'s estimate of her position at 2100 put her well to the south-east of where she actually was. Even if the U-boats had managed to reach her, it is doubtful whether they would have been of much use in the weather conditions.

14 In addition to housing the Headquarters BdU, Lorient was a well-defended tidal base and the first to service a visiting Atlantic U-boat, on 7 July, 1940. It became the most extensive U-boat port established in France by the German Navy and was home to the 2nd (Salzwedel) and the 10th U-Flotillas.

Initially U-boats were serviced in the open, either in dry dock or aground beside a slipway, camouflaged under netting and tarpaulins, but after the first serious air raid in September, 1940, two concrete bunkers, known as 'cathedrals' because of their pointed roofs, and providing protection for two Type II coastal U-boats, were constructed, followed shortly after by a tidal shelter with a concrete roof 10 feet thick built on the Scorff river bank. This was the first temporary protection for Type VII and Type IX Atlantic boats. Constructions began on two bunkers, Keroman I and II, early in 1941, and, when completed later that year, these facilities accommodated thirteen submarine pens. The bunkers fronted the esplanade with workshops at the rear and armour doors three feet thick could be closed across each pen entrance. U-boats were transported into the pens in a cradle mounted on a wide transverser on rails. The entire process of bringing a U-boat ashore and into the farthest pen in the bunker could be accomplished in about an hour. The largest bunker, Keroman III, was not fully operational until May, 1943.

Two ships, the *Crapaud* and the *Strasbourg* (formerly the German light cruiser *Regensburg*) were moored in Port Louis Bay in front of the Keroman bunkers. They were fitted with tall masts to which were tethered barrage balloons as a defence against low level torpedo and bombing attack.

15   During a television news programme many years later Hirschfeld met the former commander of *U-93*, Claus Korth. The casualty from convoy HX 126 had been the tanker *Elusa*, hit at 0522 on the morning of 21 May, 1941, by Korth's last torpedo.

16   Cdr Fischer later served for eighteen months aboard the heavy cruiser *Admiral Hipper* and was subsequently Head of the Officers' Personnel Department in Kiel in the rank of full captain until the end of the war. His subsequent whereabouts are not known.

17   Upon being attacked, Admiralty instructions required the assailant to be identified by a radio distress message indicating either SSS (submarine), RRR (regular surface warship) or QQQ (a raider in the disguise of a merchant vessel).

18   The smoke-screen may have been the effect caused by the 1914-built coal-fired steamer 'putting the pitch'. This may not have been the first occasion when German officers overestimated the armament of an adversary. Admiral Dönitz was obsessed with Q-ships as a result of his personal experience with them in the Great War, and constantly impressed upon his commanders the danger which they presented, cautioning them never to approach an apparently disabled ship too closely. On the other hand, Bleichrodt was a highly experienced officer and it is improbable that he could have been wrong about the speed of the *City of Auckland*. Even in her prime twenty-seven years earlier, she had a maximum of 12 knots and now she made 14 knots.

Probably the British vessel was a DEMS (Defensively Equipped Merchant Ship) which had been re-engined and fitted out with a few guns, hydrophones and possibly a few depth-charge throwers, but although she was aggressively handled and was an undesirable proposition for a U-boat commander, Bleichrodt's caution seems to have been a little exaggerated, as will again be amply demonstrated during the incident with the *Halcyon* on a later voyage (see page 124 et seq)

19   Neutrality is a term of international law in respect of the conduct of states not involved as belligerents in a legal state of war. The Hague Convention of 1907 codified the strict impartiality of neutral nations with regard to their coastal waters. From the opening day of the Second World War neither of the belligerents was much concerned to observe the conventions of neutrality where that conflicted with their interests, although both Britain and Germany made a great pretence of it.

20   Professor Rohwer, the German naval historian, records that eight U-boats (*U-331, U-126, U-94, U-124, U-79, U-109, U-93* and *U-371*) assembled between Gibraltar and the Azores for the purpose of attacking convoy HG69. Three Italian boats, *Finzi, Marconi* and *Viniero*, were also involved. When the attack was finally abandoned on 16 August, 1941, only *Marconi* and an FW200 aircraft had any success to report, sinking two vessels totalling 5300 tons. *Marconi* unsuccessfully attacked the sloop HMS *Deptford* and the corvette HMS *Convolvulus*.

      Germany did not pursue experiments in the shorter radar wavebands until very late in the war, while Britain developed ever shorter wavelengths leading to the construction of radar sets compact enough to be fitted into small escort vessels. This gave them an unparalleled advantage over German U-boats, which lacked any form of radar. By 1942 many patrol aircraft had been fitted with an ASV set enabling them to detect and attack U-boats proceeding on the surface under conditions which had hitherto been safe, such as under overcast skies or at night.

21   The Order of the Knight's Cross of the Iron Cross was worn on a ribbon round the neck.

22   The word *Bleihauer* is a mining term meaning a lead face-worker. Bleichrodt's corruption of the warrant officer's name was *Bleiarsch*, which translates to 'Leadarse'.

23   This was probably the large British minelaying submarine HM S/M *Rorqual* (Lt Napier), which laid mines off La Rochelle on the morning of 19 November, 1941, the day following the sighting of a British submarine by Lt Keller.

24   This ship was in fact the British freighter *Thirlby*, 4887 GRT. The purpose of the deception as to her identity is not known.

25 The *Tacoma Star* (Capt R. G. Whitehead) sailed from Montevideo for Hampton Roads and Halifax from where she would join up with a UK-bound convoy. Shore operators received her signal on 1 February saying she had been torpedoed by a U-boat in a position about 380 miles east of Hampton Roads and ships were sent to search for survivors in that area. No trace was ever found of the ship, lifebelts or wreckage, nor of her crew of ninety-four officers and men.

26 U-boat commanders frequently overestimated the size of the ships they attacked, and this was not done for propaganda purposes. The *Halcyon*, a Panamanian flag vessel proceeding from Halifax to Demerara in ballast, was of only 3531 tons gross register, whereas Bleichrodt, who had estimated her to be 6000 tons, set his torpedoes too deep.

27 It is doubtful whether the sinking of the *Empire Kingfisher*, 6038 gross tons, should be credited to *U-109*. On 18 January, 1942, the merchant vessel struck a submerged object four miles off Cape Sable. It was reported that the object (suspected to be a sunken ship) passed beneath the *Empire Kingfisher* with a rumbling sound and a muffled explosion was heard. She stopped engines and the rumbling stopped, but when the engines were restarted the sound was heard again and then the rudder jammed. The *Empire Kingfisher* was anchored and abandoned and sank the following day south of the Bantam Rock buoy before salvage tugs arrived. If the errant torpedo from *U-109* was responsible for the explosion, it seems more probable that it struck the sunken ship than the *Empire Kingfisher*.

28 The operations of German U-boats prior to May, 1941, were often considerably extended by replenishing fuel and torpedoes from supply ships drifting in remote areas of the Atlantic. As a prelude to the *Bismarck* operation, eight supply ships were sent to Atlantic waiting positions in advance of the German squadron, and, following the sinking of the *Bismarck*, the Royal Navy made a clean sweep of them, sinking seven. The only German supply vessel of the group to regain port was the naval oiler *Spichern*, which refuelled the *Prinz Eugen* on the evening of 26 May, 1941. Captain Köhlsbach of the *Spichern* only transmitted wireless signals in the very direst emergency because he had no faith in the security of codes (see Köhlsbach, *Der Blockadebrcher mit der Glücklichen Hand*,(Köhlers Verlag, Herford, 1958).

Captain Hellmuth Brinkmann of the *Prinz Eugen* became so alarmed at the wireless indiscipline of the naval supply chain, reporting their positions and requesting instructions, that he soon concluded it was too dangerous for his ship to remain at large while it continued and he made for Brest, where he arrived unannounced on the morning of 1 June, 1941.

After this disaster it became the practice for U-boats to refuel from German tankers laid up in neutral Spanish harbours, or from minelaying submarines converted to supply boats. Eventually the ten purpose-built U-tankers (*U-459* to *U-464* and *U-487* to *U-490*), which carried 205 tons of fuel for disposal to attack U-boats, were used operationally. All were depth-charged and sunk, mostly by aircraft, between August, 1942, and June, 1944. The location of refuelling meets was usually compromised because of the insecurity of the naval code. During refuelling the two or sometimes three U-boats involved were exposed on the surface for several hours during the oil transfer. The idea of underwater refuelling was not seriously considered until it was too late.

29 The ship was the J. C. Harrison Ltd's *Harpagon*, 5719 tons, from Baltimore to Barry with 5,000 tons of nitro-glycerine. She had a crew of thirty-five and six gunners.

30 A Type II boat was a 250-ton coastal submarine which was sensitive to internal movement. Her buoyancy and trim were often adjusted by moving the crew forward or astern.

31 The *La Paz* was subsequently beached near Cape Canaveral and repaired. During the operation most of her cargo of Johnny Walker Scotch Whisky disappeared.

32 This was the 5282 gross ton *Laertes* of the Nederlandsche Stoomvaart-maatschappij on voyage from New York to Bombay via the Cape. Eighteen men were lost when the third torpedo hit a lifeboat in the darkness.

33 This may have been Teddy Suhren sinking the American 3478 gross ton *Delisle* that morning.

34 This was probably the 6078 gross ton *Ohioan*, a tanker of the American-Hawaiian Steamship Company which was sunk by Teddy Suhren in *U-564* on 8 May, 1942.

35 A lifeboat containing sixteen men was picked up after two days by the *Sylvia de Larrinaga*, but when she was torpedoed shortly after, the *Vimeira* crew put to sea again in their own lifeboat. They suffered a further twenty-nine days' hardship in the open boat before being picked up by the Norwegian steamship *Siranger* and landed at Takoradi to join four other survivors there. The death toll from the *Vimeira* was nineteen crewmen and four gunners.

36 The 270-ton four-masted schooner *Maria da Gloria* was sunk on 6 June, 1942, and the *De Laes*, a four-masted auxiliary sailing ship was destroyed on 11 September, 1942. The Portuguese Government gave these sinkings as the reason why it was not possible to accede to the British request. Eventually, in October, 1943, they did give in, but by then the Battle of the Atlantic was already in its final stages.

37 The fifty surviving crew members of the *Ocean Might* came ashore at the fishing village of New Ningo, Ghana, 35 miles east of Accra, on 7 September, 1942.

38 For a survivor's view of this incident, and of Lt Cdr Bleichrodt see *The Blue Star Line at War 1939–45* by Taffrail (Foulsham, London, 1973). The details of the attack and the sinking of the *Tuscan Star* correspond with Hirschfeld's account.

39 As the fuel oil in a tank was consumed, sea water was admitted to keep the fuel, which was lighter, trapped at the top of the bunker. As all this sea water was ballast, Schewe had transferred all the fuel into a few tanks and drained the other tanks dry.

40 In his book *U-977- 66 Tage unter Wasser* (Wiesbaden, 1950, page 135) Heinz Schaeffer described the initial trials of an underwater oil refuelling operation on 7 December, 1942, involving Schnoor's boat *U-460* and *U-445*. The boats proceeded in line astern at a depth of 150 feet connected by a hawser and slack hose. Communications were exchanged by underwater telegraphy. Eberhard Rössler commented in his book *The U-boat* (Arms and Armour Press, 1981) that the failure to introduce this system immediately was unbelievable. Not until late 1943 were official trials held in the Baltic which confirmed the technique as perfectly satisfactory. By then Schnoor and his crew were dead, surprised during a surface refuelling operation north of the Azores on 4 October, 1943, depth-charged by aircraft, a fate to which eight of the ten U-tankers had similarly succumbed before 1943 was out.

41 For details of Bleichrodt's breakdown see Appendix 1, page 223 et seq.

42 *U-526* was the only U-boat ever to be lost along the Biscay coast while under the protection of a minesweeper escort. The 'escort-mine' which sank her was an experimental device designed to become activated by the strong magnetic field of a *Sperrbrecher* escort vessel after a delay of 20 seconds. Normally the *Sperrbrecher* sailed 300 yards ahead of the U-boat being escorted. (See *Deutsche Minensucher*, Reinhart Ostertag, Köhlers Verlag, Herford, 1986). The role of the minesweeper was a very important factor in U-boat operations on the French coast where British aircraft and submarines regularly laid mines at the port approaches. The principal mine protection vessels were the large purpose-built 'M'-class minsweepers, some of which were built as coal burners in 1940: *Sperrbrecher*, which were requisitioned merchant ships packed with barrels and corks to make them unsinkable and equipped with a very heavy flak armament; and the small motor minesweepers, or *Räumboote*.

43 See *Haie im Paradies-der deutsche U-bootkrieg in Asiens Gewässern 1943–45* by Jochen Brennecke, (Wilhelm Heyne Verlag, Munich,

1973, pages 26–34.) *U-180* sailed from Bordeaux for Japan in August, 1944, with a cargo including optical instruments, mercury, dismantled V-weapons, torpedoes, radar equipment, blueprints and technical personnel, and was mined off the estuary of the Gironde on 22 August, 1944. For details of the mission of the Japanese submarine *I-52* see *The Times (Overseas News)*, Wednesday 19 July, 1995, under the title *Americans Track Down Hirohito Treasure Sub.*

44 Because *U-234* was in the Canadian designated sector at the time when Fehler elected to surrender, he ought to have put in at Halifax. He chose the US sector by reason of his misguided impression that he would secure better treatment in the USA for the *U-234* crew, an error he was to bitterly regret. Fehler never forgave the Americans for their brutal treatment of himself and U-boat crews generally. His decision not to go through with the voyage had been much influenced by his experiences as a Merchant Navy officer in the Far East, where he had had the opportunity to see the Japanese Army at work.

Tomonaga and Shosi told Fehler that they were prepared to accept internment in the Irish Free State, which was considered to be a true neutral despite its close approximity to Britain. Fehler's chances of reaching Japan via Cape Horn were favourable once he had broken out into the Atlantic.

45 The American authorities deny the presence of this Me 262 jet fighter aboard *U-234*, and it is absent from their Loading List. However, the Japanese television network company NHK Tokyo, which produced a documentary in tribute to Hideo Tomonaga, showed film extracts originating from the US Archive in which *U-234* passenger August Bringewald, the Messerschmitt aeronautical engineer, is shown examining an apparently new Me 262 jet at Wright Field air force base in May, 1945. Hirschfeld asks, 'Where did the Americans get this aircraft if it was not aboard *U-234*?' In the biographical account of his career *The Warring Seas* by A V Sellwood (White Horse Publishers, 1955) Fehler told the author then that there was an Me 262 in its component parts in the hold of *U-234*. As Commander, it is hardly likely that he would have been mistaken.

46 The full story of Hirschfeld's period in captivity from 19 May, 1945, until his discharge from the German Navy the following year is recounted in his book *Das Letzte Boot-Atlantik Farewell* (Universitas Verlag, Munich 1989). His voyages aboard *U-109* appear in diary form in his work *Feindfahrten-Das Logbuch eines U-boot-Funkers* (Paul Neff Verlag, Vienna, 1982).

INDEX

about fuel shortage to War Diary, 139; curtails fifth patrol for lack of fuel, 156; considers interning boat, 158; emotional at no early refuelling, 6th patrol, 164; berates U-Boat HQ in signal, 166; under electric motors to save fuel, 168–169; uses ruse to obtain more fuel, 170; acid exchange of signals with base over severe fuel difficulties, 174; plans to rig sail, 177; refuelled by *U-460*; 177; short measure and storms cause new fuel shortage, 179; abandons seventh patrol on grounds of fuel shortage, 184, 223–224; dangers at refuelling meets, 177; *U-460* proves underwater refuelling feasible, 240.

Gill, Gordon, radio officer, *Tuscan Star*; picked up by *U-109*, 160, 177; own account of incident, 226–227.

Gugelmeier, Lt, Signals Officer, 2 U-Flotilla, Lorient; 184, 187, 190.

Gross, Walter, boatswain *U-109*; discovers field-kitchen on foredeck, 11; recalls depth-charge attack aboard *U-14*, 14; gives early warning of British bomber, 23; fishes American can from Atlantic, 26; sights British submarine periscope near Lorient, 52; lookout during *City of Auckland*

engagement, 60; promoted Senior Boatswain, *U-460*, 134–135; in charge refuelling of *U-109*, sixth patrol, 177; supplies short measure, 179; lost aboard *U-460*, 240.

Hagen, Ferdinand, telegraphist petty officer, joins *U-109*, 18: 23, 45, 52, 68, 82, 83–85, put ashore with gonorrhoea, 86; reinstated after cure, 92–93; D/F error, 121; affected by Q-ship fear, 126; 127, 167, 173, 182; confides in Hirschfeld presentiment of death, 186; lost aboard *U-109*, 187.

Halcyon, Panamanian steamer, 124–129; 238.

Hansa, German accommodation ship, 11–12.

Harpagon, British explosives ship; 141–142, 239.

Harteck, Paul, Professor; Austrian nuclear chemist; submits design for low temperature uranium oxide/dry ice nuclear reactor, 1940, 229.

Hatten, Cdr, US Navy; supervises German skeleton crew aboard *U-234*, 217–218.

Havel, North German Lloyd steamer, 191.

Hengen, Dieter, Midshipman *U-109*; 85, 113, sent for officer training, 163.

Hertha, U-Flotilla depot ship, 10–12.

Heyer, Albert, Sub-Lt (Eng) *U-109*; 135, replaces Lt

British submarine in Biscay, 107–108; opinion on Goering, 159; commander training course, 159; lost n command *U-130*, 186.

Kessler, Ulrich, Luftwaffe AA General, Air Attache Tokyo, passenger *U-234*; 203, 210, 215.

Ketty Brövig, prize, Norwegian tanker; 191–192.

Kigoishi, Japanese Military Attache, Berlin; 199.

Kleinschmidt, Lt Cdr, commander *U-111*, 11; lost in skirmish with HM A/S trawler *Lady Shirley*, 94, 126.

Laconia, British passenger/ prison ship, xvi, 174–176.

Laertes, British steamer, 152, 239.

Lansdale, John, Lt Col (US Army), chief of atomic security and intelligence, Manhattan Project, recalls disposal of *U-234* uranium cargo, 229.

La Paz, American freighter, 150–151, 239.

Leibling, telegraphist U-109; 89, 91–92, 105, 122, 128, 146–147, 166, 178–179.

Lepel, Dr, Fleet Surgeon, Carnac, 135, 179, 182.

Lützow, incomplete German heavy cruiser, 2.

Marconi, British Ammunition ship, 28–29, 235.

Maureschat, Eduard, boatswain

U-109; appointed artillery petty officer, 18; shells *City of Auckland*, 61–62; and *Halcyon*, 125–129; and *Arthur W. Sewall*, 166; reprimanded for loss of shell cases, 87; awarded EK I, 160; saves Gordon Gill, 173; remustered 185; promoted Warrant Officer, Hirschfeld meets as commander of *S-208*, 192.

Medical Treatment on *U-109*; Hirschfeld also ship's doctor, 29; treats crushed fingers 28–29; attends courses 110, 135; treats pubic infestation, 114; infestation spreads, 130; treats appendicitis case, 138; and gonorrhoea, 138–139, 152; Bleichrodt treats own eye infection, 167; but allows Hirschfeld to treat leg injury, 170; outbreak of furuncles, 171; BdU signals treatments, 139, 223; Dr Hoch of *U-463* attends Bleichrodt, 224.

Montrolite, Canadian tanker, 123–124.

MSAD, unidentified ship attacked by Bleichrodt, 115–116.

Nazro, T. W., Lt, commander USS *Sutton*, 214.

New York, USS, American battleship, 26–27, 234.

Nieschling, Kai, Luftwaffe Judge, passenger *U-234*; assignation in Japan, 200; reports attempted suicide of Japanese passengers, 211;

248

sixth patrol, *U-109*, 162, mistakes identity of British bomber, 163–164; discusses Russian Front and neutrality with Bleichrodt, 168; opinion about *Laconia* incident, 175; says Germany cannot win war without air supremacy, 180; replaces Bleichrodt as commander, 185; lost in command *U-109*, 187.

Schröder, Dr, civilian meteorologist, *U109*, 25, 38, 42.

Schütze, Viktor, Cdr, Chief 2 U-flotilla, Lorient, 87–88, 111, 180.

Schwarten, Lt Cdr (Reserve), commander *T-139*, 2–4, 8.

Schwartzkopff, Volkmar, Lt, I WO *U-109*, 9, protests to Fischer re tactics, 23, denounces Cdr Fischer 54–56; approves of Bleichrodt, 57; during *City of Auckland* incident, 59–63; at Cadiz, 65, 68, 74, 76, 79; transfers to *U-107* at own request, 87; as commander *U-520* invites Hirschfeld to be senior telegraphist, 162; lost off Newfoundland, 186–187.

Seidel, Berthold, boatswain, *U109*, amulet of Bleichrodt, 57, 87; also 80, 88, 122, 136, 147, 171, 173; awarded German Cross in Gold, 178–179; remustered, 185.

Seidel, Waldemar, Lt, Signals Officer 2 U-Flotilla, Lorient; interviews Hirschfeld over

hydrophones, 82; 83–84, 91–92, confides in Hirschfeld re short wave D/F, 130.

Shosi, Genzo, Col, Japanese Air Force, passenger *U-234*, 198, 208–209, 211–212.

Silvaplana, prize, ex-Norwegian steamer, 101–107, 109, 120–121.

Spreewald, German blockade runner, 120–121.

Strasbourg ex *Regensburg*, decommissioned French cruiser, 53, 160, 236.

Sutton, USS, American destroyer, 212–216.

T-139 ex *Pfeil*, German torpedo boat, 1–2, 6.

Tacoma Star, British steamer, 120, 238.

Texas, USS, American battleship; 26–27, 234.

Thalia, German supply ship at Cadiz, 68–69.

Thetis, HM S/M, 9.

Thirlby, British steamer, 117, 237.

Tirranna, prize, ex-Norwegian steamer, xvi, 232.

Tomonaga, Hideo, Captain, Japanese Navy, passenger *U-234*; arrives in France aboard *U-180*, 189; at loading of uranium in Kiel, 198; 208–209; suicide of, 211–212.

Tuscan Star, British steamer, 172–173.

U-boat trap, British, at 44°N 23°W: reported by *U-82*

(Rollmann) before being sunk, 130; reported by *U-252* (Lerchen) before being sunk, 159; Bleichrodt escapes from, 131; Bleichrodt evades again, 159.

Uranium oxide ore (U_3O_8): loaded aboard *U-234* at Kiel, 199; unloaded at Portsmouth, NH, 218; probable purpose, 228–231.

Valentiner, Max, Captain (Reserve), U-boat training officer; WWI ace, xiii; *U-234* snorkel instructor, 196–197.

Vimeira, British steamer, 168, 181, 239.

Waldemar Kophamel, U-boat depot ship, 193–194.

Walter, Dr, medical officer, *U-234*; 210; confirms Japanese officers still alive after suicide attempt, 211; ordered by Fehler to ensure their deaths, 212; performs emergency surgery on US Navy crewman, 215.

War Crimes Tribunals; British introduce irregularities in procedure to obtain convictions, 225; persecution of Bleichrodt as war criminal, 225.

Weber, Martin, Lt, Chief Engineer, *U-109*; endangers boat on trial dive, 9; considered incompetent by Hirschfeld, 9; 36, 39, 42–44, culpable for deep

dive off Newfoundland, 45; argues with Cdr Fischer re diesels, 47, 49; Dönitz implies his inefficiency, 53; involved in denunciation of Cdr Fischer, 56; examples of dangerous incompetence under Bleichrodt, 73, 99–100, 103–104; 144–146; 148–149; logged in War Diary as incompetent, 149; demustered, 163; lost off Lorient aboard *U-526*, 186, 240.

Weichsel, German accommodation ship, 19; Bleichrodt supervises evacuation of Gydnia aboard, 225.

Wentzel, Kuddel, boatswain *U-109*, 12, 24, 51–52; to coxswain's training course, 57; coxswain of *U-522*, 183; advises Hirschfeld against volunteering for boat, 186; lost off Madeira, 186.

Wex, Dieter, Midshipman *U-109*, 113; transferred to officers' training, 135.

Whales, show companionable interest in *U-109*, 64, 69, 114.

Wilhelm Bauer, U-boat tender, 12–13, 16.

Winkelmann, Wilhelm, Engineering Warrant Officer, *U-234*, 197, 205.

Winter, Alfred, Engineering Warrant Officer U-109, 9, 32, 44, 100, 145–146, 179, 185.

Wüsteney, control room

machinist, *U-109*, 28, 44, 46, 122.

Wissmann, Friedrich Wilhelm, Lt, IWO third and fourth patrols, *U-109*, 87, 97, 107; remonstrates with Bleichrodt over *Halcyon*, 126; to commanders' course, 134; meets Hirschfeld as captain of *Waldemar Kophamel*, 194; supplies *U-234* with Hohentwiel radar, 194.

Witte, Werner, Lt, IWO *U-109*, 5th patrol, 134, 136, 138–139, 141–142, 144, 146, 148–151, 154–155, 159; transferred to commanders' course, 163; lost off Madeira in command *U-509*, 163.

Worden, American lighter, 151.

Zähringen, pre-Dreadnought hulk, 1.

Ziemke, Dr, Fleet surgeon, Lorient; 135, 171.

AXIS SUBMARINES MENTIONED

Italian
Cappellini, 175; *Marconi*,
79;

Japanese
I-29, (Yoichi) 189; *I-52*, 189,
240-241;

German
U-A (Eckermann), 64; *U-14*
(Weingärtner) 14, 24; *U-16*
(Wellner), 24; *U-47* (Prien),
16, 221; *U-48* (Bleichrodt),
72, 214; *U-65* (von
Stockhausen), 15; *U-66*
(Zapp), 64, 112, 117-118;
U-67 (Bleichrodt), 57, 222;
U-74 (Kentrat), 30, 50,
52-53, 98; *U-79*
(Kaufmann), 73; *U-82*
(Rollmann), 130, 159; *U-93*
(Korth), 30, 37, 69, 71, 74,
236; *U-94* (Kuppisch), 30,
36, 69, 74, 80; *U-99*
(Kretschmer), 16.

U-100 (Schepke), 16; *U-107*
(Hessler), 87, 162; *U-110*
(Lemp), 25, 233; *U-111*
(Kleinschmidt), 11, 20, 94,
126; *U-116* (von Schmidt),
164-165; *U-123* (Hardegen),
65, 75-77, 112, 115,
117-118, 138; *U-124*
(Bauer), 69, 74, 80; *U-130*
(Kals), 111-112, 115, 118,
119-129; (Keller), 186;

U-156 (Hartenstein),
174-176; *U-165*
(Hoffmann), 162, 178, 182;
U-180 (Musenberg),
188-189, 240.

U-201 (Schnee), 135; *U-203*
(Mützelburg), 164; *U-235*,
199; *U-252* (Lerchen), 159.
U331 (von Tiesenhausen),
74-75, 77, 79; *U-333*
(Cremer), 121.
U-436 (Seibicke), 224; *U-442*
(Heße), 224; *U-459*
(Wilamowitz), 137, 175;
U-460 (Schnoor), 115-117,
240; *U-463* (Wolfbauer),
224.

U-506 (Würdemann), 157,
169-171, 174-176, 189; *U-507* (Schacht), 157, 164,
169, 174-175l *U-509*
(Witte), 162; *U-518*
(Wißmann), 194; *U-520*
(Schwartzkopff), 162,
186-187; *U-522* (Schneider),
183; *U-526* (Möglich), 186,
240; *U-552* (Topp), 115;
U-556 (Wohlfarth), 25, 30,
50, 55; *U-564* (Suhren), 156;
U-572 (Hirsacker) 164-165;
U-575 (Heydemann), 224.

U-752 (Schröter), 164-165.

U-1301 (Lenkheit), 202.